AMERICA'S
TEST KITCHEN

# ALSO BY AMERICA'S TEST KITCHEN

**FOR A FULL LISTING OF ALL OUR BOOKS**

CooksIllustrated.com

AmericasTestKitchen.com

# PRAISE FOR AMERICA'S TEST KITCHEN TITLES

Selected as the Cookbook Award Winner of 2019 in the Health and Special Diet Category
**INTERNATIONAL ASSOCIATION OF CULINARY PROFESSIONALS (IACP) ON *THE COMPLETE DIABETES COOKBOOK***

"Diabetics and all health-conscious home cooks will find great information on almost every page."
**BOOKLIST (STARRED REVIEW) ON *THE COMPLETE DIABETES COOKBOOK***

"This is a wonderful, useful guide to healthy eating."
**PUBLISHERS WEEKLY ON *NUTRITIOUS DELICIOUS***

"True to its name, this smart and endlessly enlightening cookbook is about as definitive as it's possible to get in the modern vegetarian realm."
**MEN'S JOURNAL ON *THE COMPLETE VEGETARIAN COOKBOOK***

"The book offers an impressive education for curious cake makers, new and experienced alike. A summation of 25 years of cake making at ATK, there are cakes for every taste."
**THE WALL STREET JOURNAL ON *THE PERFECT CAKE***

Selected as one of the 10 Best New Cookbooks of 2017
**THE LA TIMES ON *THE PERFECT COOKIE***

"The editors at America's Test Kitchen pack decades of baking experience into this impressive volume of 250 recipes. . . . You'll find a wealth of keeper recipes within these pages."
**LIBRARY JOURNAL (STARRED REVIEW) ON *THE PERFECT COOKIE***

"Cooks with a powerful sweet tooth should scoop up this well-researched recipe book for healthier takes on classic sweet treats."
**BOOKLIST ON *NATURALLY SWEET***

"Here are the words just about any vegan would be happy to read: 'Why This Recipe Works.' Fans of America's Test Kitchen are used to seeing the phrase, and now it applies to the growing collection of plant-based creations."
**THE WASHINGTON POST ON *VEGAN FOR EVERYBODY***

"The sum total of exhaustive experimentation . . . anyone interested in gluten-free cookery simply shouldn't be without it."
**NIGELLA LAWSON ON *THE HOW CAN IT BE GLUTEN-FREE COOKBOOK***

"A one-volume kitchen seminar, addressing in one smart chapter after another the sometimes surprising whys behind a cook's best practices. . . . You get the myth, the theory, the science, and the proof, all rigorously integrated as only America's Test Kitchen can do."
**NPR ON *THE SCIENCE OF GOOD COOKING***

"Some books impress by the sheer audacity of their ambition. Backed up by the magazine's famed mission to test every recipe relentlessly until it is the best it can be, this nearly 900-page volume lands with an authoritative wallop."
**CHICAGO TRIBUNE ON *THE COOK'S ILLUSTRATED COOKBOOK***

"The 21st-century *Fannie Farmer Cookbook* or *The Joy of Cooking*. If you had to have one cookbook and that's all you could have, this one would do it."
**CBS SAN FRANCISCO ON *THE NEW FAMILY COOKBOOK***

"The go-to gift book for newlyweds, small families, or empty nesters."
**ORLANDO SENTINEL ON *THE COMPLETE COOKING FOR TWO COOKBOOK***

"This book upgrades slow cooking for discriminating, 21st-century palates—that is indeed revolutionary."
**THE DALLAS MORNING NEWS ON *SLOW COOKER REVOLUTION***

"Some 2,500 photos walk readers through 600 painstakingly tested recipes, leaving little room for error."
**ASSOCIATED PRESS ON *THE AMERICA'S TEST KITCHEN COOKING SCHOOL COOKBOOK***

"If you're a home cook who loves long introductions that tell you why a dish works followed by lots of step-by-step hand holding, then you'll love *Vegetables Illustrated*."
**THE WALL STREET JOURNAL ON *VEGETABLES ILLUSTRATED***

# EASY
# EVERYDAY
# KETO

Healthy Kitchen–Perfected Recipes

AMERICA'S TEST KITCHEN

Library of Congress Cataloging-in-Publication Data

Names: America's Test Kitchen (Firm), editor.
Title: Easy everyday keto : healthy kitchen-perfected recipes
    / America's Test Kitchen.
Description: Boston, MA : America's Test Kitchen, 2020. | Includes index.
Identifiers: LCCN 2019053814 | ISBN 9781948703123 (paperback) | ISBN 9781948703130 (epub)
Subjects: LCSH: Ketogenic diet. | Low-carbohydrate diet--Recipes. | Reducing diets--Recipes. | LCGFT: Cookbooks.
Classification: LCC RC374.K46 E43 2020 | DDC 641.5/6383--dc23
LC record available at https://lccn.loc.gov/2019053814

**AMERICA'S TEST KITCHEN**
21 Drydock Avenue, Boston, MA 02210

Manufactured in the United States of America
10 9 8 7 6 5 4 3 2 1

Distributed by Penguin Random House Publisher Services
Tel: 800.733.3000

**Pictured on front cover**  Thai Chicken Lettuce Wraps (page 78)

**Pictured on back cover**  Chocolate Chip Cookies (page 220), Grilled Bacon–Wrapped Scallops with Celery Salad (page 149), Super Cobb Salad (page 156), Pan-Seared Strip Steak with Smashed Cucumber Salad (page 105), Overnight Chia Pudding with Raspberries and Almonds (page 46), Singapore Noodles (page 150)

**Featured Photography**  **Steve Klise**

Editorial Director, Books  **Adam Kowit**

Executive Food Editor  **Dan Zuccarello**

Executive Managing Editor  **Debra Hudak**

Senior Editors  **Leah Colins, Joseph Gitter, Kaumudi Marathé, Sara Mayer, and Russell Selander**

Associate Editor  **Lawman Johnson**

Test Cooks  **Samantha Block and Sarah Ewald**

Assistant Editors  **Kelly Cormier and Brenna Donovan**

Editorial Assistant  **Tess Berger**

Consulting Nutritionist
**Alicia A. Romano, MS, RD, CNSC**

Art Director, Books  **Lindsey Timko Chandler**

Deputy Art Director  **Courtney Lentz**

Photography Director  **Julie Bozzo Cote**

Photography Producer  **Meredith Mulcahy**

Senior Staff Photographers  **Steve Klise and Daniel J. van Ackere**

Staff Photographer  **Kevin White**

Food Styling  **Catrine Kelty, Chantal Lambeth, Ashley Moore, and Elle Simone Scott**

Photoshoot Kitchen Team

Photo Team Manager  **Timothy McQuinn**

Lead Test Cook  **Eric Haessler**

Assistant Test Cooks  **Hannah Fenton, Jacqueline Gochenouer, and Christa West**

Illustration  **Jay Layman**

Senior Manager, Publishing Operations
**Taylor Argenzio**

Imaging Manager  **Lauren Robbins**

Production and Imaging Specialists  **Tricia Neumyer, Dennis Noble, Jessica Voas, and Amanda Yong**

Copy Editor  **Cheryl Redmond**

Proofreader  **Patricia Jalbert-Levine**

Indexer  **Elizabeth Parson**

Chief Creative Officer  **Jack Bishop**

Executive Editorial Directors  **Julia Collin Davison and Bridget Lancaster**

# CONTENTS

# WELCOME TO AMERICA'S TEST KITCHEN

This book has been tested, written, and edited by the folks at America's Test Kitchen. Located in Boston's Seaport District in the historic Innovation and Design Building, it features 15,000 square feet of kitchen space, including multiple photography and video studios. It is the home of *Cook's Illustrated* magazine and *Cook's Country* magazine and is the workday destination for more than 60 test cooks, editors, and cookware specialists. Our mission is to test recipes over and over again until we understand how and why they work and until we arrive at the best version.

We start the process of testing a recipe with a complete lack of preconceptions, which means that we accept no claim, no technique, and no recipe at face value. We simply assemble as many variations as possible, test a half-dozen of the most promising, and taste the results blind. We then construct our own recipe and continue to test it, varying ingredients, techniques, and cooking times until we reach a consensus. As we like to say in the test kitchen, "We make the mistakes so you don't have to." The result, we hope, is the best version of a particular recipe, but we realize that only you can be the final judge of our success (or failure). We use the same rigorous approach when we test equipment and taste ingredients.

All of this would not be possible without a belief that good cooking, much like good music, is based on a foundation of objective technique. Some people like spicy foods and others don't, but there is a right way to sauté, there is a best way to cook a pot roast, and there are measurable scientific principles involved in producing perfectly beaten, stable egg whites. Our ultimate goal is to investigate the fundamental principles of cooking to give you the techniques, tools, and ingredients you need to become a better cook. It is as simple as that.

To see what goes on behind the scenes at America's Test Kitchen, check out our social media channels for kitchen snapshots, exclusive content, video tips, and much more. You can watch us work (in our actual test kitchen) by tuning in to *America's Test Kitchen* or *Cook's Country* on public television or on our websites. Download our award-winning podcast, *Proof*, which goes beyond recipes to solve food mysteries (AmericasTestKitchen.com/proof), or listen in to test kitchen experts on public radio (SplendidTable.org) to hear insights that illuminate the truth about real home cooking. Want to hone your cooking skills or finally learn how to bake—with an America's Test Kitchen test cook? Enroll in one of our online cooking classes. And you can engage the next generation of home cooks with kid-tested recipes from America's Test Kitchen Kids.

However you choose to visit us, we welcome you into our kitchen, where you can stand by our side as we test our way to the best recipes in America.

facebook.com/AmericasTestKitchen
twitter.com/TestKitchen
youtube.com/AmericasTestKitchen
instagram.com/TestKitchen
pinterest.com/TestKitchen

AmericasTestKitchen.com
CooksIllustrated.com
CooksCountry.com
OnlineCookingSchool.com
AmericasTestKitchen.com/kids

# GETTING STARTED

# A HIGH-FAT, LOW-CARB WAY TO EAT

High-fat, low-carb diets are not new. People have long chosen diets like ketogenic or Atkins for a variety of health and lifestyle reasons, but recently interest in keto has increased substantially. Maintaining the restrictions of the keto diet, however, typically requires a lot of home cooking and we learned from our fans who eat keto that there was a desire for foolproof and varied keto recipes to make home cooking easier, tastier, and even more interesting. That's where America's Test Kitchen came in. We wanted to give keto cooks a trusted source of rigorously tested recipes for flavorful meals and snacks that don't take hours to prepare and are calculated to work nutritionally.

What could we use? Meat, fish, eggs, nuts, unsweetened chocolate, coffee, butter, oil, cream, and cheese are all welcome on the keto table. What's out are the carb-rich staples that we usually rely on, like sugar, wheat, corn, oats, rice, potatoes, and pasta. So with this book, we wanted to offer the best naturally keto recipes (with high-fat, low-carb ingredients), rework some of our favorite recipes using keto-friendly ingredients, ensure that vegetables were represented, find alternatives to carb-heavy staples, and present keto options for must-have classics. Along the way, we found ingredient swaps that do the job while tasting good.

Keto guidelines recommend that eaters consume 70 to 75 percent of their daily calories from fats and 20 to 25 percent from proteins, but less than 5 percent from net carbohydrates. We used these macronutrient percentages to develop our recipes so you can mix and match them to achieve the goal of your day's macros. We wanted to make sure the food tasted delicious and not fatty, heavy, or greasy. First we tackled recipes that are a natural fit because they are traditionally made with high-fat and protein-rich ingredients—eggs, cream, cheese, butter, or meat—like our Breakfast Scramble with Gruyère and Herbs (page 33) and Butter-Basted Rib-Eye Steak (page 106).

Next, we tested recipes with low-carb, high-fiber vegetables and paired them with high-fat cheeses, nuts, and oil, as in our satisfying Grilled Vegetable Plate with Burrata and Pistachio-Tarragon Pesto (page 164) and our Super Cobb Salad (page 156).

Then there were favorites like pancakes, tacos, chicken noodle soup, and chocolate chip cookies for which we created keto options in different ways, such as reworking chicken noodle soup with zucchini noodles. It's comforting, gives you the right amount of fat from chicken thighs and olive oil, and reduces carbohydrates by using zucchini instead of conventional pasta. Some exciting recipes evolved out of the development process, like the Smoked Salmon Brunch Plate (page 37) that replaces bread with a roasted portobello mushroom base for a stunning and scrumptious open-faced sandwich. Anyone, keto or not, will want to eat it.

Finding alternatives or swaps for traditional carbohydrates was challenging. How do we make pancakes without flour and sugar? We experimented with almond flour and coconut flour, and thickeners like psyllium husk and flaxseed meal to make ingredient combos that successfully replace wheat flour. We tested a range of sweeteners like erythritol and xylitol to see if they could work in various applications, like baked goods, custards, smoothies, and frozen treats. We learned which foods contained hidden carbs (like garlic and onion) and discovered tricks to add flavor while minimizing carbohydrates. For instance, we put a whole onion into a soup base but took it out after cooking so it imparted flavor but only a negligible amount of carbs to the dish.

We consulted with nutritionist and dietician Alicia A. Romano to guide us in the creation of nutritionally balanced recipes and share her keto health tips, too. With these helpful suggestions and flavorful recipes in hand, keto cooking and eating will be surprisingly easy and very delicious.

Our helpful Five-Day Menu Plans, Keto Meal Prep ideas, and time-saving guidelines will make keto cooking, storage, and reheating convenient. Best of all, you will relish eating food that tastes both familiar and unique, nourishing and varied. Enjoy our flavorful global keto recipes and come back for more.

## Keto History

Ketogenic eating was initially developed to reduce or prevent epileptic seizures in children for whom medications had not worked. In the 1920s, Mayo Clinic doctors like Russell Wilder discovered that children with epilepsy had fewer seizures when their blood sugar was low from being on a high-fat, low-carb diet. A corollary was that because patients were not eating carbs, their bodies were tricked into thinking they were starving and they lost weight. The phenomenon of mimicking starvation to stop epilepsy had been known about for hundreds of years but the term "ketosis" was only coined in the 20th century. It refers to the metabolic process that converts fats into ketones, which are released into the bloodstream and provide the body's fuel in the place of carbohydrate-generated glucose. Current keto diets evolved from the original. These newer versions are more flexible and easier to manage and maintain.

## Who Can Eat Keto

The ketogenic diet is not appropriate for pregnant or breastfeeding women, people with chronic diseases, and athletes, unless it is especially modified or targeted. If your keto diet was medically prescribed, your care team should provide an appropriate transition protocol.

# KETO AT A GLANCE

ALICIA A. ROMANO, MS, RD, CNSC

The average daily American calorie intake comes from 50 to 60 percent carbohydrates, 20 to 30 percent fats, and 10 to 20 percent proteins. These give us the energy to think, exercise, work, play, and just keep on ticking.

**The ketogenic diet completely flips the amounts of basic macronutrients we consume. Fats now make up 70 to 75 percent of the daily calories, proteins account for 20 to 25 percent, and net carbs (total carbohydrates from which fiber and sugar alcohols are subtracted) are limited to 5 percent or less.**

How does the ketogenic diet accomplish this? It eliminates grains, most fruits, starchy vegetables, legumes, and sweets, replacing their calories with fat calories. How can that work, you wonder? The diet is grounded in historical medical research. Our cells prefer blood sugar (glucose) as their primary energy source. In fact, glucose is the main form of energy for our body, even at rest—the brain alone requires 100 grams of glucose every day, just to keep working!

The glucose we use comes from the breakdown of the carbohydrates we ingest, and our bodies store excess carbohydrates in the form of glycogen in tissue (mainly in the liver and muscle). If the body demands glucose, glycogen is converted into glucose through the process of *glycogenolysis*. But what if there are no carbohydrates left in the body to convert and glycogen stores are depleted?

**When the body does not have access to ingested glucose, it will adapt to using other nutrients.** As glycogen is used, the human body takes alternative routes of energy production through non-carbohydrate sources, using free fatty acids and amino acids through *ketosis* and *gluconeogenesis*, which occur concurrently.

**Gluconeogenesis** is the process of creating glucose from non-carbohydrate sources like certain amino acids (protein) and fatty acids (triglycerides). Essentially, gluconeogenesis ensures that critical limits of glucose are maintained for physiological function so our bodies can keep going even if carbohydrates are absent. Gluconeogenesis provides us with a very minimal amount of glucose—essentially only enough for the brain and other organs to keep working.

**Ketosis** is the process of converting stored and circulating fatty acids into ketones to fuel us. Ketosis can occur under various circumstances, including fasting, starvation, untreated type 1 diabetes, or very low-carbohydrate diets like the ketogenic diet. This process takes place in the liver and gives the body an abundant energy source.

When we shift into ketosis, ketones become our main fuel. Once our bodies have reached a point where fats are regularly being converted to ketones and we are in a state of ketosis, our cells will continue to use ketones as their primary source of energy until we start eating carbohydrates again. Then our bodies will return to converting carbs into glucose.

## ON THE
# AVERAGE AMERICAN DIET

**50–60% CARBS**
**20–30% FAT**
**10–20% PROTEIN**

ON THIS DIET, THE BODY CONVERTS CARBS TO GLUCOSE

**GLUCOSE LEVELS RISE**

**STOREHOUSE**

THE BODY STORES EXTRA GLUCOSE IN THE FORM OF GLYCOGEN UNTIL REQUIRED WHEN THERE IS A LACK OF CARBOHYDRATES

**GLUCOSE PROVIDES FUEL**

GLYCOGEN IS CONVERTED BACK TO GLUCOSE AS NEEDED

# ENERGY
**FOR THE BODY AND PHYSIOLOGICAL FUNCTION**

## WHEN YOU SWITCH TO THE
# KETO DIET

**70–75% FAT**
**20–25% PROTEIN**
**<5% NET CARBS**

AS CARBS ARE LESS ABUNDANT FOR THE BODY TO CONVERT TO GLUCOSE

**GLUCOSE LEVELS FALL**

**STOREHOUSE**

THE BODY USES UP GLYCOGEN STORED FROM A HIGH-CARB DIET

WHEN THE BODY GOES INTO KETOSIS, IT STILL REQUIRES GLUCOSE FOR THE ORGANS TO KEEP WORKING

THE BODY SWITCHES TO CONVERTING FATTY ACIDS INTO KETONES

**KETONES PROVIDE FUEL**

AS THE BODY MAKES KETONES, IT ALSO CONVERTS NON-CARB NUTRIENTS INTO SMALL AMOUNTS OF GLUCOSE

# ENERGY
**FOR THE BODY**

# ENERGY
**FOR BASIC PHYSIOLOGICAL FUNCTION**

# KNOW YOUR MACROS

On the keto diet, you will hear the word "macro" often. Macro is short for macronutrients. Macronutrients are nutrients we eat in large quantities. We divide these into three broad categories—carbohydrates, fats, and proteins. The human diet also consists of micronutrients, which are just as essential to good health. These "micros" include vitamins and minerals.

To eat keto, we substitute one macro or major fuel source—carbohydrates—for another—fats. "Knowing your macro" means knowing how many calories you need to acquire daily from each of your macronutrients to maintain ketosis. This means that of the total calories you consume each day, 70 to 75 percent should come from fats, 20 to 25 percent from proteins, but only 5 percent or less from net carbs. These macros are individually calculated in grams: Fats contain 9 calories per gram, proteins have 4 calories per gram, and carbs also contain 4 calories per gram. Our nutritional chart (page 230) offers a breakdown of each recipe so you can add up your day's meals and know if you are hitting your macros. First you need to determine how many

calories you need, which depends on age, gender, weight, activity level, and BMI (body mass index). Ask your doctor to calculate your BMI and then use a macronutrient calculator (apps or online calculators are easily available). Once you know how many calories you need to eat daily, you can determine how many grams of fats, proteins, and net carbs you need, plan your menus, and start cooking! Measure your ketones every day so you stay on track. The nutritional information in our recipes helps you get the right daily macro ratios. Our suggested menu plans show you how to put together workable recipes for the day and week. Why is this important? By limiting carbs, you maintain your body's metabolic state of ketosis, eating good fats as your primary energy source. You don't eat too much protein—it raises your insulin levels and prevents ketosis. You don't eat too little, either, or you lose muscle mass. And you avoid most carbs. Every meal doesn't have to hit your macro ratio but your day's percentages should hit your macro ratio in order to avoid bumping you out of ketosis.

# KETOGENIC FOOD PYRAMID

We created this inverted food pyramid to illustrate how to get your macros on the keto diet.

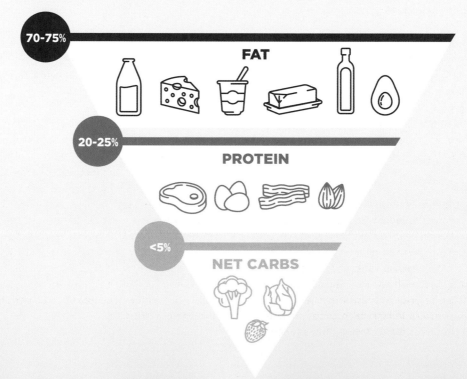

70-75% — FAT
20-25% — PROTEIN
<5% — NET CARBS

## Fats

Fats are your primary source of nutrition on the keto diet because they provide fatty acids, which the liver converts into ketones. These ketones are the body's fuel in the absence of carb-generated glucose.

Fats exist in different forms: unsaturated, saturated, and trans. We use both unsaturated and saturated fats in our keto recipes. Trans fats are unhealthy and should be avoided on any diet.

**Unsaturated fats** are derived from plant-based foods including nuts, seeds, olives, avocados and their oils, as well as from fatty fish. Diverse unsaturated fats in your diet will give you a wide range of fatty acids, vitamins, and minerals.

**Saturated fats** are mainly found in animal-based foods and include the marbling in meat, poultry skin, lard, dairy fats, and butter. Coconut oil is also a saturated fat.

Medium chain triglycerides (MCTs) are a kind of saturated fat, commonly used in the ketogenic diet because they may produce ketones more easily than long chain fats. Certain MCTs bypass the liver and convert directly into ketones, thus helping maintain ketosis. MCTs are found in coconut products (coconut oil, coconut flesh) and via commercially produced MCT oil (which may contain other additives and preservatives). For this book, we used only naturally occurring MCTs.

**Trans fats** (trans-fatty acids) occur naturally in small quantities in some meat and dairy products but most are formed when hydrogen is industrially added to vegetable oil. Trans fats are also found in nondairy creamers, margarine, and some frozen doughs and pizza crusts. These fats raise your bad cholesterol (LDL) and lower your good cholesterol (HDL); therefore, we don't use them.

## Protein

Proteins make up the next largest macronutrient in the keto diet. Proteins help build bone, muscle, cartilage, and blood. They are eaten in moderation on the keto diet because too much protein can prevent your body from going into ketosis. Choosing a variety of proteins from fresh meat, poultry, and fish rich in omega-3 fatty acids is essential to optimize your nutritional intake. You can also find healthy proteins in high-fat sources such as nuts, seeds, nut butters, cream, cheese, and whole-milk

yogurt. Highly processed meats are also proteins but it is important to limit consumption of these as they contain high levels of saturated fat, sodium, and preservatives.

## Carbohydrates

Carbohydrates should be eaten sparingly on the keto diet to maintain the production of ketones by preventing the body from falling back into the habit of converting carbs to glucose. Carbohydrates come from a variety of whole foods including grains, starches, fruits, vegetables, and dairy products as well as from processed foods like sweets, treats, soft drinks, or sugar-sweetened beverages, which are not good for your health. The most appropriate sources of carbs for the keto diet are low in sugars and high in fiber and water content: Think leafy greens; non-starchy vegetables such as broccoli, zucchini, cucumbers, bell peppers, eggplant; and some berries.

To calculate carbohydrate consumption, we consider the total amount of carbs consumed—the carbs that are absorbed by the body, referred to as net carbohydrates; and two other carbohydrates that are not absorbed—fiber and sugar alcohol.

**Fiber** is a type of carbohydrate that cannot be broken down into digestible sugar molecules and therefore passes through the intestinal tract relatively intact; this aids in digestion, causes less impact on the blood sugar response, and does not impart calories.

**Sugar alcohols** are organic compounds that can occur naturally in certain fruits and vegetables (such naturally occurring carbs are called polyols and can be found in mushrooms, cauliflower, plums, peaches, and apricots) or be produced industrially. Because they are carbs that are not fully absorbed in the digestive tract, they have a minimal impact on a person's blood sugar and glycemic response.

For the keto diet, the focus is on the artificial form of sugar alcohols (in the form of sweeteners like erythritol, xylitol, isomalt, lactitol, and maltitol) when accounting for their effect on net carbohydrates. Thanks to their incomplete absorption, added sugar alcohols can be subtracted from total grams of carbohydrates when evaluating net carbs on a nutrition label. For example, if you purchase a packaged product that contains 20 grams of carbohydrates with 16 grams of sugar alcohols, the net carbohydrates in that product would be 4 grams.

**Net carbohydrates** are carbohydrates that the body absorbs. Net carbohydrates are calculated by subtracting the carbohydrate grams of fiber (and sugar alcohols, if a low-carb sweetener is used) per serving from the total carbohydrates per serving. For example, if you eat an item that has 15 grams of carbohydrates and 7 grams of fiber, your net carb intake equals 7 subtracted from 15, which is 8 grams. If the item also contains 2 grams of sugar alcohols, subtract those as well. Your net carb intake will then be 6 grams.

*Be aware that overconsumption of sugar alcohols (more than 20 to 30 grams per day), especially in their synthetic form, can lead to digestive upset such as abdominal cramping and diarrhea, and you should monitor your intake to determine your tolerance.*

# THE CHALLENGES OF KETOSIS

Managing the new order of things on the keto diet—eating more fats and proteins, and fewer carbs—and maintaining overall dietary balance might be challenging. The recipes in this book are designed to prevent imbalance and boredom and add variety to your diet while never losing sight of your macronutrient percentages.

## Starting Off

When you start the keto diet and change your eating habits, you may face side effects that include fatigue, bad breath, nausea, vomiting, constipation, irritability, brain fog, and sleep disturbances. These symptoms, which might show up for the first several days, are commonly called the "keto flu."

## The Keto Flu

Symptoms vary greatly and depend largely on your earlier health and dietary patterns. Some people never experience symptoms as they transition into the diet but others do. The duration of keto flu symptoms may vary, but can last for the first few days of the diet. If you experience prolonged symptoms for more than seven days, seek attention from your health care team. In some cases, going "cold turkey" from a standard American diet to a ketogenic diet may not be the appropriate dietary change for you. A slower transition may help mitigate uncomfortable keto flu symptoms while helping you to adjust to the change of diet and lifestyle. Unfortunately, there is no evidence-based or universal protocol for initiating or "easing into" the ketogenic diet; however, gradually reducing carbohydrate intake while increasing fat intake over time may work.

Take the story of Mr. CQ. He ate a generally healthy diet, with a macronutrient balance of 30 percent protein, 40 percent carbohydrates, and 30 percent fat. When he tried to go headlong into the ketogenic diet, he developed keto flu symptoms. When he felt that these had persisted for too long, he consulted a medical expert, who eased him into the transition by reducing carbohydrate intake by 50 percent each week until his macro goals were reached.

| Week 1 | Week 2 | Week 3 |
|---|---|---|
| 40% PROTEIN | 40% PROTEIN | 25% PROTEIN |
| 20% CARBS | 10% CARBS | 5% CARBS |
| 40% FAT | 50% FAT | 70% FAT |

## Managing Symptoms

If you do experience keto flu symptoms, here are some ways to manage them. With the right planning, tracking, and hydration, you should be able to ease into the new diet satisfactorily.

» **STAY WELL HYDRATED.** Any drastic shifts in the diet can cause dehydration. Drink plenty of water regularly and get enough sodium. If your sodium intake is lacking and your doctor recommends supplementing electrolytes, drinking broth can help. Doctors say you should not consume more than 2300 mg of sodium daily.

» **MAINTAIN FIBER IN YOUR DIET.** Since you are eating less grain, fruits, and vegetables on this diet, you will eat less fiber. But fiber is an important nutrient that aids in proper digestion, so make sure you are eating a colorful variety of low-carbohydrate vegetables like leafy greens, broccoli, cauliflower, cucumbers, and a sprinkling of low-carbohydrate fruits like blackberries and raspberries which contain fiber, vitamins, and minerals.

» **TRACK YOUR MACROS.** Keep a log. This will be the most efficient way of making sure you are eating enough fat and staying in line with your macronutrient ranges. If your macronutrient intake is inadequate (often seen as inadequate fat intake), you may continue to lack energy during the day.

» **ADJUST YOUR CARBOHYDRATES.** The ketogenic diet is highly individualized. If your symptoms persist, especially feelings of fatigue or low energy, you may be over-restricting your carbohydrates. This may be a good time to visit with a medical professional to optimize your plan.

» **BE AWARE OF GIMMICKS.** It is not necessary to purchase expensive supplements online to help you off-set any symptoms you may be feeling. With the appropriate amount of time, hydration, and dietary manipulation, you should get through the keto flu phase.

## Intermittent Fasting

Intermittent fasting is an intentional and complete restriction of macronutrients for a length of time necessary to deplete the body's glycogen stores, so it can begin to turn fat into fuel. It may optimize the process of ketosis and the ability to maintain it. Unlike the concept of prolonged fasting for 24-plus hours, intermittent fasting restricts the eating window during the day to 6 to 12 hours, extending the fasting window to 12 to 18 hours. When integrated with the ketogenic diet, intermittent fasting may accelerate the depletion of glycogen, reducing the time it takes to achieve ketosis.

**» URINE TESTING:** The most widely available, inexpensive, and non-invasive method of ketone testing, the urine test is less accurate than the blood test for measuring ketone production and breakdown. Also, as the body adapts to excreting fewer ketones in the urine, the test can become less accurate.

**» BREATH TESTING:** A newer non-invasive technology to measure ketones, the breath test requires a device that measures acetone (metabolic waste), providing results that relate to low blood ketone levels. However, it is also less accurate than blood testing.

# EATING NATURALLY ON KETO

The basis of the ketogenic diet is to emphasize fat, moderate protein, and limit carbohydrate intake but we also want your diet to be varied and nutritionally beneficial. We encourage eating healthy varieties of the three macronutrients and offer recipes that let you eat naturally and nutritiously. You should aim to consume fiber, vitamins, and minerals every day.

With any specialized diet, it is important to be aware of the potential lifestyle challenges the diet may pose and be prepared for cooking at home and eating out. Eating at home is the easiest way to control your food choices and the ingredients you cook with.

But it can also come with its challenges. First there is the extra time and effort it takes to plan and prepare meals you are not used to cooking. Our Five-Day Menu Plans, and the Keto Meal Prep suggestions accompanying recipes will help you to plan ahead and shop for ingredients to make the recipes in this book.

## To Start

- » Establish a keto-friendly pantry
- » Stick to whole foods when possible
- » Take the time to meal plan and prep

A keto-friendly pantry (see page 13) is an excellent starting point when transitioning to a keto lifestyle. Look through the foods you have in your home, identifying those that fall in line with the ketogenic diet. It is important to remember that highly processed foods may contain hidden ingredients that may hinder your

## Tracking and Testing Ketones

Calculate your macros and use the nutritional information in our recipes to ensure you are getting 70 to 75 percent of your calories from fats, 20 to 25 percent from proteins, and 5 percent or less from carbs each day. You also need to test your ketones regularly to ensure that you are in ketosis. There are various types of ketones formed in the body, including **acetone**, **acetoacetic acid**, and **beta-hydroxybutyric acid.** While the presence of ketones can actually be detected in the breath of a person in ketosis—the breath smells characteristically fruity or acetone-like—measuring ketone levels with blood, urine, or breath tests is the most objective way to determine if you are in ketosis. Each method has its own benefits and limitations. The frequency of testing body ketones is also highly individualized and should be discussed with your healthcare team.

**» BLOOD TESTING:** This is the most accurate way to measure ketosis. This test measures beta-hydroxybutyrate, the most abundant ketone in the blood, and requires the purchase of test strips and a measuring device, and a finger prick for testing the blood.

Include recipe ingredients in your grocery list and take the time to shop to keep your refrigerator and pantry well stocked. A keto-friendly grocery list will make shopping trips easier. In general, sticking to fresh whole foods that fall in the keto guidelines (for example, fresh meats, fish and poultry, nuts and seeds, avocados, oils and other fats, leafy greens, cauliflower, and berries) is the best place to start. Pantry items such as keto-friendly sauces, marinades, and dressings and broths without added sugars may be welcome additions.

## Cooking Ahead

Preparing meals in batches on the weekend will reduce extra cooking time during the week, making it easier to stick to your diet. Use our Keto Meal Prep guidelines to decide what parts of dishes can be made ahead, reheated, or easily packed for lunch and snacks so you are prepared for each day. Weighing and measuring ingredients and foods with a kitchen scale, especially in the very beginning of the diet, is the easiest way to learn appropriate portions based on your individual dietary needs.

## Eating Out

With planning and preparation, eating out is possible on the keto diet. Be mindful of food choices and use macro ratios as a basis for picking your meal. Scanning the menu ahead of time can help you decide. Simply prepared proteins paired with non-starchy vegetables (leafy greens, crucifers, etc.) and healthy fats are easy to find. Using oil and vinegar instead of premade salad dressing, and asking for avocado, olives, slivered nuts, and cheese are great ways to optimize fats and maintain low carbs. Note that sauces, gravies, dressings, and marinades often contain hidden carbohydrates. Protein portions tend to be very large in restaurants so you can box up half of your protein to eat later.

progress on this diet. Removing all foods from your home that do not fall into keto guidelines may not be manageable, if you have young children at home or those who do not follow the diet. This may mean keeping a "keto only" section of the cabinet and refrigerator for easy access to the ingredients you need.

## Planning Time and Shopping List

Once you have established your keto-friendly pantry, take time to plan out your meals. This step is non-negotiable and is essential to reaching your macronutrient goals. Write out specific meals or recipes that you would like to prepare. Plan a full week's worth of meals, and calculate their macronutrient information, using our recipe nutritionals. You will also find a helpful nutritional chart you can use (see page 230).

## About The Nutritionist

Alicia A. Romano, MS, RD, CNSC, is a registered dietitian and nutritionist with over 10 years of experience in nutrition support, digestive health, oncology, sports nutrition, and healthy living.

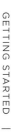

# COOKING KETO

Changing the way you think about food—eating and cooking it—can be challenging. To make the transition as easy as possible, this book provides user-friendly, appetizing, and inventive recipes that mostly use familiar everyday ingredients, as well as some new ones you will be glad to add to your cooking repertoire.

» Each recipe has nutritional information (calories, fats, proteins, net carbs, fiber, sugar alcohols, and total carbs) so you can calculate your daily macros

» Recipes offer suggestions for keto side dishes or accompaniments to help you plan complete meals

» Our Five-Day Menu Plans (see page 17) give you an idea of how to combine recipes creatively while meeting nutrition goals

» If you eat more carbs at one meal, plan to eat lower carb dishes at other meals during the day

» Keep track of your nutritional count and test yourself regularly (see page 10) to ensure that you are reaching and maintaining ketosis

# OUR KETO PANTRY

Here is a starter list of ingredients, including basic fats, proteins, carbohydrates, and flavorings (which also contain carbs) used in our recipes, with suggestions for ingredients to moderate or avoid. We also suggest ingredient substitutions in recipes, when appropriate.

## FATS

**Dairy Products
(Full Fat Only)**
Butter
Cheese: *Blue cheese,
    burrata, cheddar,
    fontina, goat cheese,
    Gruyère, mozzarella,
    Parmesan*
Cream cheese
Half & half
Heavy cream
Sour cream
Yogurt

**Non-Dairy Products**
Almond milk
Coconut (unsweetened):
*Cream, milk*

**Oils**
Avocado oil
Coconut oil
Olive oil
Sesame oil
Vegetable Oil

## PROTEINS

**Animal Proteins**
Beef: *Ground, Flank
    steak, rib-eye steak,
    steak tips*
Chicken: *Breast, ground
    chicken, thighs,
    whole chicken*
Eggs
Fish & Seafood: *Cod,
    salmon (fresh and
    smoked), scallops, sea
    bass, shrimp, tuna*
Lamb
Pork: *Bacon, chops,
    chorizo, country-style
    ribs, ground pork,
    prosciutto*
Turkey

**Other Proteins**
Nuts: *Almonds, hazel-
    nuts, macadamia nuts,
    peanuts, pine nuts,
    pecans, pistachios*
Seeds: *Pepitas, sesame*

## CARBOHYDRATES

Arugula
Asparagus
Avocado
Bell peppers
Bok choy
Broccoli
Broccoli rabe
Cabbage
Carrots
Cauliflower
Celery
Fennel
Garlic
Ginger
Lettuce
Kale
Mushrooms: *Cremini,
    portobello, shiitake*
Poblano chiles
Olives
Radish
Scallions
Shallots
Shirataki noodles
Spinach

Summer squash
Thai chiles
Zucchini

**To Moderate**
Blueberries
Lemon
Lime
Onions
Orange
Raspberries
Tomatoes: *Fresh,
    sun-dried, tomato
    paste*
Strawberries

**To Avoid**
Read nutrition informa-
tion before you buy
products like ketchup,
non-dairy creamers,
and salad dressings to
limit your consumption
of hidden carbs. See
page 14 for other foods
to avoid.

## ADDING FLAVOR

**Herbs**
Basil
Chives
Cilantro
Dill
Mint
Oregano
Parsley
Rosemary
Sage
Tarragon
Thyme

**Salt**
Kosher
Table

**Spices**
Bay leaves
Cardamom
Cayenne
Chipotle
Cinnamon
Cloves
Coriander

Cumin
Curry powder
Fennel seed
Garam masala
Mustard
Paprika
Red pepper flakes
Turmeric

**Flour/Thickeners**
Almond flour
Chia seeds

Coconut flour
Flax
Psyllium husk
Xanthan gum

**More**
Vinegar: *Red wine,
    rice, white wine*
Capers
Chocolate chips,
    sugar-free

Coconut
    (unsweetened):
    *Flaked, shredded*
Gochujang
Horseradish
Hot sauce
Kimchi
Miso
Vanilla: *Beans,
    extract*

## LOW-CARB SWEETENERS

In our tests, erythritol and Swerve proved to be the favorite low-carb sweeteners for our recipes. We defaulted to erythritol as it is the most pure sugar alcohol. Feel free to use the sweetener of your choice.

### SUGAR ALCOHOLS
#### Erythritol
This is our preferred sweetener. When used in a 1:1 ratio to replace sugar, it is a little less sweet. Erythritol is available in powdered and granulated form and was most reliable when making syrups, beverages, desserts, and baked goods. It had no noticeable aftertaste.

#### Swerve
This brand-name sugar replacement contains erythritol mixed with proprietary ingredients. It can be used in the same proportions as erythritol and is slightly sweeter. It is also available in granulated and powdered form and had no noticeable aftertaste.

#### Monk Fruit
This sugar alcohol made from monk fruit extract is available in liquid, powdered, and granulated form. The concentrated liquid requires only three drops per teaspoon of erythritol, but is hard to incorporate into baked goods. The powdered form blends monk fruit extract with erythritol, and sweetens like pure erythritol. It sometimes has an off-flavor/menthol taste that tasters did not like.

#### Xylitol
This is a 1:1 replacement for erythritol. Although the taste of xylitol was on par with other sugar alcohol products, when we used it in cheesecake and panna cotta, the desserts did not set up properly.

### OTHER SWEETENERS
#### Splenda
Splenda, made from sucralose, is slightly sweeter than erythritol. It worked for baking but it is not available in powdered form and does not dissolve as well as erythritol.

#### Stevia
Stevia ranked last in our sweetener tests. It is≈highly concentrated so it is used in very small amounts. It did not help the texture of baked goods, and tasters also noticed a chemical aftertaste. For this reason, stevia is best used to sweeten beverages, rather than in baked goods.

### Alcohol
Beer and wine contain some carbs, as does rum. Spirits like tequila, vodka, and whiskey contain none. However, according to our nutritionist, while an occasional drink may be all right, the body metabolizes alcohol differently on the keto diet.

## TO AVOID

**High-Carb Ingredients**
Apples
Bananas
Beans
Bread
Cashews
Cereal
Fruit juices
Lentils
Pasta
Peas
Pineapple
Plantains
Potatoes
Reduced-fat and nonfat
    dairy products
Sweet potatoes
Watermelon
Yams

**Processed Fats and Proteins**
Hydrogenated oils
Processed meats: *Bologna, hot dogs, salami*
Processed snacks: *Sweet and savory snacks like chips, cookies, pretzels*

# KETO KITCHEN WISDOM

Here are some of the interesting discoveries that test cooks made during the keto recipe testing process. Keeping these tips in mind will help you shop, cook, store, and eat your best keto.

## Embrace Fat

Keep good fats like butter, coconut oil, ghee, and olive oil on hand. Avocado oil, canola oil, grapeseed oil, and bacon fat work really well for our recipes, too.

We found that incorporating additional fat into dishes was not just about adding more fat or oil. Emulsified sauces made with cauliflower, cheese, high-fat dairy, or nuts are ways to keep a dish from being an oil-slick while maintaining keto's required high fat content.

## Instead of an Apple a Day, Eat...

It's what your mama told you, but you can't eat an apple a day on the keto diet! Many fruits and vegetables that are "good for you" are so carb-heavy they can throw you out of ketosis. This was challenging when we first started recipe development. But we learned that being on keto doesn't mean you can't eat any vegetables. To reduce carbs, add fiber, and still make keto eating healthy and enjoyable, we used colorful low-carb, fiber-rich vegetables like broccoli rabe, cabbage, cauliflower, and kale. We added more higher-carb ones—like tomatoes or onions—in small quantities to impart taste but not too many carbohydrates. And we made use of ingredients like coconut, chia seeds, and psyllium husk to give fiber and replace high-carb wheat and cornstarch. There will always be some carbs in ingredients but we focused on creatively using low-carb ones in small amounts to suit your nutrient quotas.

## Salt It

Another way to bring out a dish's flavors is to salt it well, especially when traditional flavorings like tomato sauce and onions are limited. We also found that sprinkling salt on sweet treats like our Dark Chocolate Clusters (page 216) heightened sweetness in much the same way that a cookie benefits from adding salt to the dough.

## Herb It Up

Herbs and spices do for salads, mains, and side dishes what vanilla does for sweet treats. Fresh or dried thyme, tarragon, dill, parsley, rosemary, mint, and cilantro; spices like turmeric, cayenne, coriander, and cumin; and spice blends like garam masala add savory flavor and a pleasant color to our recipes, without significantly impacting carb content.

## Make All Things Nice

Sometimes a low-carb sweetener does not lend enough sweetness to desserts or shakes, which can inhibit a dish's other flavors from shining through. That's when a touch of vanilla; orange, lime, or lemon zest; or cinnamon and cardamom can give the much-needed illusion of sweetness or fruity flavor.

## Be Free, Be Flexible

Since grains are rich in carbohydrates, they are not included on the keto diet. We found that almond flour, coconut flour, flaxseed meal, and quinoa flakes and flour are great low-carb alternatives to use for keto cookies, breads, pizza dough, and granola. Our test cooks discovered that a combination of flours was often best; almond flour gave texture, structure, and neutral flavor while coconut flour helped the dough or batter retain moisture and become tender after baking.

## Thicken The Thin

Since we couldn't use flour or cornstarch in our keto sauces, we tested natural thickeners—vegetable emulsions and purees, reductions of stocks, and nut butters (peanut and almond). We also tried thickeners and binders like flax meal, psyllium husk, and xanthan gum to bring together doughs and batters. We have indicated where thickeners are optional.

Thickening soups without a starch can be very difficult. High-fiber vegetables like cauliflower, broccoli, or spinach that one can puree, or even almond flour, work well as swaps. They are much more effective than simply reducing the liquid or adding ingredients like sour cream, cheese, or yogurt.

### Swaps

| In | Out |
|---|---|
| Almond, coconut, or quinoa flakes | Wheat flour |
| Pork rinds (chicharrones) Nuts + coconut flakes | Bread crumbs |
| Shallots | Onion |
| Shirataki noodles, zucchini noodles | Wheat pasta |
| Cauliflower | Pasta, potatoes, rice, sweet potatoes |

## Measure, Store, Rest

### GIVE WEIGHT SOME THOUGHT AND LET IT FLOW

» For the keto diet, more than many others, weighing ingredients is critical. When weight measurements are given, always use weight measurements over volume for the most accuracy.

» When measuring coconut oil, melting it first makes it easier to measure and more accurate.

### STORE AND CHILL

» Store nut-based flours and coconut flour in the refrigerator once opened for a longer shelf life. The oils in nut-based flours will turn the flours rancid more quickly than standard starch-based flours.

» When storing leftovers, store in individual portions for easier reheating.

### GIVE IT A REST

» When baking with nut and coconut flours, resting the dough or batter is nearly always beneficial. It allows the flours to better absorb moisture, making for a more cohesive dough. We did this with our keto bread, muffins, and cookies. A rest was not helpful with the pizza dough however.

# FIVE-DAY MENU PLANS

We offer these sample menu plans because planning ahead is key on the keto diet. Choosing meal macros that work for you personally is critical, though. Our menus provide a range of calories per day. Select what works for you. Our Keto Meal Prep tips will allow you to partially prepare dishes and keep them well chilled or frozen till needed.

## WEEK ONE

| Monday | | Cal | Total Fat (g) | Protein (g) | Net Carbs (g) | Total Carbs (g) | Fiber (g) | Sugar Alcohols (g) |
|---|---|---|---|---|---|---|---|---|
| Breakfast | Blueberry Muffin (page 41) | 200 | 16 | 6 | 5 | 16 | 3 | 8 |
| Lunch | Curried Chicken Salad with Pistachios (page 74) | 570 | 42 | 42 | 4 | 7 | 3 | 0 |
| Snack | Bacon-Ranch Cheese Balls (page 198) | 190 | 16 | 9 | 1 | 2 | 1 | 0 |
| Dinner | Vietnamese Pork and Noodle Bowls (page 125) | 790 | 63 | 40 | 8 | 16 | 8 | 0 |
| **TOTALS** | | **1750** | **137** | **97** | **18** | **41** | **15** | **8** |
| **Tuesday** | | | | | | | | |
| Breakfast | Muffin Tin Frittatas with Asparagus and Fontina Cheese (page 34) | 410 | 33 | 25 | 3 | 4 | 1 | 0 |
| Lunch | Vietnamese Pork and Noodle Bowls (page 125) | 790 | 63 | 40 | 8 | 16 | 8 | 0 |
| Snack | Spiced Nut Mix (page 202) | 230 | 22 | 6 | 2 | 6 | 4 | 0 |
| Dinner | One-Pan Steak Fajitas (without tortillas) (page 109) | 680 | 57 | 40 | 7 | 18 | 11 | 0 |
| **TOTALS** | | **2110** | **169** | **111** | **20** | **44** | **24** | **0** |
| **Wednesday** | | | | | | | | |
| Breakfast | Blueberry Muffin (page 41) | 200 | 16 | 6 | 5 | 16 | 3 | 8 |
| Lunch | One-Pan Steak Fajitas (without tortillas) (page 109) | 680 | 51 | 40 | 7 | 18 | 11 | 0 |
| Dinner | Pan-Seared Salmon with Cucumber-Ginger Relish (page 145) | 490 | 37 | 30 | 3 | 5 | 2 | 0 |
| Side | Cauliflower Rice (page 183) | 190 | 18 | 2 | 4 | 6 | 2 | 0 |
| **TOTALS** | | **1560** | **122** | **78** | **19** | **45** | **18** | **8** |
| **Thursday** | | | | | | | | |
| Breakfast | Muffin Tin Frittatas with Asparagus and Fontina Cheese (page 34) | 410 | 33 | 25 | 3 | 4 | 1 | 0 |
| Lunch | Bistro Salad with Salmon and Avocado (page 134) | 610 | 46 | 39 | 5 | 12 | 7 | 0 |
| Snack | Seeded Crackers (page 206) | 170 | 13 | 11 | 1 | 2 | 1 | 0 |
| Dinner | Chicken Zoodle Soup (page 54) | 470 | 35 | 30 | 6 | 8 | 2 | 0 |
| Treat | Chocolate Mug Cake (page 224) | 350 | 31 | 10 | 6 | 19 | 5 | 8 |
| **TOTALS** | | **2010** | **158** | **115** | **21** | **45** | **16** | **8** |
| **Friday** | | | | | | | | |
| Breakfast | Breakfast Scramble with Gruyère and Herbs (page 33) | 420 | 35 | 23 | 1 | 1 | 0 | 0 |
| Lunch | Chicken Zoodle Soup (page 54) | 470 | 35 | 30 | 6 | 8 | 2 | 0 |
| Dinner | Keto Pizza with Prosciutto, Arugula, and Ricotta (page 163) | 470 | 37 | 29 | 5 | 7 | 2 | 0 |
| Side | Kale Caesar Salad (page 192) | 420 | 38 | 13 | 4 | 6 | 2 | 0 |
| **TOTALS** | | **1780** | **145** | **95** | **16** | **22** | **6** | **0** |

# WEEK TWO

## Monday

| | | Cal | Total Fat (g) | Protein (g) | Net Carbs (g) | Total Carbs (g) | Fiber (g) | Sugar Alcohols (g) |
|---|---|---|---|---|---|---|---|---|
| Breakfast | Muffin Tin Frittatas with Sausage, Bell Pepper, and Cheddar (page 34) | 530 | 40 | 36 | 5 | 6 | 1 | 0 |
| Lunch | Chicken Salad with Fresh Herbs (page 74) | 470 | 34 | 38 | 1 | 1 | 0 | 0 |
| Snack | Mediterranean Whipped Almond Dip (page 213) | 280 | 27 | 6 | 4 | 6 | 2 | 0 |
| Snack | 3 celery stalks (4 ounces) | 20 | 0 | 1 | 2 | 4 | 2 | 0 |
| Dinner | Easy Ground Beef Chili (page 69) | 640 | 50 | 35 | 8 | 14 | 6 | 0 |
| **TOTALS** | | **1940** | **151** | **116** | **19** | **31** | **11** | **0** |

## Tuesday

| | | | | | | | | |
|---|---|---|---|---|---|---|---|---|
| Breakfast | Smoked Salmon Brunch Plate (page 37) | 470 | 39 | 22 | 7 | 10 | 3 | 0 |
| Lunch | Easy Ground Beef Chili (page 69) | 640 | 50 | 35 | 8 | 14 | 6 | 0 |
| Dinner | Nut-Crusted Pork Chops (page 117) | 670 | 53 | 42 | 5 | 9 | 4 | 0 |
| Side | Roasted Broccoli Salad (page 179) | 240 | 22 | 4 | 5 | 12 | 7 | 0 |
| **TOTALS** | | **2020** | **164** | **103** | **25** | **45** | **20** | **0** |

## Wednesday

| | | | | | | | | |
|---|---|---|---|---|---|---|---|---|
| Breakfast | Pancakes (page 38) | 420 | 37 | 15 | 6 | 17 | 5 | 6 |
| Snack | Green Smoothie (page 49) | 370 | 38 | 2 | 3 | 15 | 4 | 8 |
| Lunch | Chicken Salad with Fresh Herbs (page 74) | 470 | 34 | 38 | 1 | 1 | 0 | 0 |
| Dinner | Lemon-Thyme Pork Tenderloin with Green Beans (page 122) | 630 | 47 | 41 | 5 | 9 | 4 | 0 |
| Treat | Chocolate-Covered Peanut Butter Bites (page 219) | 110 | 11 | 3 | 3 | 17 | 0 | 14 |
| **TOTALS** | | **2000** | **167** | **99** | **18** | **59** | **13** | **28** |

## Thursday

| | | | | | | | | |
|---|---|---|---|---|---|---|---|---|
| Breakfast | Breakfast Scramble with Gruyère and Herbs (page 46) | 420 | 35 | 23 | 1 | 1 | 0 | 0 |
| Lunch | Smoked Salmon Brunch Plate (page 37) | 470 | 39 | 22 | 7 | 10 | 3 | 0 |
| Snack | Spiced Nut Mix (page 202) | 230 | 22 | 6 | 2 | 6 | 4 | 0 |
| Dinner | Chicken Baked in Foil with Fennel and Radishes (page 84) | 650 | 47 | 43 | 8 | 13 | 5 | 0 |
| **TOTALS** | | **1770** | **143** | **94** | **18** | **30** | **12** | **0** |

## Friday

| | | | | | | | | |
|---|---|---|---|---|---|---|---|---|
| Breakfast | Overnight Chia Pudding with Raspberries and Almonds (page 46) | 380 | 33 | 7 | 6 | 22 | 10 | 6 |
| Lunch | Classic Tuna Salad with Eggs, Radishes, and Capers (page 137) | 410 | 33 | 24 | 2 | 3 | 1 | 0 |
| Snack | Snack Bar (page 205) | 250 | 21 | 9 | 6 | 18 | 4 | 8 |
| Dinner | Pan-Seared Steak Tips with Rosemary-Peppercorn Pan Sauce (page 102) | 570 | 45 | 36 | 1 | 1 | 0 | 0 |
| Side | Whipped Cauliflower (page 184) | 150 | 14 | 2 | 4 | 6 | 2 | 0 |
| Treat | Chocolate Chip Cookies (page 220) | 170 | 14 | 4 | 5 | 16 | 2 | 9 |
| **TOTALS** | | **1930** | **160** | **86** | **24** | **66** | **19** | **23** |

# WEEK THREE

## Monday

| | | Cal | Total Fat (g) | Protein (g) | Net Carbs (g) | Total Carbs (g) | Fiber (g) | Sugar Alcohols (g) |
|---|---|---|---|---|---|---|---|---|
| Breakfast | Pancakes (page 38) | 420 | 37 | 15 | 6 | 17 | 5 | 6 |
| Lunch | Hearty Beef Stew with Cauliflower and Mushrooms (page 66) | 610 | 47 | 38 | 9 | 13 | 4 | 0 |
| Snack | Seeded Crackers (page 206) | 170 | 13 | 11 | 1 | 2 | 1 | 0 |
| Dinner | Creamy Shirataki Noodles with Spinach, Mushrooms, and Pecorino (page 172) | 580 | 52 | 15 | 6 | 11 | 5 | 0 |
| **TOTALS** | | **1780** | **149** | **79** | **22** | **43** | **15** | **6** |

## Tuesday

| | | | | | | | | |
|---|---|---|---|---|---|---|---|---|
| Breakfast | Muffin Tin Frittatas with Mushrooms and Gruyère (page 34) | 430 | 33 | 28 | 5 | 6 | 1 | 0 |
| Lunch | Super Cobb Salad (page 156) | 360 | 29 | 13 | 8 | 13 | 5 | 0 |
| Snack | Bacon-Ranch Cheese Balls (page 198) | 190 | 16 | 9 | 1 | 2 | 1 | 0 |
| Dinner | Thai Chicken Lettuce Wraps (page 78) | 600 | 45 | 40 | 8 | 11 | 3 | 0 |
| **TOTALS** | | **1580** | **123** | **90** | **22** | **32** | **10** | **0** |

## Wednesday

| | | | | | | | | |
|---|---|---|---|---|---|---|---|---|
| Breakfast | Toasted Coconut Porridge (page 45) | 290 | 23 | 7 | 6 | 19 | 10 | 3 |
| Snack | Green Smoothie (page 49) | 370 | 38 | 2 | 3 | 15 | 4 | 8 |
| Lunch | Thai Chicken Lettuce Wraps (page 78) | 600 | 45 | 40 | 8 | 11 | 3 | 0 |
| Dinner | Grilled Thin-Cut Pork Chops with Spicy Barbecue Coleslaw (page 121) | 740 | 53 | 54 | 4 | 7 | 3 | 0 |
| **TOTALS** | | **2000** | **159** | **103** | **21** | **52** | **20** | **11** |

## Thursday

| | | | | | | | | |
|---|---|---|---|---|---|---|---|---|
| Breakfast | Muffin Tin Frittatas with Mushrooms and Gruyère (page 34) | 430 | 33 | 28 | 5 | 6 | 1 | 0 |
| Lunch | Chicken Salad with Smoked Paprika and Almonds (page 74) | 580 | 43 | 42 | 3 | 6 | 3 | 0 |
| Snack | Bacon-Ranch Cheese Balls (page 198) | 190 | 16 | 9 | 1 | 2 | 1 | 0 |
| Dinner | Pan-Roasted Striped Bass with Red Pepper–Hazelnut Relish (page 146) | 480 | 37 | 34 | 2 | 4 | 2 | 0 |
| Side | Broiled Broccoli Rabe (page 180) | 150 | 14 | 3 | 1 | 3 | 2 | 0 |
| **TOTALS** | | **1830** | **143** | **116** | **12** | **21** | **9** | **0** |

## Friday

| | | | | | | | | |
|---|---|---|---|---|---|---|---|---|
| Breakfast | Smoked Salmon Brunch Plate (page 37) | 470 | 39 | 22 | 7 | 10 | 3 | 0 |
| Lunch | Chicken Salad with Smoked Paprika and Almonds (page 74) | 580 | 43 | 42 | 3 | 6 | 3 | 0 |
| Dinner | Butter-Basted Rib-Eye Steak (page 106) | 650 | 57 | 31 | 1 | 1 | 0 | 0 |
| Side | Pan-Roasted Asparagus with Toasted Garlic (page 176) | 160 | 15 | 3 | 3 | 5 | 2 | 0 |
| Treat | Chocolate Chip Cookies (page 220) | 170 | 14 | 4 | 5 | 16 | 2 | 9 |
| **TOTALS** | | **2030** | **168** | **102** | **19** | **38** | **10** | **9** |

**Makes** twelve 5-inch tortillas
**Total Time** 1 hour

## PER TORTILLA
**Cal** 110 | **Total Fat** 9g
**Protein** 5g | **Net Carbs** 1g
**Fiber** 3g | **Total Carbs** 4g

## Why This Recipe Works

Soft, pliable, and tasty, keto tortillas or wraps are hard to find. They either are bound with xanthan gum or have enough powerfully flavored ingredients to overwhelm the most potent fillings. We wanted chew and flexibility without chemical add-ins or off-flavors. We started with a pourable batter and made a crepe-like wrap, but flipping it was difficult and the egg-forward flavor was unpleasant. Next, we attempted a more robust tortilla. A few simple ingredients worked best—almond flour was a great base, flaxseed meal and egg gave us flexibility and chew, and salt kept the tortillas from being bland. The dough came together quickly in the food processor. Letting it rest hydrated the flaxseed meal and gave us time to prep our cooking method, identical to our corn tortilla–making method. We used a cut zipper-lock bag and olive oil spray (to prevent sticking) to flatten out our tortillas before quickly cooking them in a skillet. Leftover tortillas make great chips: Cut each tortilla into six wedges and bake in a single layer on a parchment paper–lined rimmed baking sheet in a 350-degree oven until crisp and the edges are browned, 12 to 15 minutes; let cool completely before serving.

# KETO TORTILLAS

1¼  cups (5 ounces) blanched, finely ground almond flour
½  cup (2 ounces) ground flaxseed meal
2  eggs
½  teaspoon table salt
2  tablespoons extra-virgin olive oil, divided

**1.** Process almond flour, flaxseed meal, eggs, and salt in food processor until rough dough ball forms, about 1 minute. Transfer dough to bowl and cover with plastic wrap; let rest for 10 minutes.

**2.** Pinch off and roll dough into 12 balls (about 1 ounce each). Transfer dough balls to plate and cover with damp paper towel. Cut open seams along sides of 1-gallon zipper-lock bag, leaving bottom seam intact. Spray inside of bag lightly with olive oil spray.

**3.** Heat ½ teaspoon oil in 12-inch nonstick skillet over medium-low heat until shimmering. Using paper towels, carefully wipe out oil, leaving thin film of oil on bottom of skillet. Place 1 dough ball in center of prepared bag. Fold top layer of plastic over ball. Using clear pie plate, press dough flat into 5-inch circle.

**4.** Peel top layer of plastic away from tortilla. Using plastic to lift tortilla from bottom, place exposed side of tortilla in palm of your hand and invert tortilla. Peel away plastic. Carefully flip tortilla into skillet and cook until edges lighten in color, about 2 minutes, flipping halfway through cooking. Transfer tortilla to tortilla warmer or wrap in damp dish towel. Repeat with remaining oil and remaining dough balls, lightly spraying bag with oil spray as needed. Serve.

### Spinach-Herb Tortillas

Add 1 ounce baby spinach and 1 tablespoon minced fresh basil, parsley, or tarragon to processor with almond flour.
**Per Tortilla** Cal 110; Total Fat 9g; Protein 5g; Net Carbs 1g; Fiber 3g; Total Carbs 4g

### Smoky Chipotle Tortillas

Add 1½ teaspoons chipotle chile powder and 1½ teaspoons paprika with almond flour in step 1.
**Per Tortilla** Cal 110; Total Fat 9g; Protein 5g; Net Carbs 2g; Fiber 3g; Total Carbs 5g

### *Keto Meal Prep*

» To store, stack cooled tortillas, separated by sheets of parchment paper, and wrap tightly in plastic wrap. Refrigerate for up to 2 days or freeze for up to 1 month; thaw frozen tortillas overnight in refrigerator before serving.

» To reheat, stack tortillas, separated by sheets of parchment paper, and wrap in damp paper towel. Microwave until pliable, about 30 seconds.

# SEEDED BREAD *terrible*

2¼ cups (9 ounces) blanched, finely ground almond flour

¾ cup (3 ounces) coconut flour

½ cup raw sunflower seeds, divided

6 tablespoons (1½ ounces) powdered psyllium husk, sifted

¼ cup (1 ounce) ground flaxseed meal

2 tablespoons baking powder

1 teaspoon table salt

1¼ cups water

6 large eggs

6 tablespoons unsalted butter, melted

**1.** Adjust oven rack to lowest position and heat oven to 350 degrees. Grease 8½ by 4½-inch loaf pan.

**2.** Whisk almond flour, coconut flour, 6 tablespoons sunflower seeds, psyllium husk, flaxseed meal, baking powder, and salt together in large bowl. Whisk water, eggs, and melted butter together in separate bowl. Stir egg mixture into flour mixture until well combined. Scrape batter into prepared pan. Smooth top, mounding batter slightly in center. Sprinkle with remaining 2 tablespoons sunflower seeds, pressing gently to adhere. Cover and let sit at room temperature for 30 minutes.

**3.** Bake until well browned and skewer inserted in center comes out clean, about 1½ hours, rotating pan halfway through baking.

**4.** Remove bread from oven and let cool in pan on wire rack for 10 minutes. Remove loaf from pan and let cool completely, about 3 hours, before slicing and serving.

### Cheddar-Caraway Bread

Omit sunflower seeds. Add 5 ounces shredded sharp cheddar cheese, 2 teaspoons caraway seeds, and ½ teaspoon dry mustard powder to almond flour mixture before adding egg mixture. Sprinkle loaf with additional 1 ounce shredded sharp cheddar cheese before baking.

**Per ½-inch-thick slice** Cal 230, Total Fat 18g; Protein 9g; Net Carbs 4g; Fiber 6g; Total Carbs 10g

### Cinnamon-Pecan Bread

Omit sunflower seeds. Add ¾ cup chopped toasted pecans, 2 ounces granulated erythritol, and 2 teaspoons ground cinnamon to almond flour mixture before adding egg mixture. Sprinkle loaf with additional 2 tablespoons chopped pecans and press gently to adhere before baking.

**Per ½-inch-thick slice** Cal 220; Total Fat 18g; Protein 7g; Net Carbs 5g; Fiber 6g; Sugar Alcohols 3g; Total Carbs 14g

### *Keto Meal Prep*

» Bread can be wrapped tightly in plastic wrap and refrigerated for up to 1 week. For longer storage, slice bread ½ inch thick, stack, separated by sheets of parchment paper, and wrap tightly in plastic wrap. Bread slices can be frozen for up to 1 month; thaw overnight in refrigerator or microwave for 30 to 45 seconds, flipping halfway through microwaving, before serving.

**Makes** 1 loaf
**Total Time** 2½ hours, plus 3 hours cooling time

---

**PER ½-INCH-THICK SLICE**
**Cal** 210 | **Total Fat** 16g
**Protein** 7g | **Net Carbs** 4g
**Fiber** 6g | **Total Carbs** 10g

---

### Why This Recipe Works

If you ask someone on the keto diet which food they miss most, the answer is almost always bread. There are few commercially available keto options and many recipes out there don't cut it because of the missing gluten. In a regular loaf, wheat gluten forms an elastic network within which air pockets are trapped to create an open-textured slice and a satisfying chew. Without it, you end up with delicate cake-like quick bread. We found that psyllium husk powder was the best gluten substitute—it formed a chewy web-like structure that allowed baking powder to do its job and provide lift and an open crumb. Ground flaxseed meal added an appealing wheaty flavor. With the basic formula set, we tried different mix-ins like seeds, cheese, spices, and nuts. Erythritol is our preferred low-carb sweetener. You can substitute any of your favorite low-carb sweeteners but not all can be substituted 1:1 for erythritol (see page 14). Be sure to sift the psyllium husk to remove any unevenly ground husk. The test kitchen's preferred loaf pan measures 8½ by 4½ inches; if you use a 9 by 5-inch loaf pan, start checking for doneness 5 minutes earlier than advised in the recipe.

**Makes** 8 slices
**Total Time** 35 minutes

## PER SLICE
**Cal** 150 | **Total Fat** 12g
**Protein** 10g | **Net Carbs** 2g
**Fiber** 1g | **Total Carbs** 3g

## Why This Recipe Works

To replicate the combination of starch and well-developed gluten that makes the best conventional pizza crusts chewy, crispy, and delicious, keto recipes turn to ingredients like ground chicken, cauliflower, nut flours, bacon, and cheese. We tried them too. But while we wanted the flavor of traditional pizza, it had to be easy to make. We discounted cauliflower crusts due to their moisture content; without extensive pretreatment, our crusts consistently came out soggy. But using mozzarella for the crust worked really well. It developed an exterior crispness and stayed chewy within; Parmesan aided in browning and gave both crunch and flavor. Almond flour bound the cheeses together and created a dough-like texture. An egg gave us lift; another egg white lent additional structure and height without turning the interior custardy. A preheated baking sheet enhanced crispness too. Best of all we just stirred our ingredients together into a dough, shaping it into a round before baking. Make sure to shred your own mozzarella from a block; preshredded mozzarella contains a starch divider, which impedes melting, which this recipe needs. A baking stone can be used instead of the baking sheet in step 1. Use this crust to make Keto Pizza (page 163).

# PIZZA CRUST

8 ounces whole-milk mozzarella cheese, shredded (2 cups)
⅔ cup (2⅔ ounces) blanched, finely ground almond flour
⅓ cup grated Parmesan cheese
1 large egg plus 1 large white

**1.** Adjust oven rack to lowest position, place inverted baking sheet on rack, and heat oven to 450 degrees. Using wooden spoon, stir all ingredients in bowl until fully combined.

**2.** Using your hands, press dough between 2 large sheets of greased parchment paper into 11-inch round, about ¼ inch thick. Discard top piece of parchment and tidy edges of crust.

**3.** Transfer crust, still on parchment, to pizza peel or second inverted baking sheet, then slide parchment with crust onto heated baking sheet. Bake crust until deep golden brown and edges are crisp, 12 to 15 minutes. Transfer crust to wire rack and discard parchment.

*Keto Meal Prep*

» Pizza crust can be wrapped tightly in plastic wrap and refrigerated for up to 3 days or frozen for up to 1 month; do not thaw frozen crust before reheating. To reheat, place crust on preheated rimmed baking sheet and bake in 400-degree oven for 5 minutes.

1. Toast garlic in 8-inch skillet over medium heat, shaking skillet occasionally, until softened and spotty brown, about 8 minutes. When garlic is cool enough to handle, remove and discard skins and chop coarse. Meanwhile, toast pine nuts in now-empty skillet over medium heat, stirring often, until golden and fragrant, about 4 minutes.

2. Place basil and parsley, if using, in 1-quart zipper-lock bag. Pound bag with flat side of meat pounder or with rolling pin until all leaves are bruised.

3. Process garlic, pine nuts, and herbs in food processor until finely chopped, about 1 minute, scraping down sides of bowl as needed. With processor running, slowly add oil until incorporated. Transfer pesto to bowl, stir in Parmesan, and season with salt and pepper to taste. (Pesto can be refrigerated for up to 3 days or frozen for up to 3 months. To prevent browning, press plastic wrap flush to surface or top with thin layer of olive oil. Bring to room temperature before using.)

# BASIL PESTO

*Very good!*

**Makes** about ¾ cup

## PER 1-TABLESPOON SERVING
**Cal** 120 | **Total Fat** 12g
**Protein** 2g | **Net Carbs** 1g
**Fiber** 0g | **Total Carbs** 1g

Basil pesto tastes great on any sautéed, grilled, or roasted protein, on zucchini noodles, and in our Keto Pizza with Mozzarella, Tomatoes, and Basil Pesto (page 163). Pounding the basil helps release its flavorful oils.

    2  garlic cloves, unpeeled
    ¼  cup pine nuts
    2  cups fresh basil leaves
    2  tablespoons fresh parsley leaves (optional)
    ½  cup extra-virgin olive oil
    ¼  cup grated Parmesan cheese

# PISTACHIO-TARRAGON PESTO

**Makes** about ¾ cup

## PER 1-TABLESPOON SERVING
**Cal** 120 | **Total Fat** 12g
**Protein** 1g | **Net Carbs** 1g
**Fiber** 1g | **Total Carbs** 2g

This pesto is a great alternative to basil pesto. We use it in our Grilled Vegetable Plate with Burrata and Pistachio-Tarragon Pesto (page 164).

    1  cup fresh parsley leaves
    ½  cup fresh tarragon leaves
    ½  cup shelled pistachios, toasted
    1  small garlic clove, chopped
    ⅛  teaspoon table salt
    ½  cup extra-virgin olive oil
    4  teaspoons lemon juice

Process parsley, tarragon, pistachios, garlic, and salt in food processor until finely chopped, about 1 minute, scraping down sides of bowl as needed. With processor running, slowly add oil and lemon juice until incorporated. Transfer pesto to bowl and season with salt and

pepper to taste. (Pesto can be refrigerated for up to 3 days or frozen for up to 3 months. To prevent browning, press plastic wrap flush to surface or top with thin layer of olive oil. Bring to room temperature before using.)

# SALSA VERDE

**Makes** about ¾ cup

### PER 1-TABLESPOON SERVING
**Cal** 70 | **Total Fat** 7g
**Protein** 1g | **Net Carbs** 0g
**Fiber** 1g | **Total Carbs** 1g

Salsa verde is delicious with Fish Tacos (page 142) and Chicken Mole Poblano (page 93).

| | |
|---|---|
| 2¼ | cups fresh parsley leaves |
| ¾ | cup fresh mint leaves |
| 1½ | tablespoons capers, rinsed and minced |
| 2 | anchovy fillets, rinsed and minced |
| 1 | small garlic clove, minced |
| ⅛ | teaspoon table salt |
| 6 | tablespoons extra-virgin olive oil |
| 2 | tablespoons plus 1 teaspoon white wine vinegar |

Pulse parsley, mint, capers, anchovies, garlic, and salt in food processor until coarsely chopped, about 10 pulses, scraping down sides of bowl as needed. Transfer mixture to medium bowl and stir in oil and vinegar. Cover and let sit at room temperature for at least 1 hour to allow flavors to meld. Season with salt and pepper to taste. (Sauce can be refrigerated for up to 2 days; bring to room temperature and stir to recombine before using.)

# CHIMICHURRI

**Makes** about ¾ cup

### PER 1-TABLESPOON SERVING
**Cal** 70 | **Total Fat** 7g
**Protein** 0g | **Net Carbs** 1g
**Fiber** 0g | **Total Carbs** 1g

Cauliflower Steaks with Chimichurri (page 167) makes for a satisfying vegetarian keto meal. The tangy sauce brightens the neutral vegetable.

| | |
|---|---|
| 2 | tablespoons hot tap water |
| 1 | teaspoon dried oregano |
| ½ | teaspoon table salt |
| ⅔ | cup fresh parsley leaves |
| ⅓ | cup fresh cilantro leaves |
| 3 | garlic cloves, minced |
| ¼ | teaspoon red pepper flakes |
| 6 | tablespoons extra-virgin olive oil |
| 2 | tablespoons red wine vinegar |

**1.** Combine hot water, oregano, and salt in small bowl; let sit for 5 minutes to soften oregano.

**2.** Pulse parsley, cilantro, garlic, and pepper flakes in food processor until coarsely chopped, about 10 pulses. Transfer mixture to medium bowl and stir in oil, vinegar, and water mixture. Cover and let sit at room temperature for at least 1 hour to allow flavors to meld. Season with salt and pepper to taste. (Sauce can be refrigerated for up to 2 days; bring to room temperature and stir to recombine before using.)

Pulse cilantro, garlic, cumin, paprika, cayenne, and salt in food processor until coarsely chopped, about 10 pulses. Transfer mixture to medium bowl and stir in oil and lemon juice. Cover and let sit at room temperature for at least 1 hour to allow flavors to meld. Season with salt and pepper to taste. (Sauce can be refrigerated for up to 2 days; bring to room temperature and stir to recombine before using.)

# HAZELNUT ROMESCO

**Makes** about ¾ cup

## PER 1-TABLESPOON SERVING
**Cal** 50 | **Total Fat** 5g
**Protein** 0g | **Net Carbs** 1g
**Fiber** 0g | **Total Carbs** 1g

Our hazelnut romesco is delicious on Keto Pizza (page 163) and as a dip for raw veggies.

- ⅔ cup jarred roasted red peppers, patted dry
- ¼ cup hazelnuts, toasted and skinned
- ¼ cup fresh parsley leaves
- 3 tablespoons extra-virgin olive oil
- 1 tablespoon sherry vinegar
- 1 garlic clove, minced
- ¼ teaspoon table salt

Process all ingredients in food processor until smooth, about 1 minute, scraping down sides of bowl as needed. (Sauce can be refrigerated for up to 2 days; bring to room temperature and stir to recombine before using.)

# CHERMOULA

**Makes** about ¾ cup

## PER 1-TABLESPOON SERVING
**Cal** 70 | **Total Fat** 7g
**Protein** 0g | **Net Carbs** 1g
**Fiber** 0g | **Total Carbs** 1g

Pan-Roasted Lamb Chops with Brussels Sprouts and Chermoula (page 129) is light but satisfying as a keto main course.

- 1¼ cups fresh cilantro leaves
- 4 garlic cloves, minced
- ¾ teaspoon ground cumin
- ¾ teaspoon paprika
- ¼ teaspoon cayenne pepper
- ¼ teaspoon table salt
- 6 tablespoons extra-virgin olive oil
- 3 tablespoons lemon juice

# TAHINI SAUCE

**Makes** about ¾ cup

## PER 1-TABLESPOON SERVING
**Cal** 40 | **Total Fat** 3.5g
**Protein** 1g | **Net Carbs** 2g
**Fiber** 0g | **Total Carbs** 2g

This sauce makes a great salad dressing or topping for sautéed, grilled, or roasted proteins and hearty vegetables. Our favorite brand of tahini is Ziyad. We use this sauce on our Mediterranean "Falafel" Wraps (page 160).

- ⅓ cup tahini
- ⅓ cup water
- 2 tablespoons lemon juice
- 1 garlic clove, minced
- ⅛ teaspoon table salt

Whisk all ingredients together in bowl until smooth (mixture will appear broken at first). Cover and let sit at room temperature for at least 30 minutes to allow flavors to meld. Season with salt and pepper to taste. (Sauce can be refrigerated for up to 4 days; bring to room temperature and stir to recombine before using.)

# AVOCADO CREMA

**Makes** about ¾ cup

## PER 1-TABLESPOON SERVING
**Cal** 45 | **Total Fat** 3.5g
**Protein** 1g | **Net Carbs** 1g
**Fiber** 1g | **Total Carbs** 2g

Smooth, rich avocado crema is delicious on keto sandwiches, with chicken or seafood, and with vegetable main dishes, too.

- ¾ cup sour cream
- ½ avocado, cut into 1-inch pieces
- 1 teaspoon lime juice

Process sour cream, avocado, and lime juice in food processor until smooth, scraping down sides of bowl as needed, and season with salt and pepper to taste. (Sauce can be refrigerated for up to 2 days.)

# HORSERADISH–SOUR CREAM SAUCE

**Makes** about ¾ cup

## PER 1-TABLESPOON SERVING
**Cal** 20 | **Total Fat** 1.5g
**Protein** 0g | **Net Carbs** 1g
**Fiber** 0g | **Total Carbs** 1g

This sauce is classic with roast beef, but it's also good as a dip for raw veggies. Buy refrigerated prepared horseradish, not the shelf-stable kind, which contains preservatives and additives.

6 tablespoons sour cream
6 tablespoons prepared horseradish, drained
½ teaspoon table salt
⅛ teaspoon pepper

Whisk all ingredients together in bowl. Cover and refrigerate for at least 30 minutes to allow flavors to meld. Season with salt and pepper to taste. (Sauce can be refrigerated for up to 2 days.)

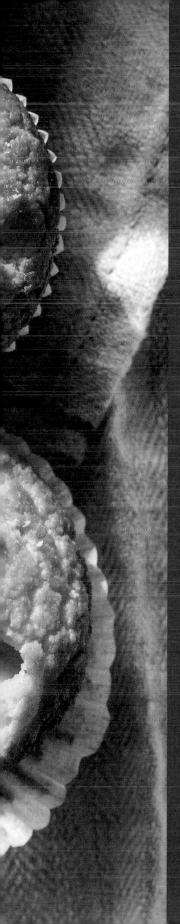

# CHAPTER 1

# BREAKFAST

# BREAKFAST SCRAMBLE WITH GRUYÈRE AND HERBS

6 large eggs
¼ teaspoon table salt
⅛ teaspoon pepper
3 tablespoons unsalted butter
1 ounce Gruyère cheese, shredded (¼ cup)
2 tablespoons minced fresh chives, dill, parsley, and/or tarragon

**1.** Beat eggs, salt, and pepper with fork in bowl until eggs are thoroughly combined and mixture is pure yellow; do not overbeat.

**2.** Melt butter in 10-inch nonstick skillet over medium-high heat, swirling to coat skillet. Add egg mixture and, using heat-resistant rubber spatula, constantly and firmly scrape along bottom and sides of skillet until eggs begin to clump and spatula leaves trail on bottom of skillet, 1½ to 2½ minutes.

**3.** Reduce heat to low and add Gruyère and herbs. Gently and constantly fold eggs until clumped and slightly wet, 30 to 60 seconds. Immediately transfer eggs to warmed plates and season with salt and pepper to taste. Serve immediately.

## Breakfast Scramble with Feta and Spinach

Omit herbs. Add 2 ounces chopped baby spinach to melted butter in step 2 before adding eggs and cook until wilted, about 1 minute. Substitute ¼ cup crumbled feta for Gruyère.
**Per Serving** Cal 410; Total Fat 34g; Protein 22g; Net Carbs 2g; Fiber 1g; Total Carbs 3g

## Breakfast Scramble with Cheddar and Bacon

Cook 3 ounces sliced bacon, chopped, in 10-inch nonstick skillet over medium heat until crispy, 5 to 7 minutes; transfer to paper towel–lined plate. Pour off all but 3 tablespoons fat from skillet; add extra-virgin olive oil as needed to yield 3 tablespoons. Reduce salt to pinch and proceed with recipe, substituting bacon fat for butter, extra-sharp cheddar for Gruyère and bacon for herbs.
**Per Serving** Cal 520; Total Fat 44g; Protein 28g; Net Carbs 2g; Fiber 0g; Total Carbs 2g

**Serves** 2
**Total Time** 15 minutes

### PER SERVING
**Cal** 420 | **Total Fat** 35g
**Protein** 23g | **Net Carbs** 1g
**Fiber** 0g | **Total Carbs** 1g

## Why This Recipe Works

Naturally keto, eggs and cheese are the stars of this any-weather scramble, which can be varied to suit your mood or the season. Gruyère and herbs like parsley, dill, or chives elevate the flavor of an easy-to-make breakfast. The feta-spinach variation has a light, summery taste but still gives you the right proportions of fat, protein, and carbs, while the scramble with cheddar and bacon is a more substantial meal. We wanted the eggs to taste clean and delicate so we cooked them gently. The quick but constant stirring gave us softly scrambled eggs, lightly melted cheese, and just-wilted greens. It is important to follow visual cues, as pan thickness will affect cooking times. If using an electric stove, heat one burner on low heat and a second on medium-high heat; move the skillet between burners when it's time to adjust the heat. Feel free to use a combination of herbs here.

**Serves** 2 (Makes 6 frittatas)
**Total Time** 50 minutes

## PER SERVING
**Cal** 530 | **Total Fat** 40g
**Protein** 36g | **Net Carbs** 5g
**Fiber** 1g | **Total Carbs** 6g

### Why This Recipe Works

Our goal was to develop a frittata that doubled as a breakfast and an easy-to-eat make-ahead keto bite. It needed the visual appeal and flavor of the traditional skillet-baked dish, and a short baking time for weekdays. A nonstick muffin tin was the solution. The individual frittatas required just 12 to 14 minutes in the oven, were flavorful, and easy to store. We half-cooked the sausage and softened the red pepper in a skillet. After the mixture cooled, we stirred in grated yellow cheddar. An earlier test kitchen recipe had recommended increasing the fat content in the mini frittatas to help them release easily from the tin. In that version, mixing the eggs with half-and-half instead of milk did the trick. But for the keto diet, half-and-half lacked enough fat so we tried heavy cream. That yielded delicate frittatas that released easily from the pan but weren't greasy when eaten warm or at room temp-erature. To bake, we divided the sausage mixture between six cups of a 12-cup muffin tin and ladled the egg-cream mixture over. Add-ins like mushrooms or asparagus were delicious substitutes for peppers, contributing a vegetable element and color contrast; scallions imparted subtle onion flavor. You will need a 12-cup nonstick muffin tin for this recipe. This recipe can easily be doubled to fill the muffin tin.

# MUFFIN TIN FRITTATAS WITH SAUSAGE, BELL PEPPER, AND CHEDDAR

1 teaspoon extra-virgin olive oil
6 ounces sweet or hot Italian sausage, casings removed
½ red bell pepper (4 ounces), stemmed, seeded, and chopped
1 scallion, white and green parts separated, sliced thin
4 large eggs
2 tablespoons heavy cream
¼ teaspoon pepper
3 ounces sharp cheddar cheese, shredded (¾ cup)

**1.** Adjust oven rack to lower-middle position and heat oven to 425 degrees. Generously spray middle 6 cups of 12-cup nonstick muffin tin with olive oil spray.

**2.** Heat oil in 10-inch nonstick skillet over medium heat until shimmering. Add sausage, bell pepper, and scallion whites and cook, breaking up sausage with wooden spoon, until sausage is no longer pink and pepper is softened, about 4 minutes. Transfer to medium bowl and let cool slightly.

**3.** Beat eggs, cream, and pepper in separate bowl with fork until thoroughly combined and mixture is pure yellow; do not overbeat. Stir cheddar and scallion greens into sausage mixture. Divide sausage mixture evenly among prepared muffin cups. Using ladle, evenly distribute egg mixture over filling in cups. Bake until frittatas are lightly puffed and set in centers, 12 to 14 minutes.

**4.** Transfer muffin tin to wire rack and let frittatas cool for 10 minutes. Run plastic knife around edges of frittatas, if necessary, to loosen from muffin tin, then gently remove. Serve.

### Muffin Tin Frittatas with Asparagus and Fontina

Increase oil to 2 teaspoons. Substitute 6 ounces trimmed asparagus, sliced ½ inch thick, for sausage and bell pepper and cook until crisp tender, 2 to 4 minutes, in step 2. Substitute fontina cheese for cheddar and add ¼ teaspoon salt to egg mixture.
**Per Serving** Cal 410; Total Fat 33g; Protein 25g; Net Carbs 3g; Fiber 1g; Total Carbs 4g

### Muffin Tin Frittatas with Mushrooms and Gruyère

Increase oil to 2 teaspoons. Substitute 6 ounces trimmed cremini mushrooms, sliced thin, for sausage and bell pepper and cook until dry and lightly browned, 6 to 8 minutes, in step 2. Substitute Gruyère cheese for cheddar and add ¼ teaspoon salt to egg mixture.
**Per Serving** Cal 430; Total Fat 33g; Protein 28g; Net Carbs 5g; Fiber 1g; Total Carbs 6g

### *Keto Meal Prep*

» Frittatas can be refrigerated for up to 5 days. To reheat, place on greased, foil-lined baking sheet and bake in 350-degree oven for 10 minutes or place on large plate and microwave for 45 to 60 seconds.

# SMOKED SALMON BRUNCH PLATE

**Serves** 2
**Total Time** 45 minutes

4   portobello mushroom caps
    (3 ounces each), gills removed
3   tablespoons extra-virgin
    olive oil, divided
⅛   teaspoon table salt
2   ounces cream cheese,
    softened
4   ounces smoked salmon
1   recipe Easy-Peel Hard-
    Cooked Eggs (recipe
    follows), sliced thin
1   tablespoon capers, rinsed
    and minced
1   tablespoon minced shallots
1   tablespoon minced fresh
    parsley and/or dill
¼   teaspoon lemon juice

**1.** Adjust oven rack to upper-middle position, place rimmed baking sheet on rack, and heat oven to 400 degrees. Using sharp knife, cut ¼-inch slits, spaced ½ inch apart, in crosshatch pattern on surface (non-gill side) of mushrooms.

**2.** Brush both sides of mushroom caps with 2 tablespoons oil and sprinkle with salt. Carefully place caps gill side up on preheated sheet and roast until mushrooms have released some of their juices and begun to brown around edges, 8 to 12 minutes. Flip caps over and continue to roast until liquid has completely evaporated and caps are golden brown, 8 to 12 minutes. Transfer mushrooms to plate and let cool slightly.

**3.** Spread cream cheese over gill side of mushroom caps and arrange on 2 individual serving plates. Top with salmon, eggs, capers, shallots, and parsley. Sprinkle with pepper to taste and drizzle with lemon juice and remaining 1 tablespoon oil. Serve.

### *Keto Meal Prep*

» Cream cheese–covered portobellos, prepared through step 3, can be refrigerated for up to 3 days; let sit at room temperature for 15 minutes before serving with toppings.

---

### Easy-Peel Hard-Cooked Eggs
#### Makes 2 eggs

Be sure to use large eggs that have no cracks and are cold from the refrigerator. If you don't have a steamer basket, gently place the eggs in the water; they can rest above the water or partially submerged. You can cook as many as 12 eggs without altering the timing, as long as you use a pot and steamer basket large enough to hold the eggs in a single layer. Eggs can be refrigerated for up to 5 days and peeled when needed.

2   large eggs

**1.** Bring 1 inch water to rolling boil in medium saucepan over high heat. Place eggs in steamer basket. Transfer basket to saucepan. Cover, reduce heat to medium (small wisps of steam should escape from beneath lid), and cook eggs for 13 minutes.

**2.** When eggs are almost finished cooking, combine 2 cups ice cubes and 2 cups cold water in medium bowl. Using tongs or spoon, transfer eggs to ice bath; let sit for 15 minutes. Peel before using.

**Per 1 Egg** Cal 70; Total Fat 5g; Protein 6g; Net Carbs 0g; Fiber 0g; Total Carbs 0g

---

### PER SERVING
**Cal** 470 | **Total Fat** 39g
**Protein** 22g | **Net Carbs** 7g
**Fiber** 3g | **Total Carbs** 10g

### Why This Recipe Works

There is no brunch dish more iconic than a New York–style smoked salmon bagel plate. But with a conventional bagel topping out at over 50 grams of net carbs, this perennial favorite is off-limits for keto. We could have used some terrific toasted Seeded Bread (page 23) as the base for this recipe but a test cook suggested portobello mushrooms. Some were skeptical about replacing bread with a mushroom until they tasted it. We used our classic method for roasting portobellos, which employs a preheated baking sheet in a moderate oven to achieve a toasty, crisp exterior. Scoring the cap was essential—it drove away excess moisture and meant that even after 20 minutes in the oven, the mushrooms did not turn tough or chewy. We loved how substantial the warm, just-crisp mushrooms were against the tangy cream cheese and fatty smoked salmon. What's more, a pair of trimmed portobellos contains less than 4 grams of net carbs. As for topping the mushrooms, capers, parsley or dill, and minced shallots were deemed essential for this classic dish and a sliced egg, while perhaps gilding the lily, made for an incredibly satisfying meal. Use portobello mushroom caps measuring 4 to 5 inches in diameter. We find it best to use a spoon to scrape the gills off the underside of the portobellos.

**Serves** 4 (Makes 8 pancakes)
**Total Time** 40 minutes

## PER SERVING

**Cal** 420 | **Total Fat** 37g
**Protein** 15g | **Net Carbs** 6g
**Fiber** 5g | **Sugar Alcohols** 6g
**Total Carbs** 17g

### Why This Recipe Works

Perfect pancakes should be fluffy, tender, lightly sweet, and easy to make. To create a keto recipe that would stand up to its traditional counterparts, we chose an acceptable non-grain flour. We settled on almond flour; its mild, subtly sweet, nutty flavor worked well in a breakfast application. Next, we focused on achieving the fluffy, light texture that's characteristic of great pancakes. Using eggs and adding baking powder provided lift, but the batter needed a bigger boost. A blender was the answer: We processed the liquid ingredients until the mixture was frothy, added the dry ingredients, and processed the batter a minute longer. The blender helped incorporate air into the batter, ensuring a smooth, pourable mix that made fluffier pancakes. Erythritol gave our pancakes just enough sweetness; a generous amount of vanilla extract offset any egginess. Erythritol is our preferred low-carb sweetener here; however, you can substitute your favorite low-carb sweetener. Be aware that not all low-carb sweeteners can be substituted 1:1 for erythritol. See page 14 for more information on low-carb sweeteners and substitutions. An electric griddle set at 350 degrees can be used in place of a skillet. Serve with butter or Keto Maple Syrup (recipe follows).

# PANCAKES

¾ cup water
3 large eggs
4 tablespoons unsalted butter, melted and cooled, divided
2 teaspoons vanilla extract
1¾ cups (7 ounces) blanched, finely ground almond flour
2 tablespoons granulated erythritol
2 teaspoons baking powder
¼ teaspoon table salt

**1.** Adjust oven rack to middle position and heat oven to 200 degrees. Set wire rack in rimmed baking sheet and spray with olive oil spray.

**2.** Process water, eggs, 3 tablespoons melted butter, and vanilla in blender until light and frothy, about 30 seconds. Add almond flour, erythritol, baking powder, and salt and process until thoroughly combined, about 1 minute.

**3.** Heat 1 teaspoon melted butter in 12-inch nonstick skillet over medium-low heat until shimmering. Using paper towels, carefully wipe out butter, leaving thin film of butter on bottom and sides of skillet. Using ⅓ cup batter per pancake, portion batter into skillet in 2 places and spread into 4-inch rounds. Cook until edges are set and first side is golden, 2 to 4 minutes.

**4.** Flip pancakes and continue to cook until second side is golden, 2 to 3 minutes. Serve immediately or transfer to prepared rack and keep warm in oven. Repeat with remaining batter, adjusting heat and using remaining 2 teaspoons melted butter as needed.

### Keto Meal Prep

» To store, stack pancakes, separated by sheets of parchment paper, and wrap tightly in plastic wrap. Refrigerate for up to 2 days or freeze for up to 1 month. To reheat, place pancakes (unthawed, if frozen) in single layer on large plate and microwave for about 2 minutes, flipping halfway through microwaving.

---

### Keto Maple Syrup
**Makes about ⅔ cup**

For the best flavor, be sure to use pure maple extract. The syrup will look opaque immediately after processing, but will turn clear as it settles.

½ cup powdered erythritol
½ cup water
1 tablespoon pure maple extract
¼ teaspoon xanthan gum

Process all ingredients in blender until combined, about 30 seconds. (Syrup can be stored at room temperature for up to 1 month. If crystals develop, microwave at 10 second intervals, until dissolved, stirring after each interval.)

**Per 1-Tablespoon Serving** Cal 5; Total Fat 0g; Protein 0g; Net Carbs 0g; Fiber 0g; Sugar Alcohols 10g; Total Carbs 10g

# BLUEBERRY MUFFINS OK

- ¾ cup (3 ounces) blanched, finely ground almond flour
- ¼ cup (1 ounce) coconut flour
- 1 teaspoon baking powder
- ⅛ teaspoon table salt
- ½ cup sour cream
- ¼ cup (2 ounces) granulated erythritol
- 2 large eggs
- 2 tablespoons unsalted butter, melted
- ½ teaspoon vanilla extract
- 1½ ounces (⅓ cup) fresh or frozen blueberries

**1.** Line middle 6 cups of 12-cup nonstick muffin tin with paper or foil liners and spray with olive oil spray. Whisk almond flour, coconut flour, baking powder, and salt together in large bowl. Whisk sour cream, erythritol, eggs, melted butter, and vanilla together in medium bowl. Stir sour cream mixture into flour mixture until fully combined. Cover and let sit at room temperature for 30 minutes.

**2.** Adjust oven rack to middle position and heat oven to 350 degrees. Fold blueberries into batter. Portion batter evenly among prepared muffin cups and smooth tops. Bake until tops are golden and toothpick inserted in center comes out clean, 30 to 35 minutes. Let muffins cool in muffin tin for 30 minutes before serving.

*Rest batter longer when doubling.*

### Keto Meal Prep

» Muffins can be stored at room temperature for up to 5 days or wrapped individually, transferred to zipper-lock bag, and frozen for up to 1 month. To serve from frozen, microwave for 30 seconds, then warm in 300-degree oven for 10 to 15 minutes.

**Serves** 6 (Makes 6 muffins)
**Total Time** 1 hour 20 minutes, plus 30 minutes cooling time

## PER SERVING
**Cal** 200 | **Total Fat** 16g
**Protein** 6g | **Net Carbs** 5g
**Fiber** 3g | **Sugar Alcohols** 8g
**Total Carbs** 16g

### Why This Recipe Works
We were skeptical about creating a good keto blueberry muffin. Muffins rely on flour and sugar for structure and flavor and we couldn't use either. Finding a flour stand-in was our biggest challenge. Many recipes use almond flour as its relatively neutral taste and slightly coarser consistency recalls a traditional muffin crumb. But just substituting almond flour for wheat created a crumbly muffin; the extra fat made it greasy. Adding coconut flour dramatically improved texture, helping the almond flour absorb extra moisture without imparting coconut flavor. Sour cream thickened the batter, built structure, and gave a pleasing tang to contrast with the sweet berries. We played with baking powder, egg, and butter amounts to find the right balance for good rise and a domed top. But the muffins were still dry and looked craggy; more liquid just made them soggy. So, inspired by established pancake methods, we rested the batter for 30 minutes. The flours absorbed more moisture, making tender, smooth muffins. Erythritol is our preferred low-carb sweetener; you can substitute your favorite low-carb sweetener. Be aware that not all low-carb sweeteners can be substituted 1:1 for erythritol. See page 14 for more information on low-carb sweeteners and substitutions. This recipe can be easily doubled to fill a 12-cup muffin tin.

**Makes** 6 cups
**Total Time** 2 hours

---

**PER ⅓-CUP SERVING**
**Cal** 240 | **Total Fat** 21g
**Protein** 6g | **Net Carbs** 7g
**Fiber** 4g | **Sugar Alcohols** 1g
**Total Carbs** 12g

---

## Why This Recipe Works

Oats and sugar, key granola ingredients, are not part of the keto diet, so we set out to make crave-worthy granola without them, replacing rolled oats with quinoa flakes, which mimicked their texture and chew. Unsweetened coconut, almonds or pecans, and sunflower seeds or pepitas provided crunch. Many recipes call for maple syrup to bind ingredients together, but egg whites and coconut oil made the perfect liquid "glue." Since almonds and coconut are high in fat, just ¼ cup of coconut oil ensured that our granola crisped nicely. We used a tried-and-true test kitchen method for superchunky granola. Instead of spreading the mixture onto a baking sheet, we pressed it into a rimmed sheet with a sturdy spatula, baking it gently at 300 degrees without stirring. This produced "bark" we could break into beautiful chunks. Cinnamon, ginger, cardamom, cloves, and freeze-dried mango made a satisfying warm spice variation. In another, we added unsweetened cocoa powder. After the granola cooled, we mixed in sugar-free dark chocolate chips. Erythritol is our preferred low-carb sweetener here; however, you can substitute your favorite low-carb sweetener. Be aware that not all low-carb sweeteners can be substituted 1:1 for erythritol. See page 14 for more information on low-carb sweeteners and substitutions. Chopping the nuts by hand is our first choice for superior texture and crunch.

# GRAIN-FREE GRANOLA

- 2  large egg whites
- 2  tablespoons granulated erythritol
- 5  teaspoons vanilla extract
- ½  teaspoon table salt
- ¼  cup coconut oil, melted and still warm
- 2  cups whole almonds, chopped coarse
- 2  cups unsweetened flaked coconut
- 1  cup quinoa flakes
- 1  cup raw sunflower seeds

**1.** Adjust oven rack to upper-middle position and heat oven to 300 degrees. Line rimmed baking sheet with parchment paper.

**2.** Whisk egg whites, erythritol, vanilla, and salt together in large bowl, then whisk in oil. Fold in almonds, coconut, quinoa flakes, and sunflower seeds until thoroughly coated. Transfer mixture to prepared sheet and spread into even layer. Using stiff metal spatula, press on almond mixture until very compact. Bake until deep golden brown, about 45 minutes, rotating sheet halfway through baking.

**3.** Let granola cool on wire rack for 1 hour, then break into pieces of desired size. Serve.

### Grain-Free Chocolate Granola

Substitute 2 cups pecans for almonds. Whisk 2 tablespoons unsweetened cocoa powder into egg white mixture. Transfer cooled granola to bowl and stir in ½ cup sugar-free dark chocolate chips before serving.

**Per ⅓-cup Serving** Cal 290; Total Fat 26g; Protein 5g; Net Carbs 6g; Fiber 6g; Sugar Alcohols 3g; Total Carbs 15g

### Grain-Free Chai Spice Granola

Substitute 1 cup pepitas for sunflower seeds. Whisk 1½ teaspoons ground cinnamon, 1½ teaspoons ground ginger, 1½ teaspoons ground cardamom, ½ teaspoon ground cloves, and ⅛ teaspoon pepper into egg white mixture. Transfer cooled granola to bowl and stir in ½ cup chopped freeze-dried mango before serving.

**Per ⅓-cup Serving** Cal 250; Total Fat 21g; Protein 8g; Net Carbs 8g; Fiber 4g; Sugar Alcohols 1g; Total Carbs 13g

## *Keto Meal Prep*

» Granola can be stored in airtight container for up to 2 weeks.

# TOASTED COCONUT PORRIDGE

¼ cup unsweetened flaked coconut
2 tablespoons raw pepitas
1 cup water
¼ cup coconut flour
3 tablespoons golden flax meal
1½ teaspoons granulated erythritol
½ teaspoon ground cinnamon
Pinch table salt
1 cup unsweetened coconut milk
1 tablespoon coconut oil
1 teaspoon vanilla extract

**1.** Toast flaked coconut and pepitas in medium saucepan over medium heat, stirring frequently, until coconut is fragrant and golden brown, about 4 minutes; transfer to bowl.

**2.** Whisk water, coconut flour, flax meal, erythritol, cinnamon, and salt together in now-empty saucepan. Bring to simmer over medium heat and cook, stirring frequently, until thick, dry paste forms, about 2 minutes. Off heat, stir in coconut milk, oil, and vanilla and let sit until heated through, about 1 minute. Sprinkle individual portions with toasted coconut mixture before serving.

### *Keto Meal Prep*

» Porridge can be refrigerated for up to 5 days. Toasted coconut topping can be stored in airtight container for up to 5 days. To reheat, cook porridge in small saucepan over medium-low heat for 2 minutes or microwave in bowl for 1 minute, adjusting consistency with up to 2 tablespoons water as needed.

**Serves** 2
**Total Time** 30 minutes

## PER SERVING
**Cal** 290 | **Total Fat** 23g
**Protein** 7g | **Net Carbs** 6g
**Fiber** 10g | **Sugar Alcohols** 3g
**Total Carbs** 19g

## Why This Recipe Works
A bowl of steaming porridge is a treat in the dead of winter—a creamy mix of grains, hot liquid, and tasty toppings. Much of the creaminess of porridge comes not from fat but from starch released from the grain, usually oats. We wanted to replicate that velvety texture in our coconut flour porridge, which contains no starch. Most keto versions rely on an egg for thickening power. We were underwhelmed by the results; egg whites fully coagulate around 180 degrees, by which time they had imparted a sulfurous off-flavor. We tried other thickeners—chia, psyllium husk, and ground flax meal, and only flax gave us the right texture—smooth and luscious without being overly set or granular. We used just a little sweetener (less than 1 teaspoon per person) but we really enjoyed the addition of cinnamon and vanilla. These hinted at sweetness without overwhelming the delicate coconut flavor, which was reminiscent of Cream of Wheat. Toasted coconut flakes and pepitas provided a deeply rounded, crunchy topping that was a snap to make in the same saucepan. Erythritol is our preferred low-carb sweetener here; however, you can substitute your favorite low-carb sweetener. Be aware that not all low-carb sweeteners can be substituted 1:1 for erythritol. See page 14 for more information on low-carb sweeteners and substitutions.

**Serves** 2
**Total Time** 20 minutes, plus
8 hours chilling time

## PER SERVING
**Cal** 380 | **Total Fat** 33g
**Protein** 7g | **Net Carbs** 6g
**Fiber** 10g | **Sugar Alcohols** 6g
**Total Carbs** 22g

## Why This Recipe Works

Chia pudding comes together by what seems like Jack and the Beanstalk magic. When chia seeds are combined with liquid and left to soak overnight they create a gel, which thickens and produces a no-cook tapioca-like pudding—a spectacular base for a simple, healthy breakfast. Before letting it rest overnight, we gave the pudding a second whisk 15 minutes after its initial mixing to prevent clumping and make sure the chia developed its luscious texture. Pudding alchemy aside, chia is great for the keto diet because it provides a thoroughly satisfying texture yet contributes very few net carbs, because it is comprised mainly of fat, with a little protein and a huge amount of fiber. You could rehydrate these little powerhouse seeds with any liquid, but tasters loved the combination of heavy cream and water for its simplicity and clean richness. Chia pudding is best enjoyed with toppings: A handful of raspberries contributed little pops of color and acidity while crunchy toasted almonds offered textural contrast. Serve with Keto Maple Syrup (page 38), if desired. Erythritol is our preferred low-carb sweetener here, however, you can substitute your favorite low-carb sweetener. Be aware that not all low-carb sweeteners can be substituted 1:1 for erythritol. See page 14 for more information on low-carb sweeteners and substitutions.

# OVERNIGHT CHIA PUDDING WITH RASPBERRIES AND ALMONDS

½  cup water
½  cup heavy cream
¼  cup chia seeds
 1  tablespoon granulated
    erythritol
½  teaspoon vanilla extract
⅛  teaspoon table salt
½  cup (2½ ounces) raspberries
 2  tablespoons chopped
    toasted almonds

**1.** Whisk water, cream, chia seeds, erythritol, vanilla, and salt together in bowl. Let mixture sit for 15 minutes, then whisk again to break up any clumps.

**2.** Cover and refrigerate until pudding is set, about 8 hours. Top individual portions with raspberries and almonds before serving.

### Keto Meal Prep
» Pudding can be refrigerated for up to 1 week. Adjust consistency with up to 2 tablespoons water as needed.

# GREEN SMOOTHIE

¾ cup unsweetened plain
  almond milk
2 tablespoons extra-virgin
  olive oil
2 teaspoons granulated
  erythritol
¼ teaspoon grated orange zest
  Pinch table salt
¼ avocado (2 ounces)
1 ounce (1 cup) baby spinach
½ cup ice cubes

Add all ingredients in blender
(in order listed) and process until
smooth, about 30 seconds. Serve.

**Serves** 1
**Total Time** 10 minutes

## PER SERVING
**Cal** 370 | **Total Fat** 38g
**Protein** 2g | **Net Carbs** 3g
**Fiber** 4g | **Sugar Alcohols** 8g
**Total Carbs** 15g

## Why This Recipe Works

Smoothie-making's a breeze, right?
Just blend fruits, vegetables, and juice
together for a refreshing, healthy
drink. But anyone who's on the keto
diet knows it's challenging to make
a delicious protein- and fat-enriched
smoothie without fruit to impart
sweetness and texture. Carb-heavy
juice and bananas were out, so we
tried kale, switching to spinach, which
had a more delicate flavor, and adding
olive oil for fat. To bolster the smoothie's nutritional value, we experimented
coconut milk yogurt for good fat
and texture, finally choosing almond
milk for its neutral taste. We thought
cocoa might enhance flavor and
sweetness but it only muddied the
smoothie's color. Then we tried lemon
juice, which gave brightness, but
using enough meant adding too many
carbs. Fresh ginger was brightly floral
and tasters liked the drink but found
the ginger overpowering. A test cook
suggested orange zest, which imparted
the citrus aroma everyone loved and
created a perfect sense of fruitiness
without the carbs. Blending in ice
cooled the drink pleasantly. Erythritol
is our preferred low-carb sweetener
here; however, you can substitute your
favorite low-carb sweetener. Be aware
that not all low-carb sweeteners can be
substituted 1:1 for erythritol. See page
14 for more information on low-carb
sweeteners and substitutions. This
recipe can easily be doubled.

_I can drink it._

# CHOCOLATE-ALMOND SHAKE

**Serves** 1
**Total Time** 10 minutes

## PER SERVING
**Cal** 470 | **Total Fat** 46g
**Protein** 8g | **Net Carbs** 6g
**Fiber** 4g | **Sugar Alcohols** 8g
**Total Carbs** 18g

## Why This Recipe Works

Shakes are a perennial favorite, and it's no wonder: A sweet, creamy shake is an indulgent liquid treat. To create one that tasted delicious and chocolaty as a breakfast drink, we started with plain unsweetened almond milk. Its neutral flavor and silky consistency replaced milk, and added fiber. We mixed in unsweetened cocoa powder and tried avocado as a thickener because it also lent fat and flavor. Ultimately, though, unsweetened almond butter proved a better complement to the shake's rich chocolatiness. For sweetness, we enlisted a modest amount of erythritol; a touch of salt helped balance that and further draw out rich taste. Finally, to boost fat without compromising net carbs, taste, or texture, we blended in naturally sweet coconut oil. Erythritol is our preferred low-carb sweetener here; however, you can substitute your favorite low-carb sweetener. Be aware that not all low-carb sweeteners can be substituted 1:1 for erythritol. See page 14 for more information on low-carb sweeteners and substitutions. This recipe can easily be doubled.

¾  cup unsweetened plain almond milk
2  tablespoons unsweetened creamy almond butter
2  teaspoons granulated erythritol
1½  teaspoons unsweetened cocoa powder
Pinch table salt
½  cup ice cubes
2  tablespoons coconut oil, melted

Process almond milk, almond butter, erythritol, cocoa, salt, and ice cubes in blender until smooth, about 30 seconds. With blender running, slowly add coconut oil, and process until combined, about 10 seconds. Serve.

_good if you add peanut butter instead of Almond butter._

# CHAPTER 2

# SOUPS AND STEWS

**Serves** 4
**Total Time** 1 hour

## PER SERVING

**Cal** 470 | **Total Fat** 35g
**Protein** 30g | **Net Carbs** 6g
**Fiber** 2g | **Total Carbs** 8g

## Why This Recipe Works

Chicken noodle soup is the ultimate comfort food, easy to make at home. To make it keto-friendly, we upped the fat content and reduced the carbs from pasta and onion. At the test kitchen, we start the base for our chicken noodle soup with store-bought broth—a timesaver—but enhance it with aromatics and fond built by browning chicken pieces in a Dutch oven. For this version, we browned fatty chicken thighs, removed them, and added broth, onion, carrots, and thyme to the fat left in the pot, scraping up the delicious browned bits. Then we put the thighs back in to finish cooking and deepen the broth's flavor. And that onion? We discovered a neat trick—adding a halved onion during cooking enhanced the taste and we could easily discard it before serving. For the noodles, we turned to tried-and-true low-carb zucchini, spiralizing them and then cutting the noodles into 2-inch lengths. These only needed a few moments in the simmering soup to become tender. A quick sprinkle of chopped parsley gave pleasant freshness to our finished soup. Our Southwestern- and Japanese-inspired variations bring new twists of flavor to a comforting standard. We prefer to spiralize our own zucchini, but you can substitute store-bought spiralized zucchini, though they tend to be drier and less flavorful. Avoid buying large zucchini, which have thicker skins and more seeds.

# CHICKEN ZOODLE SOUP  *very good*

- 3  zucchini (8 ounces each), ends trimmed
- 2  pounds bone-in chicken thighs, trimmed
- 6  tablespoons extra-virgin olive oil, divided
- 6  cups chicken broth
- 1  onion (8 ounces), halved through root end
- 2  carrots (5 ounces), peeled and cut into ½-inch pieces
- 1  tablespoon minced fresh thyme or 1 teaspoon dried
- ¼  teaspoon table salt
- ¼  teaspoon pepper
- 2  tablespoons chopped fresh parsley

**1.** Using spiralizer, cut zucchini into ⅛-inch-thick noodles, then cut noodles into 2-inch lengths; set aside. (You should have 1 pound of zucchini noodles after spiralizing; reserve extra noodles for another use.)

**2.** Pat chicken dry with paper towels. Heat 2 tablespoons oil in Dutch oven over medium-high heat until just smoking. Brown chicken on both sides, 8 to 10 minutes; transfer to plate.

**3.** Stir broth, onion, carrots, thyme, salt, and pepper into fat left in pot, scraping up any browned bits. Return chicken and any accumulated juices to pot and bring to simmer. Reduce heat to low, cover, and cook until chicken registers 165 degrees, about 10 minutes.

**4.** Discard onion. Transfer chicken to cutting board, let cool slightly, then shred into bite-size pieces using 2 forks; discard skin and bones.

**5.** Return soup to boil over medium-high heat. Stir in chicken and zucchini and cook until zucchini is tender, about 1 minute. Season with salt and pepper to taste. Drizzle each portion with 1 tablespoon oil and sprinkle with parsley. Serve.

### Chipotle Chicken Zoodle Soup

Omit carrots and thyme. Before adding broth in step 3, add 1½ teaspoons minced canned chipotle chile in adobo sauce, 1½ teaspoons minced fresh oregano, and 1 teaspoon ground cumin to fat left in pot; cook until fragrant, about 30 seconds. Substitute cilantro for parsley and top individual portions with 2 ounces thinly sliced radishes before serving.

**Per Serving** Cal 460; Total Fat 35g; Protein 30g; Net Carbs 5g; Fiber 1g; Total Carbs 6g

### Miso Chicken Zoodle Soup

Omit thyme, salt, and pepper. Before adding broth in step 3, add 1 tablespoon white miso and 1 tablespoon grated fresh ginger to fat left in pot; cook until fragrant, about 30 seconds. Substitute 4 ounces thinly sliced shiitake mushrooms for carrots. Substitute toasted sesame oil for olive oil and 1 thinly sliced scallion green for parsley in step 5.

**Per Serving** Cal 470; Total Fat 35g; Protein 31g; Net Carbs 7g; Fiber 2g; Total Carbs 9g

### *Keto Meal Prep*

» Spiralized zucchini can be placed in zipper-lock bag and refrigerated for up to 5 days.
» Soup can be refrigerated for up to 3 days. To reheat, bring to gentle simmer in saucepan or microwave in bowl until steaming.

# BROCCOLI-CHEDDAR SOUP WITH CHICKEN

*Very good.*

**Serves** 4
**Total Time** 1 hour

## PER SERVING
**Cal** 630 | **Total Fat** 47g
**Protein** 43g | **Net Carbs** 7g
**Fiber** 3g | **Total Carbs** 10g

- 2 pounds bone-in chicken thighs, trimmed
- 6 tablespoons extra-virgin olive oil, divided
- 1¼ pounds broccoli, florets chopped into ½-inch pieces, stalks peeled and sliced ¼ inch thick
- 3 garlic cloves, minced
- 1 teaspoon dry mustard
- ¼ teaspoon table salt
  Pinch cayenne pepper
- 3 cups chicken broth
- 1 ounce (1 cup) baby spinach
- 4 ounces sharp cheddar cheese, shredded (1 cup)
- 1½ ounces Parmesan cheese, grated (¾ cup)
- 1 tablespoon minced fresh chives

**1.** Pat chicken dry with paper towels. Heat 2 tablespoons oil in Dutch oven over medium-high heat until just smoking. Brown chicken on both sides, 8 to 10 minutes; transfer to plate.

**2.** Add broccoli florets to fat left in pot and cook until tender and just beginning to brown, about 4 minutes. Transfer 1 cup broccoli florets to bowl and set aside for serving. Stir broccoli stalks, garlic, mustard, salt, and cayenne into pot and cook until fragrant, about 1 minute. Stir in broth, scraping up browned bits. Return chicken and any accumulated juices to pot and bring to simmer. Reduce heat to low, cover, and cook until chicken registers 165 degrees, about 10 minutes.

**3.** Transfer chicken to cutting board, let cool slightly, then shred into bite-size pieces using 2 forks; discard skin and bones.

**4.** Working in 2 batches, process soup, spinach, cheddar, Parmesan, and remaining ¼ cup oil in blender until smooth, about 30 seconds for each batch. Return soup and chicken to now-empty pot and bring to brief simmer over medium-low heat. Season with salt and pepper to taste. Top individual portions evenly with chives and reserved broccoli before serving.

### Keto Meal Prep
» Soup and reserved broccoli can be refrigerated separately for up to 3 days. To reheat, bring soup to gentle simmer in saucepan, stirring often, or microwave in bowl until steaming. Bring broccoli to room temperature before serving.

## Why This Recipe Works
You might not think that a vegetable-driven soup makes an ideal keto meal but then you might not have considered broccoli-cheddar soup! Rich, hearty, and packed with low-carb broccoli and fat-rich cheese, it's both satisfying and filling. We wanted to increase the protein content so we used chicken thigh meat in our version; the fond created by browning the meat also flavored the chicken broth. When the soup was blended, the broccoli did not give it enough of a green hue. So we blended in a little spinach the next time. That helped and had the extra benefit of increasing fiber. We also gave the soup a subtle hint of Parmesan to balance the richness of cheddar. Once the soup was smooth, we stirred our chicken back in and warmed everything through. A sprinkling of reserved broccoli florets and chives added vibrant color and an aromatic finish to our creamy soup. We start with 1¼ pounds broccoli, which is trimmed to 1 pound after cutting off the tough outer part of the stalk and the base.

## PER SERVING

**Cal** 550 | **Total Fat** 44g
**Protein** 34g | **Net Carbs** 2g
**Fiber** 2g | **Total Carbs** 4g

### Why This Recipe Works

This Korean-inspired dish gets a triple dose of fat from beef, coconut oil, and toasted sesame oil, but the richness is balanced by tangy kimchi, a traditional condiment of spicy pickled vegetables. Kimchi serves another purpose too, helping the meatballs stay tender. At the test kitchen, we use a panade (a mixture of bread crumbs and liquid) to keep meatballs and meatloaf juicy and moist, but a panade was out for this book. Since we didn't want tough meatballs and wanted to highlight Korean flavors in this soup, we considered kimchi instead as a swap for traditional panade. We made meatballs by combining beef with a mixture of minced kimchi and scallions, which prevented the shaped meat from becoming dense during cooking and added delicious texture and crunch. A poaching liquid of beef broth, kimchi, garlic, and ginger also contributed abundant flavor. We gently poached our meatballs until they were just done; we then finished the dish with a sprinkle of scallion greens and a drizzle of potent sesame oil to enhance the Korean nuances of this simple but satisfying soup.

# KIMCHI BEEF MEATBALL SOUP

1½ pounds 80 percent lean ground beef
2½ cups cabbage kimchi (1½ cups minced, 1 cup chopped), divided
3 scallions, white parts minced, green parts sliced thin on bias, divided
2 tablespoons coconut oil
3 garlic cloves, minced
1 tablespoon grated fresh ginger
4 cups beef broth
2 teaspoons toasted sesame oil, divided

**1.** Add ground beef, minced kimchi, 1 tablespoon scallion whites, and 1 tablespoon scallion greens to bowl and gently knead with your hands until combined. Pinch off and roll meat mixture into 1¾-inch balls (you should have about 30 balls).

**2.** Heat coconut oil in Dutch oven over medium heat until shimmering. Add remaining scallion whites, garlic, and ginger and cook until fragrant, about 1 minute. Stir in chopped kimchi and cook until softened, about 2 minutes. Stir in broth, then gently add meatballs and bring to simmer. Reduce heat to low, cover, and cook until meatballs are cooked through, 4 to 6 minutes, gently stirring to redistribute meatballs halfway through cooking. Season with salt and pepper to taste. Drizzle each portion with ½ teaspoon sesame oil and sprinkle with remaining scallion greens before serving.

### *Keto Meal Prep*

» Shaped meatballs, prepared through step 1, can be refrigerated for up to 24 hours.
» Soup can be refrigerated for up to 3 days. To reheat, bring soup to gentle simmer in saucepan or microwave in bowl until steaming.

# THAI COCONUT SOUP WITH SHRIMP AND BOK CHOY

- 5 tablespoons coconut oil
- 1 pound bok choy, stalks sliced ¼ inch thick, leaves cut into 1-inch pieces
- 2 tablespoons grated fresh ginger
- 1 tablespoon Thai red curry paste
- 1 lemongrass stalk, trimmed to bottom 6 inches and minced
- 2½ cups chicken broth
- 1 (14-ounce) can unsweetened coconut milk
- 1 tablespoon fish sauce
- 1½ pounds extra-large shrimp (21 to 25 per pound), peeled, deveined, tails removed, and cut into ½-inch pieces
- 1 tablespoon lime juice
- 1 tablespoon toasted sesame oil
- ¼ cup fresh cilantro leaves

1. Heat coconut oil in Dutch oven over medium heat until shimmering. Add bok choy stalks and cook until softened, about 3 minutes. Stir in ginger, curry paste, and lemongrass and cook until fragrant, about 1 minute. Stir in broth, coconut milk, and fish sauce, scraping up any browned bits, and bring to simmer. Reduce heat to medium-low, partially cover, and cook until flavors meld, about 15 minutes.

2. Stir in shrimp, return to simmer, and cook until opaque throughout, about 3 minutes. Off heat, stir in bok choy leaves and let sit until wilted, about 2 minutes. Stir in lime juice and sesame oil. Season with salt and pepper to taste. Top individual portions evenly with cilantro before serving.

## Keto Meal Prep

» Soup can be refrigerated for up to 24 hours. To reheat, bring to gentle simmer in saucepan, stirring often, or microwave in bowl, until steaming.

**Serves** 4
**Total Time** 1 hour

## PER SERVING
**Cal** 330 | **Total Fat** 25g
**Protein** 20g | **Net Carbs** 8g
**Fiber** 1g | **Total Carbs** 9g

## Why This Recipe Works

The wonderful thing about Thai coconut soup is its velvety richness dancing with aromatic heat, and fresh-tasting add-ins. As in many Southeast Asian dishes, a lively interplay of ingredients and flavors is essential: Fragrant lemongrass, pungent fish sauce, tart citrus juice, and floral ginger blend into a tantalizing, mouthwatering dish. Thai curry paste, which packs a spicy (and convenient) punch and fruity flavors, was a good substitute for a more time-consuming homemade blend. While chicken is the traditional protein for this soup, we chose shrimp, cutting it into bite-size pieces, and added crunch, color, and texture with bok choy. We first sautéed just the bok choy stems along with aromatics to infuse the soup with their flavor, and added the leaves and shrimp at the end so they maintained their delicate texture. After a final garnish of cilantro leaves and lime juice we were ready to devour this delectable, fragrant soup.

**Serves** 4
**Total Time** 30 minutes

## PER SERVING

**Cal** 300 | **Total Fat** 25g
**Protein** 8g | **Net Carbs** 8g
**Fiber** 4g | **Total Carbs** 12g

### Why This Recipe Works

The fresh taste of garden vegetables can be hard to showcase in a cooked dish like soup. Their delicate flavors become diluted by liquid or the vegetables themselves get overcooked and turn to mush. We got around these concerns by cooking our soup only briefly after first sautéing our vegetables in some olive oil. We chose the spring flavors of low-carb asparagus, zucchini, and cabbage. After adding the aromatics and broth, we simmered the vegetables for just a few minutes until crisp-tender, so they were able to maintain their characteristic taste and texture. Many traditional recipes use water for the soup base, but because we weren't simmering the soup for long, we used mostly vegetable broth to boost the flavor. We added a swirl of basil pesto just before serving; the heat of the broth released the aromas of basil and garlic, and tasters loved both the taste of the pesto and the buttery goodness of the pine nuts and Parmesan. Fresh snap peas and radishes offered a flourish of spring crunch and color. You should have about 12 ounces of asparagus after trimming.

# HEARTY SPRING VEGETABLE SOUP

- 3 tablespoons extra-virgin olive oil
- 1 pound asparagus, trimmed and cut into ½-inch lengths
- 12 ounces zucchini, cut into ½-inch pieces
- 2 cups (8 ounces) chopped green cabbage
- ¼ teaspoon table salt
- ¼ teaspoon pepper
- 2 garlic cloves, minced
- 2½ cups vegetable broth
- 1 cup water
- ¼ cup Basil Pesto (page 26)
- 1 ounce Parmesan cheese, grated (½ cup)
- 2 ounces snap peas, strings removed, sliced thin on bias
- 2 radishes (2 ounces), trimmed, halved, and sliced thin

**1.** Heat oil in Dutch oven over medium-high heat until just smoking. Add asparagus, zucchini, cabbage, salt, and pepper and cook until vegetables are softened, about 3 minutes. Stir in garlic and cook until fragrant, about 30 seconds.

**2.** Stir in broth and water, bring to simmer, and cook until vegetables are tender and bright green, 3 to 5 minutes. Season with salt and pepper to taste. Dollop each portion with 1 tablespoon pesto and sprinkle evenly with Parmesan, snap peas, and radishes.

### *Keto Meal Prep*

» Soup can be refrigerated for up to 3 days. To reheat, bring to gentle simmer in saucepan or microwave in bowl until steaming.

# ROASTED EGGPLANT AND KALE SOUP

- 6 tablespoons extra-virgin olive oil, divided
- 1¼ pounds eggplant, cut into ½-inch pieces
- 2 garlic cloves, minced
- 1½ teaspoons ground coriander
- 1½ teaspoons ground cumin
- 1 teaspoon grated fresh ginger
- ¾ teaspoon ground dried Aleppo pepper, divided
- ¼ teaspoon ground cinnamon
- ½ teaspoon table salt
- ¼ teaspoon pepper
- 3 cups vegetable broth
- 1½ cups water
- 2 ounces (2 cups) baby kale, chopped coarse
- ½ cup whole Greek yogurt
- 2 tablespoons sliced almonds, toasted
- 2 tablespoons minced fresh cilantro

**1.** Heat ¼ cup oil in Dutch oven over medium-high heat until just smoking. Add eggplant and cook, stirring occasionally, until tender and deeply browned, 6 to 8 minutes; transfer to bowl.

**2.** Combine garlic, coriander, cumin, ginger, ½ teaspoon Aleppo pepper, cinnamon, salt, and pepper in small bowl. Add remaining 2 tablespoons oil and garlic mixture to now-empty pot and cook over medium heat until fragrant, about 30 seconds. Stir in broth and water, scraping up any browned bits, and bring to simmer. Reduce heat to medium low, cover partially, and cook until flavors meld, about 15 minutes.

**3.** Off heat, stir in kale and eggplant along with any accumulated juices. Let sit until wilted, about 2 minutes. Season with salt and pepper to taste. Dollop each portion with 2 tablespoons yogurt and sprinkle evenly with almonds, cilantro, and remaining ¼ teaspoon Aleppo pepper before serving.

## Keto Meal Prep

» Soup can be refrigerated for up to 3 days. To reheat, bring to gentle simmer in saucepan or microwave in bowl until steaming.

**Serves** 4
**Total Time** 45 minutes

## PER SERVING
**Cal** 310 | **Total Fat** 27g
**Protein** 5g | **Net Carbs** 8g
**Fiber** 6g | **Total Carbs** 14g

## Why This Recipe Works

For a quick but hearty, deeply flavored vegetarian soup, we combined the meaty taste of eggplant with a potent combination of spices: cumin, coriander, ginger, garlic, and Aleppo pepper. We diced the eggplant and browned it before setting it aside. Adding more oil to the Dutch oven, we bloomed the spices, garlic, and ginger in it. Then we cooked the broth and spices together until the flavors melded. We added the eggplant back in off the heat and also stirred in baby kale for its fiber, color, and pleasant texture. Sliced almonds added a pleasant crunch, cilantro lent freshness, and the pleasant tang of Greek yogurt made for a rich, nuanced topping. Finally, a sprinkle of Aleppo pepper gave us a pop of bright red color. If you can't find Aleppo pepper, you can substitute ½ teaspoon paprika mixed with ¼ teaspoon minced red pepper flakes.

**Serves** 4
**Total Time** 3½ hours  *Very good*

## PER SERVING
**Cal** 610 | **Total Fat** 47g
**Protein** 38g | **Net Carbs** 9g
**Fiber** 4g | **Total Carbs** 13g

### Why This Recipe Works

Few things are as soul-satisfying as a steaming hot bowl of beef stew. This recipe uses the oven and stovetop and takes time, so it's perfect for weekend cooking when you have some leisure. You can pack the leftovers for a work lunch during the week. Many stew recipes rely on flour or potatoes as a thickener. Both are delicious but do not work on the keto eating plan. Since we still wanted a rich, hearty stew, we used fatty boneless beef short ribs because they turn meltingly tender with long, slow cooking and chunks of portobello mushrooms for their meatiness. We also decided to add low-carb cauliflower to thicken the stew and make it creamy. First we browned the meat to create flavorful fond, and then we mixed in the mushrooms and cauliflower. We cooked them with the meat in the oven with chicken broth. Finally, since cauliflower purees really easily because of its low carb content, we whizzed it up with some broth to give our stew a creamy consistency, keeping some cauliflower florets whole for diners to bite into. A drizzle of red wine vinegar and sprinkle of minced parsley made a bright, fresh accent to this comforting winter favorite.

# HEARTY BEEF STEW WITH CAULIFLOWER AND MUSHROOMS

1½ pounds boneless beef short ribs, trimmed and cut into 1½-inch pieces
½ teaspoon table salt
½ teaspoon pepper
¼ cup extra-virgin olive oil, divided
12 ounces portobello mushroom caps, gills removed, cut into 1½-inch pieces
½ onion (4 ounces), chopped fine
1 tablespoon tomato paste
1 tablespoon minced fresh thyme or 1 teaspoon dried
4 cups chicken broth
2 bay leaves
1 pound cauliflower florets, cut into 1½-inch pieces
2 teaspoons red wine vinegar
¼ cup chopped fresh parsley

**1.** Adjust oven rack to lower-middle position and heat oven to 300 degrees. Pat beef dry with paper towels and sprinkle with salt and pepper. Heat 2 tablespoons oil in Dutch oven over medium-high heat until just smoking. Brown beef on all sides, 5 to 10 minutes; transfer to bowl.

**2.** Add mushrooms, onion, and remaining 2 tablespoons oil to fat left in pot, cover, and cook over medium heat until mushrooms have released their liquid, about 5 minutes. Uncover and continue to cook until mushrooms are dry and onion is lightly browned, 5 to 10 minutes. Stir in tomato paste and thyme and cook until fragrant, about 1 minute.

**3.** Stir in broth and bay leaves, scraping up any browned bits. Stir in beef and any accumulated juices and bring to simmer. Cover, transfer pot to oven, and cook for 2 hours. Stir in cauliflower and continue to cook until meat and vegetables are tender, about 30 minutes.

**4.** Remove stew from oven and discard bay leaves. Transfer 1 cup cooking liquid and 1 cup cauliflower to blender and process until smooth, about 30 seconds, scraping down sides of blender jar as needed. Stir cauliflower puree and vinegar into stew and season with salt and pepper to taste. Sprinkle individual portions evenly with parsley before serving.

### Keto Meal Prep

» Stew can be refrigerated for up to 3 days. To reheat, bring to gentle simmer in covered saucepan, stirring often, or microwave in covered bowl, until steaming. Adjust consistency with hot water as needed.

# EASY GROUND BEEF CHILI

1 tablespoon extra-virgin olive oil

1½ pounds 80 percent lean ground beef

1 green bell pepper (8 ounces), stemmed, seeded, and cut into ½-inch pieces

2 tablespoons blanched, finely ground almond flour

1½ tablespoons chili powder

2 garlic cloves, minced

2 teaspoons ground coriander

2 teaspoons ground cumin

1 teaspoon dried oregano

1 teaspoon minced canned chipotle chile in adobo sauce

2 cups beef broth

1 (15-ounce) can diced tomatoes, drained

¼ cup sour cream

1 avocado (8 ounces), halved, pitted, and cut into ½-inch pieces

¼ cup chopped fresh cilantro

**1.** Heat oil in Dutch oven over medium-high heat until just shimmering. Add beef and bell pepper and cook, breaking up meat with wooden spoon, until any liquid has evaporated and fond begins to form on bottom of pot, 10 to 12 minutes. Stir in almond flour, chili powder, garlic, coriander, cumin, oregano, and chipotle and cook until fragrant, about 30 seconds.

**2.** Stir in broth and tomatoes, scraping up any browned bits, and bring to simmer. Reduce heat to medium-low, cover partially, and cook, stirring occasionally, until flavors meld, about 15 minutes. Season with salt and pepper to taste. Dollop 1 tablespoon sour cream on each serving and top evenly with avocado and cilantro.

## Keto Meal Prep

» Chili can be refrigerated for up to 3 days. To reheat, bring to gentle simmer in covered saucepan, stirring often, or microwave in covered bowl, until steaming. Adjust consistency with hot water as needed.

Serves 4
**Total Time** 45 minutes

### PER SERVING

**Cal** 640 | **Total Fat** 50g
**Protein** 35g | **Net Carbs** 8g
**Fiber** 6g | **Total Carbs** 14g

### Why This Recipe Works

A quick and easy chili is something all cooks should have in their repertoire because it is a satisfying, meaty dinner you can make in less than an hour. We tried first quickly browning the ground beef on its own in oil to build flavor but found that this resulted in a pebbly, dry texture we didn't like. Then we tried sautéing the beef with a green bell pepper for moisture. That worked. Once a fond was just beginning to form at the bottom of the pot, we added a spicy Southwest punch with chipotle chile, garlic, and other aromatic spices bloomed in the same hot oil. We cooked the meat and spices with broth and bright tomatoes, adding almond flour to thicken the chili. Since we love avocado, sour cream, and cilantro with our Southwestern food, it's wonderful that they are ideal keto fixings for this hearty weeknight meal.

**Serves** 4
**Total Time** 45 minutes

## PER SERVING

**Cal** 550 | **Total Fat** 40g
**Protein** 40g | **Net Carbs** 6g
**Fiber** 2g | **Total Carbs** 8g

## Why This Recipe Works

New England–style fish chowders are often loaded with carbs, which is part of what makes them thick, creamy, and delicious. We wanted a keto version that still gave us the characteristic texture of the original. After testing different ways to thicken our soup, we found that pureeing cooked cauliflower into our base re-created the velvety consistency of chowders thickened by flour. We rendered a few strips of bacon in our pot, saved the crispy bacon bits for serving, then sautéed a bit of thyme in the remaining bacon fat. We stirred half of our cauliflower into the pot and poured in clam juice, which reinforced the soup's seafood flavor and allowed us to scrape up the flavorful browned bits at the bottom of the pot. Then we simmered the mixture until the cauliflower began to break down and processed it with cream in a blender. After pouring the puree back into the pot and adding the remaining cauliflower florets, we slid in large chunks of cod. The fish cooked gently over medium-low heat and we stirred fresh lemon juice into the soup for brightness just before serving. Sprinkling crisp bacon and parsley over individual bowls provided a rich, crunchy finishing touch. Halibut and haddock are good substitutes for the cod.

# NEW ENGLAND SEAFOOD CHOWDER

6 ounces bacon, chopped
1 teaspoon minced fresh thyme or ¼ teaspoon dried
1 pound cauliflower florets, cut into ½-inch pieces, divided
2 (8-ounce) bottles clam juice
¾ teaspoon table salt
½ teaspoon pepper
1 bay leaf
1 cup heavy cream
1½ pounds skinless cod fillets, 1 inch thick, cut into 2-inch pieces
1 teaspoon lemon juice
3 tablespoons chopped fresh parsley

**1.** Cook bacon in Dutch oven over medium heat until crispy, 5 to 7 minutes. Using slotted spoon, transfer bacon to paper towel–lined plate; set aside for serving.

**2.** Add thyme to fat left in pot and cook until fragrant, about 30 seconds. Stir in half of cauliflower, clam juice, salt, pepper, and bay leaf and bring to simmer. Reduce heat to medium-low and simmer until cauliflower falls apart easily when poked with fork 10 to 12 minutes.

**3.** Discard bay leaf. Process cauliflower mixture and cream in blender until smooth, about 1 minute; return to now-empty pot and bring to simmer over medium heat. Stir in remaining cauliflower and cook for 2 minutes. Nestle cod into soup, cover, and reduce heat to medium-low. Simmer gently until cod flakes apart when gently prodded with paring knife and registers 140 degrees, 6 to 8 minutes.

**4.** Off heat, gently stir in lemon juice and season with salt and pepper to taste. Break any remaining large pieces of cod in half. Sprinkle individual portions evenly with parsley and crisp bacon before serving.

### *Keto Meal Prep*

» Chowder and reserved bacon can be refrigerated separately for up to 24 hours. To reheat, bring to gentle simmer in covered saucepan, stirring often, or microwave in covered bowl, until steaming. Adjust consistency with hot water as needed. Bring bacon to room temperature before serving.

**Makes** about 4 cups
**Total Time** 1¼ hours

## PER 1-CUP SERVING

**Cal** 470 | **Total Fat** 34g
**Protein** 38g | **Net Carbs** 1g
**Fiber** 0g | **Total Carbs** 1g

### Why This Recipe Works

Since grandma's chicken salad is a fond memory for many of us and chicken salad is naturally keto, we had to include it here and add two flavorful make-ahead variations. In many of this book's chicken recipes, we bump up the fat content by using chicken thighs. But for this classic recipe, chicken breasts were more flavorful. To make sure they stayed moist (because it is easy to overcook and dry out breasts), we used the test kitchen's easy, gentle poaching method. The moist breasts then readily took on the flavor of creamy mayonnaise, crunchy celery, and bright green herbs (we're huge fans of a combination of chives, tarragon, and dill). A squeeze of lemon juice gave a bright finish to the salad. For our Spanish variation, we used smoked paprika, warm cumin, a splash of sherry vinegar, and toasted almonds. We also played with classic curried chicken salad, using shallot, aromatic curry powder, cumin, coriander, fresh cilantro, lime juice, and toasted pistachios. (We promise you won't miss the raisins.) Chicken salad is great to make ahead, grab, and go because it tastes better the longer it sits. Serve it over leafy greens, in our Keto Tortillas (page 20), or with Seeded Bread (page 23). To ensure that the chicken cooks through, start with cold water in step 1 and don't use breasts that weigh more than 8 ounces or are thicker than 1 inch.

# CHICKEN SALAD WITH FRESH HERBS

¼ teaspoon table salt, plus salt for poaching chicken
1½ pounds boneless, skinless chicken breasts, trimmed
¾ cup mayonnaise
¼ cup finely chopped celery
¼ cup chopped fresh chives, dill, and/or tarragon
2 teaspoons lemon juice
⅛ teaspoon pepper

**1.** Dissolve 2 tablespoons salt in 6 cups cold water in Dutch oven. Submerge chicken in water. Heat pot over medium heat until water registers 170 degrees. Turn off heat, cover pot, and let sit until chicken registers 165 degrees, 15 to 17 minutes. Transfer chicken to paper towel–lined plate and refrigerate until cool, about 30 minutes.

**2.** Stir mayonnaise, celery, herbs, lemon juice, salt, and pepper together in bowl. Transfer chicken to cutting board, pat dry with paper towels, and cut into ½-inch pieces. Add chicken to bowl with mayonnaise mixture and toss to combine. Season with salt and pepper to taste. Serve.

### Chicken Salad with Smoked Paprika and Almonds

Substitute 4 ounces chopped red bell pepper for celery, fresh parsley for chives, and 1 tablespoon sherry vinegar for lemon juice. Stir 1 teaspoon smoked paprika, ¼ teaspoon ground cumin, and ½ cup chopped toasted almonds into mayonnaise mixture before adding chicken.

**Per 1-cup Serving** Cal 580; Total Fat 43g; Protein 42g; Net Carbs 3g; Fiber 3g; Total Carbs 6g

### Curried Chicken Salad with Pistachios

Substitute 1 minced shallot for celery, fresh cilantro for chives, and 4 teaspoons lime juice for lemon juice. Stir 1 tablespoon curry powder, ½ teaspoon ground cumin, ½ teaspoon ground coriander, and ½ cup chopped toasted pistachios into mayonnaise mixture before adding chicken.

**Per 1-cup Serving** Cal 570; Total Fat 42g; Protein 42g; Net Carbs 4g; Fiber 3g; Total Carbs 7g

### *Keto Meal Prep*

» Salad can be refrigerated for up to 2 days.

# GREEN GOODNESS BOWL

Pinch table salt, plus salt for poaching chicken

2 (6-ounce) boneless, skinless chicken breasts, trimmed

6 tablespoons mayonnaise

2 tablespoons sour cream

3 tablespoons chopped fresh basil, parsley, and/or tarragon

2 teaspoons water

1½ teaspoons lemon juice

1 small garlic clove, chopped

2 tablespoons chopped fresh chives

1 teaspoon extra-virgin olive oil

8 ounces asparagus, trimmed and cut into 1-inch pieces

⅛ teaspoon pepper

4 cups (4 ounces) baby spinach

½ avocado (4 ounces), sliced thin

2 tablespoons chopped toasted pistachios

**1.** Dissolve 2 tablespoons salt in 6 cups cold water in Dutch oven. Submerge chicken in water. Heat pot over medium heat until water registers 170 degrees. Turn off heat, cover pot, and let sit until chicken registers 165 degrees, 15 to 17 minutes. Transfer chicken to paper towel–lined plate and refrigerate until cool, about 30 minutes. Transfer chicken to cutting board, pat dry with paper towels, and shred into bite-size pieces.

**2.** Process mayonnaise, sour cream, herbs, water, lemon juice, and garlic in blender until smooth, scraping down sides of blender jar as needed. Stir in chives and season with salt and pepper to taste; set aside.

**3.** Heat oil in 10-inch nonstick skillet over medium-high heat until shimmering. Add asparagus, pepper, and pinch salt and cook, stirring frequently, until crisp-tender, 5 to 7 minutes; transfer to bowl.

**4.** Toss spinach with half of dressing and divide among individual serving bowls. Top evenly with chicken, asparagus, and avocado. Drizzle with remaining dressing and sprinkle with pistachios. Serve.

## *Keto Meal Prep*

» Shredded chicken, dressing, and asparagus, prepared through step 3, can be refrigerated separately for up to 4 days. Bring asparagus to room temperature and whisk dressing to recombine before serving.

**Serves** 2
**Total Time** 1½ hours

## PER SERVING
**Cal** 680 | **Total Fat** 51g
**Protein** 45g | **Net Carbs** 6g
**Fiber** 8g | **Total Carbs** 14g

## Why This Recipe Works

People believe that eating keto means not eating enough vegetables. We've developed recipes that disprove that notion, and this is one of them. Our stunning textured green bowl showcases chicken but also offers keto goodness in other shapes and forms, from an herbaceous green goddess dressing with mayonnaise and sour cream to silky avocados, crunchy pistachios, fiber-rich spinach, and crisp asparagus. Herbs lent a pretty green hue to our dressing and spinach was sturdy enough to hold up to its bold flavors; we tossed the greens with half the dressing and reserved the rest to drizzle over individual servings. Look for avocados with dark skin that yield to gentle pressure. We prefer to poach our own chicken to shred. This means it is moist and well seasoned. To ensure that the chicken cooks through, start with cold water in step 1 and don't use breasts that weigh more than 8 ounces or are thicker than 1 inch. You should have about 6 ounces of asparagus after trimming.

**Serves** 4
**Total Time** 1¼ hours

## PER SERVING

**Cal** 600 | **Total Fat** 45g
**Protein** 40g | **Net Carbs** 8g
**Fiber** 3g | **Total Carbs** 11g

### Why This Recipe Works

Thai cuisine, with its use of rich, fatty coconut; peanuts; and complex, aromatic spices and fresh herbs, is a perfect way for keto eaters to add some global variety to their diet. We developed this easy, flavorful recipe to evoke Thai food without the need for that great Asian staple, rice. Our recipe is also a time-saver: You can start it on the weekend and finish assembling it when you are ready to eat. We first combined coconut milk, fresh cilantro, nutty sesame oil, fish sauce, curry powder, and cayenne in the food processor to make a spice mixture. We used some of the paste to marinate our chicken thighs and turned the rest into a creamy sauce with the help of peanut butter; some lime juice balanced the spicy richness. While our chicken marinated, we prepared the cabbage slaw to top the chicken. Since salt extracts moisture from cabbage, shrinking the shreds and making them easier to eat, we salted red cabbage and let it rest. When it was time to bring all the elements of the wraps together, broiling the marinated chicken thighs cooked them quickly and gave us some crispy charred bits (our favorite). We finished the slaw with more cilantro and scallions, and assembled our wraps on crisp, sweet Bibb lettuce leaves. Don't forget a sprinkling of roasted peanuts for added crunch. With three wraps per person, you will feel incredibly satisfied.

# THAI CHICKEN LETTUCE WRAPS

- ½ cup unsweetened canned coconut milk
- ½ cup fresh cilantro leaves, divided
- ¼ cup toasted sesame oil
- 1 tablespoon fish sauce
- ½ teaspoon curry powder
- ⅛ teaspoon cayenne pepper
- 1½ pounds boneless, skinless chicken thighs, trimmed
- ½ cup creamy unsweetened peanut butter
- 1 tablespoon coconut oil
- ¼ cup water
- 2 tablespoons lime juice, divided
- 2 cups (8 ounces) shredded red cabbage
- ¼ teaspoon table salt
- 2 scallions, sliced thin
- 12 large Bibb lettuce leaves
- 3 tablespoons dry-roasted unsalted peanuts, chopped

**1.** Process coconut milk, ¼ cup cilantro leaves, sesame oil, fish sauce, curry powder, and cayenne in blender until smooth, about 1 minute, scraping down sides of blender jar as needed. Transfer ¼ cup coconut mixture to medium bowl, add chicken, and toss to coat. Cover and refrigerate for 30 minutes.

**2.** Add peanut butter, coconut oil, water, and 1 tablespoon lime juice to remaining coconut mixture in blender and process until smooth, about 1 minute. Transfer sauce to bowl and set aside for serving.

**3.** Toss cabbage with salt and remaining 1 tablespoon lime juice in separate bowl. Cover and refrigerate for 30 minutes.

**4.** Adjust oven rack 6 inches from broiler element and heat broiler. Set wire rack in aluminum foil–lined rimmed baking sheet and spray with olive oil spray. Transfer chicken to prepared rack and broil until chicken is evenly charred and registers 175 degrees, 16 to 20 minutes, flipping chicken halfway through broiling. Transfer chicken to cutting board, tent with aluminum foil, and let rest for 5 minutes.

**5.** Drain cabbage and return to now-empty bowl. Stir in scallions and remaining ¼ cup cilantro. Slice chicken ½ inch thick, transfer to separate bowl, and toss with ½ cup sauce. Divide chicken evenly among lettuce leaves and top with remaining sauce, cabbage slaw, and peanuts. Serve.

### *Keto Meal Prep*

» Chicken, peanut sauce, and cabbage, prepared through step 3, can be refrigerated for up to 12 hours. To reheat, place chicken in covered nonstick skillet and cook over medium heat, stirring occasionally, for about 5 minutes, or place in covered bowl and microwave for 1 to 2 minutes. Let peanut sauce come to room temperature before serving.

# TURKEY-VEGGIE BURGERS

6 tablespoons mayonnaise
¼ cup extra-virgin olive oil, divided
¼ cup sour cream
½ teaspoon grated lemon zest plus 1 tablespoon lemon juice
1 pound ground turkey
1 small zucchini (6 ounces), shredded
1 carrot (3 ounces), peeled and shredded
1 ounce Parmesan cheese, grated (½ cup)
¼ teaspoon pepper
¼ teaspoon table salt
5 ounces cherry tomatoes, halved
1 tablespoon chopped fresh basil
8 large iceberg lettuce leaves
1 avocado (8 ounces), halved, pitted, and sliced ¼ inch thick

**1.** Combine mayonnaise, 1 tablespoon oil, sour cream, and lemon zest and juice in bowl. Season with salt and pepper to taste. Cover and refrigerate until ready to serve.

**2.** Break ground turkey into small pieces in large bowl. Add zucchini, carrot, Parmesan, 1 tablespoon oil, and pepper and gently knead with your hands until well combined. Divide turkey mixture into 4 equal portions, then gently shape each portion into ¾-inch-thick patty. Using your fingertips, press center of each patty down until about ½-inch thick, creating slight divot.

**3.** Sprinkle patties with salt. Heat 1 tablespoon oil in 12-inch nonstick skillet over medium heat until just smoking. Transfer patties to skillet, divot side up, and cook until well browned on first side, 4 to 6 minutes. Flip patties, reduce heat to medium-low, and continue to cook until browned on second side and burgers register 160 degrees, 5 to 7 minutes. Transfer burgers to plate, tent with aluminum foil, and let rest for 5 minutes.

**4.** Toss tomatoes and basil with remaining 1 tablespoon oil and season with salt and pepper to taste. Using 2 lettuce leaves stacked together, create 4 lettuce wraps. Serve burgers on wraps, topped evenly with sauce, tomato mixture, and avocado.

## *Keto Meal Prep*
» Sauce and shaped patties, prepared through step 2, can be refrigerated for up to 24 hours.

**Serves** 4
**Total Time** 45 minutes

### PER SERVING
**Cal** 540 | **Total Fat** 43g
**Protein** 34g | **Net Carbs** 6g
**Fiber** 5g | **Total Carbs** 11g

### Why This Recipe Works
Turkey burgers often get a bad reputation due to their dry, crumbly texture and lackluster flavor. With a few tricks, though, we were able to turn this keto-friendly dish into a rich, moist, flavor-packed burger you'll want to add to your weekly routine. To give the sauce's flavors time to meld, we made it first. A combination of mayonnaise, olive oil, and sour cream was brightened up with some lemon juice and zest (we love the zest for its concentrated lemon flavor that's not too sour or carb-heavy). Then, we worked on the patties. To add moisture to ground turkey, we mixed in grated zucchini and sweet carrot. Grated Parmesan (think meatballs) not only helped to bind the patties, but also gave them texture and the perfect salty bite. Shaping a slight depression or divot in the center of the patty helped the meat expand evenly over heat rather than swelling up in the middle. Searing the patties first resulted in proper browning and a crisp exterior; we made sure to give them lots of oil to soak up so they were rich and deliciously keto. For "buns" we used crisp iceberg lettuce leaves, satisfyingly crunchy and subtly sweet. Finally, fresh cherry tomatoes and sliced avocado brought everything together. Be sure to use ground turkey, not ground turkey breast (also labeled 99 percent fat-free), in this recipe.

**PER SERVING**
**Cal** 650 | **Total Fat** 47g
**Protein** 43g | **Net Carbs** 8g
**Fiber** 5g | **Total Carbs** 13g

## Why This Recipe Works

Nothing beats the simplicity of a complete meal wrapped and cooked in a foil packet. We could be camping. Food baked in foil packets, or *en papillote,* has been lauded for its healthfulness and ease, but our first attempts gave us overcooked chicken, mushy vegetables, and overall blandness. We started over by softening fennel in the microwave with olive oil, pepper flakes, and thinly sliced garlic; we then tossed in crunchy radishes. The seasoned veggies made a moist, flavorful "rack" on which we set the chicken so it would steam evenly. We chose quick-cooking boneless chicken breasts, and to ensure that the seasoning permeated the flesh, we refrigerated the prepared meat and vegetable packages for 30 minutes before cooking. Leaving headroom at the top of the packets allowed maximum steam circulation for even cooking, and checking the temperature of the chicken through the foil let us monitor its progress. For added flavor, we topped the chicken with Pistachio-Tarragon Pesto (page 26). The chicken is juicy on its own, and you can use it to sop up every last bit of this incredibly flavorful sauce. You should have about 4 ounces of fennel after trimming.

# CHICKEN BAKED IN FOIL WITH FENNEL AND RADISHES

½ fennel bulb (6 ounces), stalks discarded, cored, and cut into ½-inch-thick wedges, layers separated
1 tablespoon extra-virgin olive oil
4 radishes (4 ounces), trimmed and quartered
2 (6-ounce) boneless, skinless chicken breasts, trimmed
½ teaspoon table salt
½ teaspoon pepper
6 tablespoons Pistachio-Tarragon Pesto (page 26)

**1.** Microwave fennel and oil in large bowl, stirring occasionally, until softened, about 5 minutes. Add radishes and toss to coat.

**2.** Spray two 20 by 12-inch sheets of heavy-duty aluminum foil with olive oil spray. Pound thicker end of chicken breasts between 2 sheets of plastic to uniform ½-inch thickness. Sprinkle chicken with salt and pepper. Position prepared foil sheets on counter with long sides parallel to counter edge. Arrange vegetable mixture into 2 shallow piles in center of sheets. Lay 1 chicken breast on top of each vegetable pile.

**3.** Bring short sides of each foil sheet together and crimp to seal tightly. Crimp remaining open ends of packets, leaving as much headroom as possible inside packet. Refrigerate packets for 30 minutes.

**4.** Adjust oven rack to lowest position and heat oven to 475 degrees. Arrange packets on rimmed baking sheet and bake until chicken registers 165 degrees, 15 to 20 minutes. (To check temperature, poke thermometer through foil and into chicken.)

**5.** Transfer sheet with packets to wire rack and let sit for 5 minutes. Transfer chicken packets to individual dinner plates, open carefully (steam will escape), and slide contents onto plates. Top each portion with 3 tablespoons pesto and serve.

### *Keto Meal Prep*
» Packets, prepared through step 3, can be refrigerated for up to 24 hours.

# PROSCIUTTO-WRAPPED CHICKEN WITH ASPARAGUS

**Serves** 2
**Total Time** 1 hour

### PER SERVING
**Cal** 830 | **Total Fat** 63g
**Protein** 57g | **Net Carbs** 5g
**Fiber** 3g | **Total Carbs** 8g

2   (6-ounce) boneless, skinless chicken breasts, trimmed
½   teaspoon pepper
4   thin slices prosciutto (2 ounces)
6   tablespoons extra-virgin olive oil, divided
2   ounces fontina cheese, shredded (½ cup)
12  ounces thin asparagus, trimmed
2   tablespoons toasted chopped pecans
1   tablespoon white wine vinegar
1   small shallot, minced
1   teaspoon Dijon mustard
1   teaspoon minced fresh thyme

**1.** Adjust oven rack to middle position and heat oven to 350 degrees. Pound thicker end of chicken breasts between 2 sheets of plastic to uniform ½-inch thickness. Pat chicken dry with paper towels and sprinkle with pepper. Slightly overlap 2 prosciutto slices on cutting board, lay 1 chicken breast in center, and fold prosciutto over chicken. Repeat with remaining 2 prosciutto slices and remaining chicken breast.

**2.** Heat 1 tablespoon oil in 12-inch nonstick ovenproof skillet over medium-high heat until just smoking. Brown chicken lightly, about 2 minutes per side. Transfer to cutting board and top with fontina.

**3.** Add asparagus to skillet. Using tongs, toss asparagus with 1 tablespoon oil. Arrange half of asparagus with tips pointed in 1 direction and remaining asparagus with tips pointed in opposite direction. Arrange chicken breasts on top of asparagus and bake until chicken registers 160 degrees and asparagus is tender and bright green, about 12 minutes.

**4.** Transfer chicken and asparagus to individual serving plates. Whisk remaining ¼ cup oil, pecans, vinegar, shallot, mustard, and thyme into juices left in skillet until thoroughly combined. Season with salt and pepper to taste. Drizzle chicken and asparagus with dressing and serve.

## Why This Recipe Works
Step aside, boring weeknight chicken; our fabulous prosciutto-wrapped chicken breast is here! We seasoned it with black pepper and wrapped it in thin slices of salty-sweet, nutty prosciutto. Searing the chicken on both sides in a nonstick skillet crisped up the prosciutto, enhancing its salty bite. We rested the chicken briefly, topping it with fontina (perfect for its luscious melting quality). In the skillet, we arranged a healthy portion of asparagus, placed our cheese-topped chicken breasts over it, and baked till done. Once the cooked chicken and asparagus were portioned, we made our dressing right in the skillet, whisking the residual flavors into the bright vinaigrette. We topped the chicken and asparagus with dressing and toasted pecans for a luscious, juicy, crunchy, tangy meal. Be sure to use thin asparagus spears to ensure that they finish cooking in the same time as the chicken breasts. Look for asparagus spears that are between ¼ and ½ inch near the base. You should have about 8 ounces of asparagus after trimming.

**Serves** 4
**Total Time** 45 minutes

## PER SERVING

**Cal** 380 | **Total Fat** 24g
**Protein** 38g | **Net Carbs** 0g
**Fiber** 0g | **Total Carbs** 0g

## Why This Recipe Works

Bone-in chicken thighs are more flavorful than lean breasts, meatier than drumsticks, and, thanks to their uniform size and thickness, less prone to overcooking, which eliminates any need for brining or salting. They are also suited to keto because of the fat layer underneath their skin. This fat helps keep the meat moist during cooking too, making chicken thighs the perfect protein for a quick keto weeknight supper. We simply flavored the chicken with salt and pepper before putting it into the oven. To mix things up but still keep them easy, we created a barbecue-rubbed variation with a hint of smoked paprika, and a Cajun-inspired version with cayenne and cinnamon. The chicken can be served with one of our vegetable sides, like Whipped Cauliflower (page 184), Sautéed Green Beans with Mustard Vinaigrette (page 188), or Quick Collard Greens with Chorizo (page 191). For best results, trim all visible fat from the thighs.

# OVEN-ROASTED CHICKEN THIGHS

8  (5- to 7-ounce) bone-in chicken thighs, trimmed
½  teaspoon table salt
½  teaspoon pepper

Adjust oven rack to upper-middle position and heat oven to 450 degrees. Sprinkle thighs with salt and pepper and arrange skin side up on rimmed baking sheet. Roast until chicken registers 175 degrees, 25 to 30 minutes. Transfer chicken to platter and let rest for 5 minutes. Serve.

### Barbecue-Rubbed Oven-Roasted Chicken Thighs

Combine 2 teaspoons chili powder, 2 teaspoons smoked paprika, and ¼ teaspoon cayenne pepper with salt and pepper in bowl. Rub mixture over thighs before arranging on baking sheet.
**Per Serving** Cal 390; Total Fat 24g; Protein 38g; Net Carbs 0g; Fiber 1g; Total Carbs 1g

### Cajun-Rubbed Oven-Roasted Chicken Thighs

Combine 1½ teaspoons ground coriander, 1½ teaspoons ground celery seeds, 1½ teaspoons paprika, ⅛ teaspoon cinnamon, and ⅛ teaspoon cayenne pepper with salt and pepper in bowl. Rub mixture over thighs before arranging on baking sheet.
**Per Serving** Cal 390; Total Fat 24g; Protein 38g; Net Carbs 0g; Fiber 1g; Total Carbs 1g

# ONE-PAN ROAST CHICKEN THIGHS WITH CAULIFLOWER AND TOMATOES

Serves 4
**Total Time** 1 hour

## PER SERVING
**Cal** 620 | **Total Fat** 46g
**Protein** 42g | **Net Carbs** 7g
**Fiber** 4g | **Total Carbs** 11g

1 head cauliflower (2 pounds)
6 tablespoons extra-virgin olive oil, divided
2 tablespoons chopped fresh sage, divided
1 teaspoon table salt, divided
1 teaspoon pepper, divided
8 (5- to 7-ounce) bone-in chicken thighs, trimmed
2 garlic cloves, minced
1 teaspoon grated lemon zest
6 ounces cherry tomatoes, halved
1 tablespoon coarsely chopped fresh parsley

**1.** Adjust 1 oven rack to lower middle position and second rack 8 inches from broiler element and heat oven to 475 degrees. Trim outer leaves of cauliflower and cut stem flush with bottom of head. Cut head into 8 equal wedges, keeping core and florets intact.

**2.** Gently toss cauliflower with ¼ cup oil, 1 tablespoon sage, ½ teaspoon salt, and ½ teaspoon pepper on rimmed baking sheet. Position cauliflower cut sides down in single layer in center of sheet.

**3.** Pat chicken dry with paper towels. Using sharp knife, make 2 parallel diagonal slashes across each thigh (each slash should reach bone). Sprinkle chicken with remaining ½ teaspoon salt and remaining ½ teaspoon pepper. Place 2 chicken thighs, skin side up, in each corner of sheet (chicken should rest directly on sheet, not on vegetables).

**4.** Whisk remaining 2 tablespoons oil, remaining 1 tablespoon sage, garlic, and lemon zest together in bowl. Brush skin side of chicken with seasoned oil mixture. Transfer sheet to lower rack and roast until cauliflower is browned and chicken registers 175 degrees, 25 to 30 minutes.

**5.** Remove sheet from oven and heat broiler. Scatter tomatoes over cauliflower and place sheet on upper rack. Broil until chicken skin is browned and crisp and tomatoes have started to wilt, about 3 minutes. Transfer sheet to wire rack and let chicken rest for 5 minutes. Sprinkle with parsley and serve.

## Why This Recipe Works

Tired after a hard day at work? This quick chicken, cauliflower, and tomato dinner reduces your prep time and gives you a complete meal with abundant flavor and color. We roasted keto-friendly chicken thighs along with low-carb cauliflower, then finished them under the broiler for crisp golden-brown chicken and nicely charred vegetables. Making deep slashes in each chicken thigh allowed flavor to penetrate deeply by creating more surface area to hold the earthy seasoning of sage, lemon zest, and salt. We cut the cauliflower into thick wedges so it wouldn't dry out easily while roasting with the chicken. Arranging the vegetables in the middle of the sheet (where it's cooler) and positioning the chicken thighs around the perimeter (where it's hotter) ensured that everything cooked at the same rate. Cherry tomatoes added a pop of color and tartness. You should have about 1½ pounds of cauliflower after trimming.

**Serves** 4
**Total Time** 1¼ hours

## PER SERVING

**Cal** 730 | **Total Fat** 54g
**Protein** 52g | **Net Carbs** 5g
**Fiber** 2g | **Total Carbs** 7g

## Why This Recipe Works

Summertime means farm-fresh produce, citrus, and lots of great food on the grill. And what could be better to cook outdoors than chicken thighs? They are very forgiving when it comes to overcooking, a boon to inexperienced grillers. To develop more flavor, we started with a simple paste of spicy, tangy Dijon mustard, a little garlic, and lemon zest to rub on the chicken (juice would fall off but the zest clings). We first cooked the chicken thighs on the cooler side of the grill. Grilling them skin side down thoroughly rendered the fat under the skin's surface, turning the skin paper-thin, while the collagen in the skin broke down and softened. The two reactions allowed the chicken skin to get nicely crisp when we seared it over high heat at the end of cooking. We paired the chicken with a cool, refreshing zucchini salad, for which we shaved ribbons from four zucchini with a vegetable peeler. This gave us thin, crunchy strips, and we used the same trick on Parmesan. The slight crunch of the raw zucchini pairs perfectly with the cheese's salty umami. Extra-virgin olive oil and a sprinkling of fresh mint complement the deep char of the chicken thighs. The perfect keto-friendly summer meal is well within reach! Avoid buying large zucchini, which have thicker skins and more seeds. You should have 1½ pounds zucchini ribbons after peeling; reserve any extra ribbons for another use.

# GRILLED CHICKEN THIGHS WITH SHAVED ZUCCHINI SALAD

- 2 tablespoons Dijon mustard
- 2 garlic cloves, minced
- 1½ teaspoons grated lemon zest plus 2 tablespoons juice
- ½ teaspoon water
- ¼ teaspoon pepper
- 8 (5- to 7-ounce) bone-in chicken thighs, trimmed
- ½ teaspoon table salt, divided
- 4 zucchini (8 ounces each), ends trimmed
- 6 tablespoons extra-virgin olive oil
- 2 tablespoons chopped fresh mint
- 4 ounces Parmesan cheese, shaved

**1.** Combine mustard, garlic, lemon zest, water, and pepper in bowl. Place chicken, skin side up, on large plate. Sprinkle skin side with ¼ teaspoon salt and brush with one-third of mustard paste. Flip chicken and brush with remaining mustard paste; refrigerate while preparing grill.

**2.** Using vegetable peeler, shave each zucchini lengthwise into ribbons. Peel off 3 ribbons from 1 side, then turn zucchini 90 degrees and peel off 3 more ribbons. Continue to turn and peel ribbons until you reach seeds. Discard cores. Refrigerate zucchini ribbons until needed.

**3A. For a charcoal grill** Open bottom vent halfway. Light large chimney starter mounded with charcoal briquettes (7 quarts). When top coals are partially covered with ash, pour evenly over half of grill. Set cooking grate in place, cover, and open lid vent halfway. Heat grill until hot, about 5 minutes.

**3B. For a gas grill** Turn all burners to high, cover, and heat grill until hot, about 15 minutes. Leave primary burner on high and turn off other burner(s). (Adjust primary burner [or, if using 3-burner grill, primary burner and second burner] as needed to maintain grill temperature around 350 degrees.)

**4.** Clean and oil cooking grate. Place chicken skin side down on cooler side of grill. Cover and cook for 20 minutes. Rotate chicken, keeping skin side down, so that pieces that were closest to edge are now closer to heat source and vice versa. Cover and continue to cook until chicken registers 185 to 190 degrees, 15 to 20 minutes.

**5.** Move all chicken, keeping skin side down, to hotter side of grill and cook until skin is well charred, about 5 minutes. Flip chicken and continue to cook until flesh side is lightly browned, 1 to 2 minutes. Transfer to platter and let rest while preparing salad.

**6.** Whisk oil, mint, lemon juice, and remaining ¼ teaspoon salt in large bowl. Add zucchini and Parmesan and gently toss to combine. Serve immediately with chicken.

# CHICKEN MOLE POBLANO

*Pretty good.*

**Serves** 4
**Total Time** 1 hour

## PER SERVING

**Cal** 500 | **Total Fat** 33g
**Protein** 38g | **Net Carbs** 7g
**Fiber** 3g | **Total Carbs** 10g

1   dried ancho chile, stemmed, seeded, and torn into ½-inch pieces (¼ cup)
¼   cup extra-virgin olive oil, divided
3   scallions, white and green parts separated and sliced thin
1   garlic clove, minced
2   tablespoons tomato paste
2   tablespoons creamy unsweetened peanut butter
1   teaspoon unsweetened cocoa powder
¼   teaspoon ground cinnamon
1½  cups chicken broth
½   teaspoon table salt
½   teaspoon pepper
8   (5- to 7-ounce) bone-in chicken thighs, skin removed, trimmed
½   cup Avocado Crema (page 29)

**1.** Toast ancho in Dutch oven over medium heat, stirring frequently, until fragrant, 2 to 4 minutes; transfer to bowl. Add 2 tablespoons oil, scallion whites, and garlic to now-empty skillet and cook over medium heat until fragrant, about 1 minute. Stir in tomato paste, peanut butter, cocoa, and cinnamon and cook until mixture is emulsified and bubbly, about 2 minutes.

**2.** Stir in broth, salt, pepper, and ancho, scraping up any browned bits. Cook, stirring occasionally, until chile pieces are tender and mixture is slightly thickened, about 5 minutes. Transfer mixture to blender and add remaining 2 tablespoons oil. Process until smooth, 30 to 60 seconds, scraping down sides of blender jar as needed.

**3.** Return sauce to now-empty pot. Nestle chicken into pot and spoon some of sauce over top. Bring to simmer over medium-low heat, then cover and cook until thighs register 185 degrees, 25 to 30 minutes.

**4.** Transfer chicken to platter, tent with aluminum foil, and let rest while finishing sauce. Bring sauce to simmer over medium heat and cook until thickened and reduced to 1 cup, about 5 minutes. Return chicken and any accumulated juice to sauce and turn to coat. Serve chicken with mole, drizzling individual portions evenly with avocado crema and sprinkling with scallion greens.

## *Keto Meal Prep*

» Sauce, prepared through step 2, can be refrigerated for up to 4 days; adjust consistency with water as needed before proceeding with recipe.

## Why This Recipe Works:

A mole sauce is part of a family of sauces native to the Oaxaca and Puebla regions of Mexico. Its complex, layered flavors come from intricate blends of dried chiles, spices, and fruits. For a quick keto version, we chose mole poblano, which uses spices, nuts, and unsweetened chocolate, with a little dried ancho to keep the dish's deep, earthy flavor. We lightened our work by using easily available cocoa powder instead of purchasing unsweetened chocolate, and added unsweetened peanut butter—no nut grinding needed— for the mole's smooth texture. We did make the effort to blend toasted sesame seeds in with the other sauce ingredients, though, to replicate the nuttiness that usually comes from a longer simmering time. We opted not to brown the chicken that would be cooked in the mole, as the sauce's boldness eclipses any caramelized notes acquired through browning. We simply covered the skinned chicken thighs with the mole and simmered the sauce until the thighs came to temperature. A sprinkling of remaining sesame seeds and scallions and a drizzle of bright lime crema were the perfect adornment to a deeply flavorful dish. Serve it on its own, with Whipped Cauliflower (page 184), or with Cauliflower Rice (page 183).

**Serves** 4
**Total Time** 1¼ hours

## PER SERVING

**Cal** 560 | **Total Fat** 42g
**Protein** 36g | **Net Carbs** 5g
**Fiber** 2g | **Total Carbs** 7g

### Why This Recipe Works

Indian butter chicken (*murgh makhani*) literally means pieces of chicken cooked in a sauce flavored with spices that have been bloomed in butter rather than in the classic ghee or oil used in South Asian cooking. The dish should taste rich and creamy but also vibrant and complex, so we started by softening some onion, garlic, ginger, and chile in butter and then added aromatic spices such as garam masala, coriander, cumin, and black pepper. Since we couldn't use the carb-heavy chopped or crushed tomatoes that are typical of this recipe, we used a hefty amount of tomato paste and water instead, which lent the sauce bright acidity, punch, and deep color without making it too liquidy. A half-cup of cream gave the sauce lush, velvety body, and we finished it by stirring in another 4 tablespoons of butter for extra richness. To imitate the deep charring produced by a tandoor oven, we broiled chicken thighs coated in yogurt (its milk proteins and lactose brown quickly and deeply) before cutting them into chunks and stirring them into the sauce. Traditionally, butter chicken is mildly spiced. If you prefer a spicier dish, reserve, mince, and add the ribs and seeds from the chile. Serve it with Cauliflower-Almond Rice Pilaf (page 183).

# INDIAN BUTTER CHICKEN

- 8 tablespoons unsalted butter, divided
- ½ onion, chopped fine
- 3 garlic cloves, minced
- 2 teaspoons grated fresh ginger
- 2 teaspoons minced serrano chile
- 1½ teaspoons garam masala
- ½ teaspoon ground coriander
- ¼ teaspoon ground cumin
- ¼ teaspoon pepper
- ¾ cup water
- ¼ cup tomato paste
- ¾ teaspoon table salt, divided
- ½ cup heavy cream
- 1½ pounds boneless, skinless chicken thighs, trimmed
- ¼ cup plain Greek yogurt
- 2 tablespoons chopped fresh cilantro, divided

**1.** Melt 2 tablespoons butter in medium saucepan over medium heat. Add onion, garlic, ginger, and serrano and cook, stirring frequently, until mixture is softened and onion begins to brown, 6 to 8 minutes. Add garam masala, coriander, cumin, and pepper and cook, stirring frequently, until very fragrant, about 1 minute.

**2.** Add water and tomato paste and whisk until no lumps of tomato paste remain. Add ½ teaspoon salt and bring to boil. Off heat, stir in cream and remaining 6 tablespoons butter. Transfer mixture to blender and process until smooth, 30 to 60 seconds, scraping down sides of blender jar as needed. Return sauce to now empty skillet; set aside.

**3.** Adjust oven rack 6 inches from broiler element and heat broiler. Set wire rack in aluminum foil–lined rimmed baking sheet and spray with olive oil spray. Combine chicken, yogurt, and remaining ¼ teaspoon salt in bowl and toss well to coat. Transfer chicken to prepared rack and broil until chicken is evenly charred and registers 175 degrees, 16 to 20 minutes, flipping chicken halfway through broiling. Transfer chicken to cutting board and let rest for 5 minutes.

**4.** Meanwhile, warm sauce over medium-low heat. Cut chicken into ¾-inch pieces and stir into sauce. Stir in 1 tablespoon cilantro and season with salt to taste. Sprinkle with remaining 1 tablespoon cilantro. Serve.

### *Keto Meal Prep*

» Sauce, prepared through step 2, can be refrigerated for up to 4 days.

» Butter chicken can be refrigerated for up to 3 days. To reheat, place in covered nonstick skillet and cook over medium heat, stirring occasionally, for about 5 minutes, or place in covered bowl and microwave for 1 to 2 minutes.

# THREE-CHEESE ZUCCHINI NOODLES WITH CHICKEN

- 3 zucchini (8 ounces each), ends trimmed
- 1 tablespoon extra-virgin olive oil
- 1 garlic clove, minced
- 1 teaspoon ground fennel
- ¼ teaspoon red pepper flakes
- 8 ounces ground chicken
- ¼ cup heavy cream
- ⅛ teaspoon table salt
- ⅛ teaspoon pepper
- 2 ounces blue cheese, crumbled (½ cup)
- 1 ounce Parmesan cheese, grated (½ cup)
- 2 tablespoons minced fresh chives, divided
- 2 ounces fresh mozzarella, sliced thin and patted dry

**1.** Using spiralizer, cut zucchini into ⅛-inch-thick noodles, then cut noodles into 12-inch lengths. (You should have 1 pound zucchini noodles after spiralizing; reserve any extra noodles for another use.)

**2.** Microwave zucchini in covered bowl until almost softened, about 4 minutes, tossing halfway through microwaving. Transfer zucchini to paper towel–lined plate and thoroughly pat dry.

**3.** Heat oil, garlic, fennel, and pepper flakes in 10-inch broiler-safe skillet over medium heat until fragrant, about 1 minute. Add chicken and cook, breaking up meat with wooden spoon, until no longer pink, about 5 minutes; transfer to bowl.

**4.** Adjust oven rack 6 inches from broiler element and heat broiler. Add cream, salt, and pepper to now-empty skillet and bring to simmer over medium heat. Whisking constantly, gradually add blue cheese and Parmesan, and cook until cheese has melted and sauce has thickened, about 2 minutes. Off heat, stir in 1 tablespoon chives.

**5.** Add zucchini and chicken mixture to sauce and gently toss to coat. Spread zucchini into even layer and top with mozzarella. Transfer skillet to broiler and broil until mozzarella is melted and spotty brown, about 6 minutes. Let zucchini noodles cool slightly, then sprinkle with remaining 1 tablespoon chives. Serve.

## Keto Meal Prep

» Spiralized zucchini, prepared through step 1, can be placed in zipper-lock bag and refrigerated for up to 1 week.

**Serves** 2
**Total Time** 45 minutes

## PER SERVING
**Cal** 600 | **Total Fat** 47g
**Protein** 39g | **Net Carbs** 7g
**Fiber** 3g | **Total Carbs** 10g

### Why This Recipe Works

When it comes to comfort food, there's really nothing like mac and cheese, one of those dishes you might miss on the keto diet. We had to develop a low-carb version of a three cheese "noodle" bake, our grown-up take on mac and cheese. Replacing wheat noodles with zucchini noodles was a given, so now we could focus on the flavor profile. We treated ground chicken with sausage flavorings, pepper flakes, ground fennel seeds, and garlic. Then it was time to develop the sauce. We melted tangy blue cheese and salty, nutty Parmesan in heavy cream, finishing the sauce with minced chives. We tossed the noodles and chicken with the sauce in the pan and topped the mixture with our third cheese, mozzarella. Finally, we put the pan under the broiler until the cheese was bubbly and golden. The best part of this dish, other than eating it, is that it can be made in one pan, so it's easy to quickly throw together and makes a delicious and decadent dinner for two. We prefer to spiralize our own zucchini, but you can substitute 1 pound of store-bought spiralized zucchini, though they tend to be drier and less flavorful. Avoid buying large zucchini, which have thicker skins and more seeds. Be sure to use ground chicken, not ground chicken breast (also labeled 99 percent fat free) in this recipe.

**Serves** 4
**Total Time** 1½ hours

## PER SERVING

**Cal** 660 | **Total Fat** 49g
**Protein** 49g | **Net Carbs** 2g
**Fiber** 0g | **Total Carbs** 2g

### Why This Recipe Works

Roast chicken is often described as a simple dish and when made correctly, the rich flavor and juicy chicken meat need little embellishment. But the actual process of preparing and roasting chicken is anything but simple; recipes often call for complicated trussing techniques and for rotating the bird multiple times during cooking. The most time-consuming part is salting or brining the bird, a step that ensures juiciness and well-seasoned meat. After systematically testing the various components of a typical recipe, we found that instead of trussing, we could tie the legs together and tuck the wings underneath. We also discovered we could skip both the V-rack and flipping the chicken by using a preheated skillet and placing the chicken breast side up; this method gave the thighs a jump start on cooking. Starting the chicken in a 450-degree oven and then turning the oven off while the chicken finished cooking slowed the evaporation of juices, ensuring moist, tender meat. If roasting a larger bird, increase the time that the oven is on in step 2 to 35 to 40 minutes. Cooking the chicken in a preheated skillet will ensure that the breast and thigh meat finish cooking at the same time. The pan sauce is keto-friendly and you can eat it with the darker, richer meat for added fat. Broiled Broccoli Rabe (page 180) makes a great side. Feel free to use a combination of herbs in the sauce to vary flavor.

# WEEKNIGHT SKILLET ROAST CHICKEN WITH LEMON-HERB PAN SAUCE

- 1 tablespoon kosher salt
- ½ teaspoon pepper
- 1 (3½- to 4-pound) whole chicken, giblets discarded
- 1 tablespoon extra-virgin olive oil
- 1 shallot, minced
- 1 cup chicken broth
- 2 teaspoons Dijon mustard
- 2 tablespoons unsalted butter
- 2 teaspoons minced fresh chives, parsley, tarragon, and/or thyme
- 2 teaspoons lemon juice

**1.** Adjust oven rack to middle position, place 12-inch ovensafe skillet on rack, and heat oven to 450 degrees. Combine salt and pepper in bowl. Pat chicken dry with paper towels. Rub oil all over chicken. Sprinkle salt mixture evenly over surface of chicken, then rub mixture in with your hands to coat evenly. Tie legs together with kitchen twine and tuck wingtips behind back.

**2.** Transfer chicken, breast side up, to skillet in oven. Roast until breast registers 120 degrees and thighs register 135 degrees, 25 to 35 minutes. Turn off oven and leave chicken in oven, opening door as little as possible, until breast registers 160 degrees and thighs register 175 degrees, 25 to 35 minutes.

**3.** Using potholder (skillet handle will be hot), remove skillet from oven. Transfer chicken to carving board and let rest, uncovered, for 20 minutes.

**4.** Meanwhile, add shallot to fat left in skillet and cook over medium-high heat until softened, about 2 minutes. Stir in broth and mustard, scraping up any browned bits. Simmer until reduced to ¾ cup, about 3 minutes. Off heat, whisk in butter, herbs, and lemon juice. Season with pepper to taste. Carve chicken and serve with sauce.

# CHAPTER 4

# BEEF, PORK, AND LAMB

**Serves** 2
**Total Time** 30 minutes

## PER SERVING

**Cal** 570 | **Total Fat** 45g
**Protein** 36g | **Net Carbs** 1g
**Fiber** 0g | **Total Carbs** 1g

## Why This Recipe Works

Sirloin steak tips have a rich, beefy flavor and satisfying texture, and since they're quick-cooking, we thought they'd be a good option for an easy weeknight meal. Steak is keto-friendly, of course, but adding a buttery sauce makes it even friendlier. We cooked the steak tips over medium-high heat, which gave them well-seared exteriors and allowed the meat to cook through in a matter of minutes. Once the tips were browned on all sides, we rested them and prepared the simple pan sauce. We cooked a small shallot in butter as well as the fat left behind by the steak tips in the skillet. When the shallot had softened, we stirred in beef broth and simmered the sauce until it was slightly reduced. Then we slowly whisked in some chilled butter off the heat. Because cold butter melts slowly and creates a stable emulsion, this made our sauce silky, not greasy. Using Dijon mustard or porcini mushrooms to flavor the butter instead of rosemary gave us two more flavor options. We coated the meat with rich, savory sauce just before serving it with Whipped Cauliflower (page 184). Steak tips, also known as flap meat, are sold as whole steak, cubes, and strips. To ensure evenly sized pieces, we prefer to purchase whole steak tips and cut them ourselves. We prefer these steak tips cooked to medium-rare, but if you prefer them more or less done, see our guidelines on page 238.

# PAN-SEARED STEAK TIPS WITH ROSEMARY-PEPPERCORN PAN SAUCE

12 ounces sirloin steak tips, trimmed and cut into 2-inch pieces
½ teaspoon table salt
½ teaspoon finely ground pepper, plus ¼ teaspoon coarsely ground pepper
1 tablespoon extra-virgin olive oil
4 tablespoons unsalted butter, cut into 4 pieces and chilled, divided
1 small shallot, minced
½ teaspoon minced fresh rosemary
½ cup beef broth
1 teaspoon red wine vinegar

**1.** Pat beef dry with paper towels and sprinkle with salt and finely ground pepper. Heat oil in 12-inch skillet over medium-high heat until just smoking. Add beef and cook until well browned on all sides and meat registers 120 to 125 degrees (for medium-rare), 5 to 7 minutes. Transfer beef to plate, tent with aluminum foil, and let rest while preparing sauce.

**2.** Add 1 tablespoon butter to fat left in skillet and melt over medium heat. Add shallot, rosemary, and coarsely ground pepper and cook until shallot is softened and mixture is fragrant, about 2 minutes. Stir in broth, scraping up any browned bits. Bring to simmer and cook until reduced slightly, about 2 minutes. Stir in vinegar and any accumulated meat juices and simmer for 30 seconds.

**3.** Off heat, whisk in remaining 3 tablespoons butter, 1 piece at a time, until incorporated. Season with salt and pepper to taste. Return steak tips to skillet and turn to coat with sauce. Serve.

### Pan-Seared Steak Tips with Mustard-Cream Pan Sauce

Omit coarsely ground pepper and vinegar. Substitute minced fresh thyme for rosemary and chicken broth for beef broth. Reduce butter to 2 tablespoons in step 3. Add 2 tablespoons heavy cream and 1½ tablespoons Dijon mustard to pan with butter.

**Per Serving** Cal 580; Total Fat 45g; Protein 36g; Net Carbs 2g; Fiber 0g; Total Carbs 2g

### Pan-Seared Steak Tips with Porcini Mushroom–Sage Pan Sauce

Omit coarsely ground pepper. Substitute 1 teaspoon minced fresh sage for rosemary and white wine vinegar for red wine vinegar. Add ¼ ounce dried porcini mushrooms, rinsed and minced, to skillet with shallot.

**Per Serving** Cal 580; Total Fat 45g; Protein 37g; Net Carbs 2g; Fiber 1g; Total Carbs 3g

# PAN-SEARED STRIP STEAK WITH SMASHED CUCUMBER SALAD

**Serves** 2
**Total Time** 35 minutes

### PER SERVING
**Cal** 650 | **Total Fat** 53g
**Protein** 37g | **Net Carbs** 2g
**Fiber** 2g | **Total Carbs** 4g

½  English cucumber (8 ounces),
   quartered lengthwise and cut
   into 2-inch lengths
1  teaspoon kosher salt, divided
1  (12-ounce) strip steak,
   1½ inches thick, trimmed
¼  teaspoon pepper
1  tablespoon coconut oil
1  tablespoon soy sauce,
   divided
2  teaspoons unseasoned
   rice vinegar
1  teaspoon toasted sesame
   seeds
1  small garlic clove, minced
¼  teaspoon red pepper flakes
2  tablespoons chopped fresh
   basil
4  tablespoons unsalted butter,
   melted and cooled

**1.** Combine cucumber and
½ teaspoon salt in 1-gallon zipper-
lock bag, seal bag, and turn to
distribute salt. Using rolling pin or
small skillet, gently smash cucumber
pieces in bag; set aside.

**2.** Pat steak dry with paper towels
and sprinkle with remaining
½ teaspoon salt and pepper. Heat
coconut oil in 12-inch skillet over
medium-high heat until just smoking. Brown steak on first side, about
4 minutes. Flip steak and continue
to cook until meat registers 120 to
125 degrees (for medium-rare), 4 to
6 minutes. Transfer steak to cutting
board, tent with aluminum foil, and
let rest while finishing salad.

**3.** Drain cucumber. Whisk
1 teaspoon soy sauce, vinegar,
sesame seeds, garlic, and pepper
flakes together in large bowl. Add
cucumber and basil and toss to
combine. Combine melted butter
and remaining 2 teaspoons soy
sauce in separate bowl. Slice steak
½ inch thick and drizzle with soy
sauce–butter mixture. Serve with
cucumber salad.

## Why This Recipe Works

We love a good pan-seared steak.
But since the usual fixings—like
baked potatoes—are out for keto,
we decided to give our steak dinner
a fresh spin. We wanted a light,
low-carb side we could serve alongside the rich meat and butter sauce.
Smashed cucumbers, or *pai huang
gua*, came to mind. This Sichuan
dish is typically served with rich,
spicy food and though our steak
isn't spicy, it is hearty—we thought
cucumbers would make a crunchy,
refreshing accompaniment. Given
the origins of the cucumber dish,
soy sauce, rice vinegar, sesame seeds,
and pepper flakes seemed like the
perfect dressing ingredients. First,
we smashed our cucumber pieces in
a zipper-lock bag to expel extra water
and create craggy ends that would
hold on to the dressing. Then we
cooked the strip steak, making sure
to pat it dry first so that its exterior
would brown properly. We also made
sure the skillet was really hot: Cooking steak in a pan that isn't properly
preheated leads to meat that is overcooked before it can develop a good
crust. While the cooked steak rested,
we prepared the cucumber dressing
and stirred a little soy sauce into the
melted butter for the steak, to echo
the Asian flavors of the salad. We
prefer this steak cooked to medium-
rare, but if you prefer it more or less
done, see our guidelines on page 238.

**Serves** 2
**Total Time** 30 minutes

## PER SERVING

**Cal** 650 | **Total Fat** 57g
**Protein** 31g | **Net Carbs** 1g
**Fiber** 0g | **Total Carbs** 1g

## Why This Recipe Works

There's steak and then there's butter-basted, pan-seared rib eye. This rich and satisfying recipe calls for simultaneous searing, basting, and flipping, but the tender, quickly cooked meat is worth the effort. Searing involves cooking the surface of meat at a high temperature to create a brown crust. Basting requires continuously spooning hot fat over the steak, to cook it and add flavor. We combined the two techniques so the steak developed a nice crust, cooked quickly, and stayed moist. While the bottom of the steak seared in the hot skillet, the top kept cooking, thanks to the hot basting liquid. To prevent the gray band under the crust that indicates overcooked, dried-out meat, we also repeatedly flipped the steak throughout the searing process. A hot skillet cooks food from the bottom up. When a protein is flipped, the seared side, now facing up, is also hot. While some heat dissipates into the air so the meat cools slightly and doesn't overcook, lingering residual heat continues to cook the protein from the top down. The more a protein is flipped, the more it cooks from both sides. Our basting liquid—butter infused with shallot, garlic, and thyme—enhanced the cooked meat's flavor and made a rich sauce. We prefer this steak cooked to medium-rare, but if you prefer it more or less done, see our guidelines on page 238.

# BUTTER-BASTED RIB-EYE STEAK

- 1 **(12-ounce) boneless rib-eye steak, 1½ inches thick, trimmed**
- ½ **teaspoon table salt**
- 1 **teaspoon pepper**
- 1 **tablespoon extra-virgin olive oil**
- 3 **tablespoons unsalted butter**
- 1 **shallot, peeled and quartered through root end**
- 2 **garlic cloves, lightly crushed and peeled**
- 5 **sprigs fresh thyme**

**1.** Pat steak dry with paper towels and sprinkle with salt and pepper. Heat oil in 12-inch skillet over medium-high heat until just smoking. Place steak in skillet and cook for 30 seconds. Flip steak and continue to cook for 30 seconds. Continue flipping steak every 30 seconds for 3 more minutes.

**2.** Slide steak to back of skillet, opposite handle, and add butter to front of skillet. Once butter has melted and begun to foam, add shallot, garlic, and thyme sprigs. Holding skillet handle, tilt skillet so butter pools near base of handle. Use metal spoon to continuously spoon butter and aromatics over steak, concentrating on areas where crust is less browned. Baste steak, flipping it every 30 seconds, until steak registers 120 to 125 degrees (for medium-rare), 1 to 2 minutes.

**3.** Remove skillet from heat and transfer steak to cutting board; tent with aluminum foil and let rest for 10 minutes. Discard aromatics from pan and transfer butter mixture to small bowl. Slice steak thin and serve with butter mixture.

### Butter-Basted Rib-Eye Steak with Coffee-Chile Butter

Substitute 2 tablespoons whole coffee beans, cracked, for garlic and ½ teaspoon red pepper flakes for thyme.
**Per Serving** Cal 650; Total Fat 57g; Protein 31g; Net Carbs 1g; Fiber 0g; Total Carbs 1g

### Butter-Basted Rib-Eye Steak with Rosemary-Orange Butter

Substitute 8 (2-inch) strips orange zest for garlic and 1 sprig fresh rosemary for thyme.
**Per Serving** Cal 650; Total Fat 57g; Protein 31g; Net Carbs 1g; Fiber 0g; Total Carbs 1g

# ONE-PAN STEAK FAJITAS

2 green bell peppers (1 pound), stemmed, seeded, and cut into ½-inch-wide strips

6 tablespoons extra-virgin olive oil, divided

2 garlic cloves, sliced thin

1 teaspoon table salt, divided

1 teaspoon pepper, divided

1½ tablespoons chipotle chili powder

1 (1½-pound) flank steak, trimmed

8 Keto Tortillas (optional; page 20)

1 tablespoon lime juice

2 avocados (1 pound), halved, pitted, and cut into ½-inch pieces

1 tomato (6 ounces), cored and cut into ½-inch pieces

¼ cup fresh cilantro leaves

**1.** Adjust oven rack to lower-middle position and heat oven to 475 degrees. Toss bell peppers with 2 tablespoons oil, garlic, ½ teaspoon salt, and ½ teaspoon pepper on rimmed baking sheet and spread into even layer. Roast until peppers are lightly browned around edges, about 10 minutes.

**2.** Meanwhile, combine 2 tablespoons oil, chili powder, remaining ½ teaspoon salt, and remaining ½ teaspoon pepper in bowl. Cut steak lengthwise with grain into 4 equal pieces. Pat steaks dry with paper towels, then brush with spice mixture. Stack tortillas, if using, separated by sheets of parchment paper, on sheet of aluminum foil. Wrap tightly and set aside.

**3.** Remove sheet from oven. Using rubber spatula, push vegetables to 1 half of sheet. Place steaks on other half of sheet, leaving space between steaks. Roast until vegetables are spotty brown and meat registers 130 to 135 degrees (for medium), about 8 minutes.

**4.** Remove sheet from oven, transfer steaks to cutting board, tent with aluminum foil, and let rest for 5 minutes. Place tortilla packet in oven until warm, about 5 minutes. Transfer vegetables to serving platter and toss with lime juice and remaining 2 tablespoons oil. Slice steaks thin against grain and transfer to dish with vegetables. Serve with wraps, passing avocados, tomato, and cilantro separately.

### *Keto Meal Prep*

» Fajita filling can be refrigerated for up to 3 days. To reheat, place in covered nonstick skillet and cook over medium heat, stirring occasionally, for about 5 minutes, or place in covered bowl and microwave for 1 to 2 minutes.

» To reheat tortillas, stack, separated by sheets of parchment paper, and wrap in damp paper towel. Microwave until pliable, about 30 seconds.

**Serves** 4
**Total Time** 45 minutes

### PER SERVING (WITH TORTILLAS)
**Cal** 900 | **Total Fat** 68g
**Protein** 49g | **Net Carbs** 11g
**Fiber** 16g | **Total Carbs** 27g

### PER SERVING (WITHOUT TORTILLAS)
**Cal** 680 | **Total Fat** 51g
**Protein** 40g | **Net Carbs** 7g
**Fiber** 11g | **Total Carbs** 18g

### Why This Recipe Works

Mexican fajitas are a popular choice when dining out. But to avoid high-carb extras like flour tortillas, we developed a recipe you can make easily at home. For the filling, we used flank steak—it's beefy, tender, and easily available. To reduce our work and cook our peppers and meat together, we decided to employ the oven, so searing the meat in a skillet was out. Instead, we gave the meat a similar color and flavor by using a potent, dark-colored spice rub of chipotle chili powder, salt, and pepper. After tossing bell pepper strips in olive oil, garlic, salt, and pepper, we roasted them on a baking sheet in the oven. After 10 minutes, we added the rubbed steak, cut into four equal pieces, to the other side of the same sheet. In just 8 minutes, the meat was at the target temperature range of 130 to 135 degrees. Cooking the steak to medium instead of medium-rare made it less chewy when sliced. Our fajitas are delicious on their own or in our Keto Tortillas. We prefer this steak cooked to medium, but if you prefer it more or less done, see our guidelines on page 238.

## PER SERVING
**Cal** 820 | **Total Fat** 75g
**Protein** 29g | **Net Carbs** 5g
**Fiber** 3g | **Total Carbs** 8g

### Why This Recipe Works

Chinese restaurant stir-fries are beloved for their thin strips of meat in succulent sauce. But those sauces often contain thickeners like cornstarch as well as sugar, both keto no-nos. For our satisfying keto-friendly version, we chose sumptuous shiitake mushrooms and the big meaty flavor and high fat content of boneless short ribs. Bok choy added color and fiber. Briefly marinating the meat with soy sauce enhanced its rich taste and echoed its flavors in the simple sauce of soy sauce, sesame oil, rice vinegar, and red pepper flakes without any thickener. After quickly searing the fatty meat in a nonstick skillet, we rested it and stir-fried the mushrooms before adding the bok choy stalks. Then the bok choy leaves got a short stint in the pan just to wilt them. Finally, we stirred the browned beef and vegetables back into the sauce. Served over Cauliflower Rice (page 183), our stir-fry is a satisfying meal. To make slicing the steak easier, freeze it for 15 minutes. This dish progresses quickly after step 1; it's important that your ingredients are ready to go by then.

# BEEF STIR-FRY WITH BOK CHOY AND SHIITAKES

1½ pounds boneless beef short ribs, trimmed
3 tablespoons soy sauce, divided
2 teaspoons sesame oil
1½ tablespoons unseasoned rice vinegar
¼ teaspoon red pepper flakes
3 tablespoons coconut oil, divided
8 ounces shiitake mushrooms, stemmed and quartered
1 pound bok choy, stalks and greens separated, stalks sliced ¼ inch thick on bias and greens cut into ½-inch-wide strips
1 tablespoon grated fresh ginger
3 garlic cloves, minced
2 scallions, sliced thin on bias

**1.** Cut each rib crosswise with grain into 3 equal pieces. Slice each piece against grain ¼ inch thick. Toss beef with 2 tablespoons soy sauce, cover, and marinate for 10 minutes. Whisk remaining 1 tablespoon soy sauce, sesame oil, vinegar, and pepper flakes together in separate bowl; set aside.

**2.** Drain beef. Heat 1½ teaspoons coconut oil in 12-inch nonstick skillet over medium-high heat until just smoking. Add half of beef, breaking up any clumps, and cook, without stirring, for 2 minutes. Stir beef and continue to cook until browned, about 3 minutes; transfer to clean bowl. Repeat with 1½ teaspoons coconut oil and remaining beef; transfer to bowl.

**3.** Heat 1 tablespoon coconut oil in now-empty skillet over high heat until just smoking. Add mushrooms and cook until beginning to brown, about 2 minutes. Add bok choy stalks, cover, and cook for 3 minutes. Uncover and continue to cook, stirring frequently, until vegetables are spotty brown and crisp-tender, 3 to 4 minutes.

**4.** Push vegetables to sides of skillet. Add remaining 1 tablespoon coconut oil, ginger, and garlic to center and cook, mashing mixture into skillet, until fragrant, about 30 seconds. Stir ginger-garlic mixture into vegetables. Stir in bok choy greens and cook until wilted, about 2 minutes. Stir in beef and any accumulated juices. Off heat, add sauce and toss to coat. Sprinkle with scallions and serve.

### *Keto Meal Prep*

» Marinated beef and sauce, prepared through step 1, can be refrigerated for up to 24 hours.

» Stir-fry can be refrigerated for up to 3 days. To reheat, place in covered nonstick skillet and cook over medium heat, stirring occasionally, for about 5 minutes, or place in covered bowl and microwave for 1 to 2 minutes.

# GRILLED BEEF AND VEGETABLE KEBABS

**Serves** 4
**Total Time** 2 hours

### PER SERVING
**Cal** 720 | **Total Fat** 59g
**Protein** 37g | **Net Carbs** 7g
**Fiber** 2g | **Total Carbs** 9g

¾ cup extra-virgin olive oil
6 garlic cloves, minced
1 tablespoon minced fresh thyme
2 teaspoons grated lemon zest plus 1 tablespoon juice
1 teaspoon table salt
¾ teaspoon pepper
1½ pounds sirloin steak tips, trimmed and cut into 2-inch pieces
2 zucchini (8 ounces each), halved lengthwise and sliced 1 inch thick
1 red bell pepper (8 ounces), stemmed, seeded, and cut into 1½-inch pieces
¼ cup chopped fresh parsley

**1.** Whisk oil, garlic, thyme, lemon zest, salt, and pepper together in medium bowl. Combine beef and 2 tablespoons of marinade in 1-gallon zipper-lock bag and toss to coat; press out as much air as possible and seal bag. Toss zucchini and bell pepper with 2 tablespoons of marinade in second bowl and cover with plastic wrap. Refrigerate beef and vegetables for 1 hour, flipping bag after 30 minutes.

**2.** Stir parsley and lemon juice into remaining marinade and let sit at room temperature while beef and vegetables marinate.

**3.** Remove beef from bag, pat dry with paper towels, and thread tightly onto three 12-inch metal skewers. Thread vegetables onto three 12-inch metal skewers in alternating pattern of zucchini and bell pepper.

**4A. For a charcoal grill** Open bottom vent completely. Light large chimney starter mounded with charcoal briquettes (7 quarts). When top coals are partially covered with ash, pour evenly over center of grill, leaving 2-inch gap between grill wall and charcoal. Set cooking grate in place, cover, and open lid vent completely. Heat grill until hot, about 5 minutes.

**4B. For a gas grill** Turn all burners to high, cover, and heat grill until hot, about 15 minutes. Leave primary burner on high and turn other burner(s) to medium-low.

**5.** Clean and oil cooking grate. Place beef kebabs on grill, directly over coals if using charcoal or over hotter side if using gas. Place vegetable kebabs on cooler part(s) of grill (near edge of coals if using charcoal). Cook (covered if using gas), turning kebabs every 3 to 4 minutes, until beef is well browned and registers 120 to 125 degrees (for medium-rare), 12 to 16 minutes. Transfer beef kebabs to serving platter and tent with aluminum foil. Continue to cook vegetable kebabs until tender and lightly charred, about 5 minutes.

**6.** Remove beef and vegetables from skewers using fork. Serve, passing sauce separately.

### *Keto Meal Prep*

» Marinated beef and vegetables and sauce can be refrigerated for up to 24 hours. Bring sauce to room temperature and whisk to recombine before serving.

## Why This Recipe Works
This keto recipe lets you enjoy grilled fare with your friends while sticking to your eating plan. We wanted pieces of beef with a thick char and juicy interior, paired with browned, tender-firm pepper and zucchini. We chose well-marbled steak tips and cut the meat into generous 2-inch cubes. For the marinade, we steered clear of acids like lemon juice; although they weaken collagen, acids only affect the meat's surface and, if left on too long, can actually make the meat mushy. Instead we added bright flavor with lemon zest, which we combined with salt, garlic, thyme, pepper, and oil to elevate the fat content. Grilling the beef and vegetables on separate skewers over a two-level fire allowed the vegetables to cook at a lower temperature while the beef seared over the hotter center area. Both came out perfectly cooked within minutes of each other. Mixing fresh parsley and lemon juice into the reserved marinade created a bold sauce for the kebabs. Steak tips, also known as flap meat, are sold as whole steak, cubes, and strips. To ensure evenly sized pieces, we prefer to purchase whole steak tips and cut them ourselves. If you have long, thin pieces of meat, roll or fold them into approximate 2-inch pieces. We prefer these steak tips cooked to medium-rare, but if you prefer them more or less done, see our guidelines on page 238. You will need six 12-inch metal skewers for this recipe.

**Serves** 2
**Total Time** 45 minutes

## PER SERVING

**Cal** 690 | **Total Fat** 60g
**Protein** 30g | **Net Carbs** 7g
**Fiber** 3g | **Total Carbs** 10g

### Why This Recipe Works

We wanted to develop a keto spaghetti and meatballs recipe because this comfort food favorite is usually packed with high-carb ingredients like pasta and tomato sauce. To make it keto-friendly, we needed tender meatballs topped with a delicious low-carb sauce and served on a wheat pasta replacement. Of all the vegetable noodles we tested, tasters most liked spiralized zucchini, which could be twirled around a fork like spaghetti. Roasting the noodles removed excess moisture to keep the sauce flavorful. Since we couldn't use a traditional marinara, we chose a richly flavored basil pesto and topped it with cherry tomatoes as a nod to the classic. Now for the meatballs. In the test kitchen, we often use a mixture of starch and liquid called a panade to help meatballs hold their shape and stay moist. Simply leaving it out gave us tough, rubbery meatballs. Using fattier beef and shaping larger meatballs helped a little but we still weren't satisfied with the texture. We revisited the panade idea and used our pesto as a swap for bread and water; the additional fat kept the meatballs juicy and tender. We prefer to spiralize our own zucchini, but you can substitute 1 pound of store-bought spiralized zucchini, though they tend to be drier and less flavorful. Avoid buying large zucchini, which have thicker skins and more seeds.

# ZUCCHINI NOODLES WITH PESTO MEATBALLS

- 3 zucchini (8 ounces each), ends trimmed
- 8 ounces 80 percent lean ground beef
- 5 tablespoons Basil Pesto (page 26), divided
- ½ teaspoon table salt, divided
- ¼ teaspoon red pepper flakes
- 2 teaspoons extra-virgin olive oil
- ¼ teaspoon pepper
- 2 ounces cherry tomatoes, halved
- 2 tablespoons grated Parmesan cheese

**1.** Using spiralizer, cut zucchini into ⅛-inch-thick noodles, then cut noodles into 12-inch lengths. (You should have 1 pound zucchini noodles after spiralizing; reserve any extra noodles for another use.)

**2.** Adjust oven rack to middle position and heat oven to 375 degrees. Add ground beef, 2 tablespoons pesto, ¼ teaspoon salt, and pepper flakes to large bowl and knead with your hands until well combined. Pinch off and roll mixture into 1¾-inch meatballs (you should have 6 meatballs).

**3.** Toss zucchini with oil, pepper, and remaining ¼ teaspoon salt on rimmed baking sheet and spread into even layer. Roast for 5 minutes. Push zucchini to sides of sheet, arrange meatballs in center, and roast until zucchini is tender and meatballs are cooked through, 10 to 15 minutes.

**4.** Remove zucchini and meatballs from oven. Transfer zucchini to colander and shake to remove any excess liquid. Toss zucchini with 1 tablespoon pesto in bowl, then divide among individual serving bowls. Top with meatballs, tomatoes, Parmesan, and remaining 2 tablespoons pesto. Serve.

### Keto Meal Prep

» Spiralized zucchini, prepared through step 1, can be placed in zipper-lock bag and refrigerated for up to 5 days.
» Shaped meatballs, prepared through step 2, can be refrigerated for up to 24 hours.

# NUT-CRUSTED PORK CHOPS

6 tablespoons coconut oil, divided
2 garlic cloves, minced
1½ cups sliced almonds, chopped fine
½ cup unsweetened shredded coconut
1 tablespoon minced fresh thyme
¾ cup coconut flour
2 large eggs
3 tablespoons water
1¼ teaspoons table salt, divided
¼ teaspoon cayenne pepper
4 (6-ounce) boneless pork chops, ¾ inch thick, trimmed
½ teaspoon pepper
4 lemon wedges

**1.** Adjust oven rack to middle position and heat oven to 200 degrees. Set wire rack in rimmed baking sheet. Heat 2 tablespoons oil in 12-inch nonstick skillet over medium-low heat until shimmering. Add garlic and cook until fragrant, about 30 seconds. Add almonds and coconut and cook, stirring often, until golden brown, about 4 minutes.

**2.** Transfer almond mixture to shallow dish and stir in thyme. Spread coconut flour in second shallow dish. Lightly beat eggs, water, ¾ teaspoon salt, and cayenne together in third shallow dish.

**3.** Pat pork chops dry with paper towels. With sharp knife, cut ¹⁄₁₆-inch-deep slits on both sides of chops, spaced ½ inch apart, in crosshatch pattern. Sprinkle chops with remaining ½ teaspoon salt and pepper. Dredge each chop in flour, dip in egg mixture, letting excess drip off, then coat with almond mixture, pressing gently to adhere; transfer to plate.

**4.** Wipe skillet clean with paper towels. Heat 2 tablespoons oil in skillet over medium heat until shimmering. Place 2 chops in skillet and cook until deep golden brown and crisp, turning once, and pork registers 140 degrees, 3 to 5 minutes per side, adjusting heat as needed.

**5.** Drain chops briefly on paper towels, then transfer to prepared rack and keep warm in oven. Wipe skillet clean with paper towels and repeat with remaining 2 tablespoons oil and remaining chops. Serve with lemon wedges.

## Nut-Crusted Pork Chops with Caraway and Dill
Add 2 tablespoons caraway seeds to skillet with almonds in step 1. Add 1 tablespoon Dijon mustard to egg mixture. Substitute 2 tablespoons minced fresh dill for thyme.
**Per Serving** Cal 670; Total Fat 53g; Protein 43g; Net Carbs 5g; Fiber 5g; Total Carbs 10g

## Nut-Crusted Pork Chops with Sesame and Scallion
Add 2 tablespoons sesame seeds to skillet with almonds in step 1. Omit salt in egg mixture and substitute 2 tablespoons soy sauce for water. Substitute 2 thinly sliced scallions for thyme.
**Per Serving** Cal 680; Total Fat 54g; Protein 43g; Net Carbs 5g; Fiber 5g; Total Carbs 10g

Serves 4
**Total Time** 50 minutes

## PER SERVING
**Cal** 670 | **Total Fat** 53g
**Protein** 42g | **Net Carbs** 5g
**Fiber** 4g | **Total Carbs** 9g

### Why This Recipe Works
A crunchy bread-crumb coating is a great way to add flavor and texture to mild, juicy pork chops—unless you're on the keto diet. So we set out to create a crunchy keto coating with nuts, which are high in both protein and fat. Nut coatings can be dense and leaden, however, with the rich flavor of the nuts rarely coming through. So although our chopped toasted sliced almonds worked well as a coating, they tasted heavy. To lighten the flavor, we added some toasted shredded coconut, which had the added benefit of keeping the coating crisp. We replaced the all-purpose flour for dredging with coconut flour, which holds moisture well. Two eggs and a bit of water provided structure and a little more moisture. We also found that scoring the chops before dredging helped the coating adhere and not flake off when the pork was cut. Our almond coating was now just right, but its neutral flavor also lent itself to variations. We created one using caraway seeds and fresh dill; we added hints of Asian flavor to another with sesame seeds and soy sauce. These chops are delicious with our Sautéed Green Beans with Sesame-Miso Vinaigrette (page 188).

## PER SERVING
**Cal** 630 | **Total Fat** 50g
**Protein** 37g | **Net Carbs** 7g
**Fiber** 2g | **Total Carbs** 9g

### Why This Recipe Works

To "smother" meat is to cook it low and slow in rich gravy until the meat, usually pork chops, is ridiculously tender and mouthwateringly juicy. Recipes that use this method can take hours, which doesn't lend itself easily to weeknight cooking. To achieve the same results quickly, we turned to country-style pork ribs, which are meatier than many other cuts of pork. Quick browning and 15 minutes of braising were all the cooking they needed. We flavored the melt-in-your-mouth ribs with a simple mixture of paprika, salt, and pepper. Once the ribs had browned, we used the leftover fond for a sauce to smother them in. We couldn't use carb-rich onions here so a shallot was our flavor stand-in. Mushrooms, thyme, and parsley added earthiness. To imitate the tang of classic smothered pork, we added some cider vinegar, which cut the rich heartiness of the ribs. This comforting Southern classic can be served with our Pan-Roasted Asparagus (page 176) or Whipped Cauliflower with Fennel, Garlic, and Lemon (page 184).

# SMOTHERED BONELESS PORK RIBS

½  teaspoon paprika
½  teaspoon pepper
¼  teaspoon table salt
4  (3-ounce) boneless country-style pork ribs, trimmed
1  tablespoon extra-virgin olive oil
4  tablespoons unsalted butter, cut into 4 pieces and chilled
8  ounces cremini mushrooms, trimmed and sliced thin
1  shallot, sliced thin
½  teaspoon minced fresh thyme or ⅛ teaspoon dried
1  cup chicken broth
1  teaspoon cider vinegar
2  tablespoons minced fresh parsley

**1.** Combine paprika, pepper, and salt in bowl. Pat pork dry with paper towels and season with spice mixture. Heat oil in 12-inch skillet over medium-high heat until just smoking. Brown pork on all sides, about 8 minutes; transfer to plate.

**2.** Add 2 tablespoons butter, mushrooms, and shallot to now-empty skillet. Cover and cook, stirring occasionally, until mushrooms release their liquid, about 5 minutes. Uncover and continue to cook until vegetables are lightly browned, about 5 minutes. Stir in thyme and cook until fragrant, about 30 seconds. Stir in broth, scraping up any browned bits, and bring to simmer.

**3.** Nestle pork into skillet and add any accumulated juices. Cover, reduce heat to low, and cook until tender, about 15 minutes. Transfer pork to serving platter, tent with aluminum foil, and let rest while finishing sauce.

**4.** Bring sauce to simmer over medium-high heat and cook until liquid has reduced to about ¼ cup, about 4 minutes. Off heat, whisk in remaining 2 tablespoons butter, 1 piece at a time, until incorporated. Whisk in vinegar and parsley and season with salt and pepper to taste. Spoon sauce over pork and serve.

# GRILLED THIN-CUT PORK CHOPS WITH SPICY BARBECUE COLESLAW

Serves 4
**Total Time** 1 hour

## PER SERVING
**Cal** 740 | **Total Fat** 53g
**Protein** 54g | **Net Carbs** 4g
**Fiber** 3g | **Total Carbs** 7g

- 8 (6-ounce) bone-in rib or center-cut pork chops, about ½ inch thick, trimmed
- 1 teaspoon table salt, divided
- ¾ cup mayonnaise
- 1 tablespoon prepared horseradish
- ½ teaspoon dry mustard
- ¼ teaspoon cayenne pepper
- 1½ tablespoons distilled white vinegar
- ½ teaspoon pepper
- ½ head green cabbage (1 pound), quartered lengthwise through core
- 2 scallions, sliced thin

**1.** Set wire rack in rimmed baking sheet. Pat chops dry with paper towels. Cut 2 slits, about 2 inches apart, through outer layer of fat and silverskin on each chop. Sprinkle chops with ½ teaspoon salt. Arrange on prepared rack and freeze until chops are firm, at least 15 minutes or up to 1 hour.

**2.** Whisk mayonnaise, horseradish, mustard, and cayenne together in large bowl. Measure out and reserve 6 tablespoons mayonnaise mixture. Whisk vinegar, pepper, and remaining ½ teaspoon salt into remaining mayonnaise mixture, cover, and refrigerate until needed.

**3A. For a charcoal grill** Open bottom vent completely. Light large chimney starter filled with charcoal briquettes (6 quarts). When top coals are partially covered with ash, pour evenly over grill. Set cooking grate in place, cover, and open lid vent completely. Heat grill until hot, about 5 minutes.

**3B. For a gas grill** Turn all burners to high, cover, and heat grill until hot, about 15 minutes. Leave all burners on high.

**4.** Clean and oil cooking grate. Brush chops and cabbage with reserved mayonnaise mixture. Grill chops until well browned and meat registers 140 degrees, 6 to 8 minutes, flipping chops halfway through grilling. Grill cabbage until slightly wilted and charred, 5 to 7 minutes per side. Transfer chops and cabbage to large plate as they finish cooking and tent with aluminum foil. Let chops rest while finishing slaw.

**5.** Cut cabbage crosswise into thin strips, discarding core. Transfer cabbage and scallions to bowl with dressing and toss to combine. Serve with chops.

## Why This Recipe Works
Thin-cut pork chops are widely available and perfect for a quick, tasty dinner but we wanted to make a grilled summer meal out of them with a crunchy, tart slaw. To make our work easier, we used the grill for both parts of this dish. Grilling the cabbage added a nice char to a vegetable that can be bland. Using mayonnaise in the dressing and to brush on our chops before grilling was another tangy way to tie the two elements together and get nice browning on the meat. We also ensured that our thin-cut pork chops would brown quickly by partially freezing them first; this eliminated excess moisture from their exteriors. Salting the chops before freezing prevented them from drying out, so we could skip the step of brining them. The result was a delicious dinner of moist pork and crunchy, zesty cabbage.

**PER SERVING**
**Cal** 630 | **Total Fat** 47g
**Protein** 41g | **Net Carbs** 5g
**Fiber** 4g | **Total Carbs** 9g

## Why This Recipe Works

For a restaurant-worthy dinner you can make on a weeknight, we turned to quick-cooking pork tenderloin. We rubbed a mixture of lemon zest and thyme all over the pork to add bright flavor and then started the cooking on the stovetop, searing the pork in the skillet to give it rich color before roasting. We tossed green beans with oil, salt, and pepper and added them to the skillet; we then roasted the pork and beans in the oven until the pork was perfectly cooked and the green beans were tender. To make sure this dinner met keto standards, we made a fresh olive oil–based dressing to drizzle over the meal. The dressing added savory notes and fat, and garlic and lemon balanced the richness of the extra-virgin olive oil. A sprinkle of crunchy sliced almonds and tangy goat cheese finished this elegant but easy-to-prepare dish. While skinny pork tenderloin doesn't need to be trussed to cook evenly, the tight silverskin striping its exterior must be trimmed away. To remove silverskin, simply slip a knife under it, angle the knife slightly upward, and use a gentle back-and-forth motion.

# LEMON-THYME PORK TENDERLOIN WITH GREEN BEANS

- 2 (12-ounce) pork tenderloins, trimmed
- 1½ tablespoons chopped fresh thyme
- 1 tablespoon grated lemon zest, divided, plus 2 teaspoons lemon juice
- ¾ teaspoon plus ⅛ teaspoon table salt, divided
- ¾ teaspoon pepper, divided
- 1 pound green beans, trimmed
- 10 tablespoons extra-virgin olive oil, divided
- 1 garlic clove, minced
- ¼ cup sliced almonds, toasted
- 2 ounces goat cheese, crumbled (½ cup)

**1.** Adjust oven rack to middle position and heat oven to 450 degrees. Pat pork dry with paper towels and sprinkle with thyme, 2 teaspoons lemon zest, ½ teaspoon salt, and ½ teaspoon pepper. Toss green beans with 3 tablespoons oil, ¼ teaspoon salt, and remaining ¼ teaspoon pepper in bowl.

**2.** Heat 1 tablespoon oil in 12-inch ovensafe skillet over medium-high heat until just smoking. Brown pork on all sides, 5 to 7 minutes. Off heat, center tenderloins in skillet, alternating thicker and thinner ends, and arrange green beans around sides. Transfer skillet to oven and roast until pork registers 140 degrees and green beans are tender, 10 to 12 minutes.

**3.** Transfer pork to cutting board, tent with aluminum foil, and let rest for 10 minutes. Whisk garlic, lemon juice, remaining 1 teaspoon lemon zest, remaining ⅛ teaspoon salt, and remaining 6 tablespoons oil in bowl until combined. Drizzle 1 tablespoon dressing over green beans and toss to combine. Transfer to serving platter and sprinkle with almonds and goat cheese. Slice pork ½ inch thick and serve with green beans, passing remaining dressing separately.

# VIETNAMESE PORK AND NOODLE BOWLS

¼ cup unsweetened creamy peanut butter

3 tablespoons water

4 teaspoons fish sauce, divided

1½ teaspoons grated lime zest, divided, plus 1 tablespoon juice

1 teaspoon toasted sesame oil

½ small Thai chile, stemmed and minced

1 garlic clove, minced

1 small shallot, minced

¼ teaspoon pepper

12 ounces ground pork

1 tablespoon coconut oil

2 (7- to 8-ounce) packages shirataki noodles, drained

3 ounces Boston lettuce, torn into bite-size pieces

¼ English cucumber (4 ounces), peeled, quartered lengthwise, seeded, and sliced thin on bias

¼ cup fresh cilantro leaves

¼ cup chopped fresh mint

1. Whisk peanut butter, water, 1 tablespoon fish sauce, ½ teaspoon lime zest, lime juice, oil, chile, and garlic together in bowl; set aside.

2. Combine shallot, pepper, remaining 1 teaspoon fish sauce, and remaining 1 teaspoon lime zest in large bowl. Add pork and gently mix with your hands until thoroughly combined. Pinch off and roll mixture into 6 balls. Gently flatten balls into round disks, about ½ inch thick and 3 inches in diameter.

3. Heat coconut oil in 12-inch nonstick skillet over medium-high heat until just smoking. Add patties and cook until well browned on first side and crust forms, 3 to 4 minutes. Flip patties, reduce heat to medium, and continue to cook until well browned and crust forms on second side, about 5 minutes. Transfer patties to paper towel–lined plate.

4. Meanwhile, bring 2 quarts water to boil in large pot. Stir in noodles and cook until heated through, about 2 minutes. Drain noodles well, then divide among individual serving bowls. Top with lettuce, cucumber, and patties. Drizzle with sauce and top with cilantro and mint. Serve.

## Keto Meal Prep

» Sauce and patties, prepared through step 3, can be refrigerated separately for up to 3 days. To reheat patties, place on greased, foil-lined baking sheet and bake in 350-degree oven for 10 minutes or place on large plate and microwave for 45 to 60 seconds. Bring sauce to room temperature and whisk to recombine before serving.

---

Serves 2
**Total Time** 45 minutes

## PER SERVING

**Cal** 790 | **Total Fat** 63g
**Protein** 40g | **Net Carbs** 8g
**Fiber** 8g | **Total Carbs** 16g

---

### Why This Recipe Works

Based on the traditional Vietnamese street food, *bun cha*, these pork and noodle bowls consist of flavorful pork patties atop soft noodles, eaten with fragrant herbs, crisp lettuce, cucumber, and a rich, tangy sauce. Happily, we discovered *shirataki* noodles—a Japanese noodle made from the roots of the konjac plant. They have a pleasant chew and a neutral taste (as long as you rinse them first) and, best of all, they contain zero net carbs. These noodles formed a delicate background for our bold pork patties, flavored with black pepper, minced shallot, and lime zest. Bun cha is traditionally accompanied by a light vinegar dressing. To add more fat for keto, we turned to peanut butter, whisking it with lime juice, fish sauce, chile, and garlic to make a deep, complex sauce. We seared the patties quickly in a skillet until well browned and cooked through, then served them on a bed of soft noodles with crispy cucumber slices and crunchy Boston lettuce, a flavorful dinner that's ready in under an hour. A sprinkle of fresh cilantro and mint is all you need to bring this Vietnamese specialty home. Shirataki noodles are often sold precooked in 7- to 8-ounce packages. Thoroughly drain and rinse the noodles before using them. You can find shirataki noodles in the international aisle of most well-stocked supermarkets or at your local Asian market. For a less spicy sauce, use only one-quarter of the Thai chile.

## PER SERVING

**Cal** 520 | **Total Fat** 44g
**Protein** 23g | **Net Carbs** 8g
**Fiber** 4g | **Total Carbs** 12g

### Why This Recipe Works

*Involtini* is an Italian dish of eggplant planks rolled around a creamy seasoned cheese filling. We wanted to develop a version that was impressive enough to serve a crowd, yet fit within the keto diet guidelines. Traditional recipes require a multi-step process of salting the eggplant, breading and frying it, and rolling it around a cheese filling. We couldn't use bread crumbs so we avoided breading and frying completely, instead brushing the eggplant planks with oil, seasoning with salt and pepper, and baking them until light brown and tender. We combined creamy ricotta cheese and nutty Parmesan with cooked ground pork, lemon juice, and fresh basil for a filling that was rich and balanced, not greasy or heavy. After rolling the eggplant around the filling, we arranged the shaped eggplant rolls in the same skillet where we had cooked the ground pork, which saved on cleanup. We added a sprinkle of mozzarella and Parmesan and then ran the eggplant bundles under the broiler until the cheese bubbled and browned. Instead of tomato sauce, we added tomato flavor with cherry tomatoes and basil sprinkled over the finished dish. Select shorter, wider eggplants for this recipe. You should have about 2¼ pounds of eggplant after trimming. Do not use part-skim or fat-free ricotta in this recipe.

# ITALIAN EGGPLANT ROLLS

- 2 large eggplants (1½ pounds each), peeled
- ½ cup extra-virgin olive oil, divided
- 1 teaspoon table salt, divided
- ½ teaspoon pepper, divided
- 6 garlic cloves, minced
- 1 teaspoon dried oregano
- ¼ teaspoon red pepper flakes
- 1 pound ground pork
- 4 ounces (½ cup) whole-milk ricotta cheese
- 1 ounce Parmesan cheese, grated (½ cup), divided
- ½ cup chopped fresh basil, divided
- 2 teaspoons lemon juice
- 4 ounces whole-milk mozzarella, shredded (1 cup)
- 4 ounces cherry tomatoes, quartered

**1.** Adjust 1 oven rack to lower-middle position and second rack 8 inches from broiler element. Heat oven to 375 degrees. Line 2 rimmed baking sheets with parchment paper and spray generously with olive oil spray.

**2.** Slice eggplants lengthwise into ½-inch-thick planks (you should have 12 planks). Trim rounded surface from each end piece so it lies flat. Arrange eggplant slices in single layer on prepared sheets. Brush 1 side of eggplant slices with 3 tablespoons oil and sprinkle with ½ teaspoon salt and ¼ teaspoon pepper. Flip and repeat. Bake until tender and lightly browned, 30 to 35 minutes, switching and rotating sheets halfway through baking. Let cool for 5 minutes. Using thin spatula, flip each slice over.

**3.** While eggplant bakes, cook 1 tablespoon oil, garlic, oregano, and pepper flakes in 12-inch broiler-safe skillet over medium heat until fragrant, about 1 minute. Add pork and cook, breaking up meat with wooden spoon, until no longer pink, about 5 minutes. Transfer to large bowl and let cool slightly. Stir in ricotta, ¼ cup Parmesan, ¼ cup basil, and lemon juice.

**4.** With widest ends of eggplant slices facing you, evenly distribute ground pork mixture on bottom third of each slice. Gently roll up each eggplant slice.

**5.** Heat broiler. Place eggplant rolls seam side down in now-empty skillet. Sprinkle with mozzarella cheese and remaining ¼ cup Parmesan. Transfer skillet to oven and broil until cheese is melted and browned and filling is heated through, 5 to 10 minutes. Sprinkle with tomatoes and remaining ¼ cup basil and drizzle with remaining 1 tablespoon oil. Serve.

### *Keto Meal Prep*

» Stuffed eggplant, prepared through step 4, can be refrigerated for up to 24 hours. Proceed as directed with step 5.

» To reheat cooked eggplant rolls, place on greased, foil-lined baking sheet and bake in 350-degree oven for 10 minutes, or place on large plate and microwave for 45 to 60 seconds.

# PAN-ROASTED LAMB CHOPS WITH BRUSSELS SPROUTS AND CHERMOULA

4 (4-ounce) lamb rib or loin chops, 1½ inches thick, trimmed

¼ teaspoon plus ⅛ teaspoon table salt, divided

¼ teaspoon pepper

1 tablespoon extra-virgin olive oil

8 ounces Brussels sprouts, trimmed and halved

6 tablespoons Chermoula (page 28)

**1.** Adjust oven rack to middle position and heat oven to 425 degrees. Pat chops dry with paper towels and sprinkle with ¼ teaspoon salt and pepper. Heat oil in 12-inch ovensafe skillet over medium-high heat until just smoking. Brown chops well, 3 to 5 minutes per side; transfer to plate.

**2.** Arrange Brussels sprouts cut side down in fat left in skillet and sprinkle with remaining ⅛ teaspoon salt. Cook over medium-high heat, without moving, until lightly browned, about 2 minutes.

**3.** Arrange chops on top of Brussels sprouts and transfer skillet to oven. Roast until lamb registers 120 to 125 degrees (for medium-rare) and sprouts are well browned and tender, 8 to 10 minutes. Transfer chops to plate, tent with aluminum foil, and let rest for 5 minutes. Season Brussels sprouts with salt and pepper to taste. Serve lamb and Brussels sprouts with Chermoula.

**Serves** 2
**Total Time** 45 minutes

## PER SERVING
**Cal** 800 | **Total Fat** 69g
**Protein** 33g | **Net Carbs** 7g
**Fiber** 4g | **Total Carbs** 11g

## Why This Recipe Works

Lamb is tender, juicy, fatty, and flavorful—the perfect keto protein. Given the right cut, it can cook quickly, too, so we chose rib or loin chops. Unlike leg of lamb, chops are smaller and take less time to cook so they can be made on a weeknight and you won't have to worry about left-overs. For a flavorful dinner that could be ready in under an hour, we paired the chops with skillet-roasted Brussels sprouts and North African chermoula. We pan-seared the chops in a skillet and then set them aside. Next, we arranged the Brussels sprouts in the skillet so they could cook in the remaining fat until lightly browned. We then arranged the chops on the Brussels sprouts to finish cooking together in a hot oven. We prefer the milder taste and bigger size of domestic lamb chops. If using lamb from New Zealand or Australia, the chops will probably be smaller and cook more quickly. We prefer these chops cooked to medium-rare, but if you prefer them more or less done, see our guidelines on page 238.

**Serves** 4
**Total Time** 1 hour

## PER SERVING

**Cal** 630 | **Total Fat** 51g
**Protein** 35g | **Net Carbs** 5g
**Fiber** 2g | **Total Carbs** 7g

### Why This Recipe Works

Greek gyros are classic sandwiches of seasoned, marinated lamb, tomato, lettuce, and cucumber-yogurt tzatziki sauce in soft pita bread. The traditional method for cooking the meat employs an electric vertical rotisserie on which layers of sliced and marinated leg of lamb are stacked. After cooking for hours, the meat is shaved with a long slicing knife, creating pieces with crisp exteriors and moist interiors infused with garlic and oregano. We wanted to translate this recipe for the keto home cook. Using ground lamb—which we formed into patties—made the work easy and came close to reproducing the texture of rotisserie lamb. Incorporating lemon juice and garlic in our patties gave them a fuller, more savory flavor. For a crisp outside and moist inside, we browned our shaped patties in a skillet until a crust formed on each side. For our keto wraps, we reimagined the pita component by utilizing iceberg lettuce cups. Toppings of tangy tzatziki, tomatoes, and creamy feta offered a fresh counterpoint to the rich lamb. Since both the patties and tzatziki can be made ahead, you can plan for the work week and pack some for lunch. The skillet may appear crowded when you begin cooking the patties, but they will shrink slightly as they cook.

# GREEK-STYLE LAMB WRAPS WITH TZATZIKI

### TZATZIKI
- ½ cucumber (8 ounces), peeled, halved lengthwise, seeded, and shredded
- ¼ teaspoon table salt
- ½ cup plain whole Greek yogurt
- 2 tablespoons extra-virgin olive oil
- 2 tablespoons minced fresh mint and/or dill
- 1 small garlic clove, minced

### WRAPS
- 4 teaspoons lemon juice
- 1 tablespoon minced fresh oregano or 1 teaspoon dried
- 2 garlic cloves, minced
- ½ teaspoon table salt
- ¼ teaspoon pepper
- 1½ pounds ground lamb
- 2 teaspoons extra-virgin olive oil
- 12 large iceberg lettuce leaves
- 1 large tomato (8 ounces), cored and cut into ½-inch pieces
- 2 ounces feta cheese, crumbled (½ cup)

**1. For the tzatziki** Toss cucumber with salt in colander and let drain for 15 minutes. Whisk yogurt, oil, mint, and garlic together in bowl, then stir in cucumber. Cover and refrigerate for at least 30 minutes to allow flavors to meld. Season with salt and pepper to taste.

**2. For the wraps** Combine lemon juice, oregano, garlic, salt, and pepper in large bowl. Add lamb and gently mix with your hands until thoroughly combined. Pinch off and roll mixture into 12 balls. Gently flatten balls into round disks, about ½ inch thick and 3 inches in diameter.

**3.** Heat oil in 12-inch nonstick skillet over medium-high heat until just smoking. Add patties and cook until lightly browned, 6 to 8 minutes, flipping halfway through cooking. Transfer patties to paper towel–lined plate.

**4.** Using spoon, spread tzatziki evenly inside each lettuce leaf. Divide patties among leaves and top with tomato pieces and feta. Serve.

### *Keto Meal Prep*

» Tzatziki can be refrigerated for up to 2 days.

» Patties, prepared through step 3, can be refrigerated separately for up to 3 days. To reheat patties, place on greased foil-lined baking sheet and bake in 350-degree oven for 5 to 10 minutes or place on large plate and microwave for about 30 seconds.

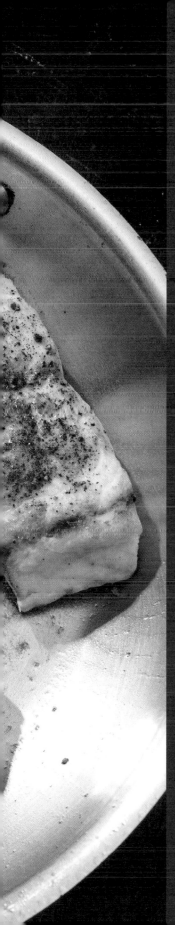

# SEAFOOD

## PER SERVING

**Cal** 610 | **Total Fat** 46g
**Protein** 39g | **Net Carbs** 5g
**Fiber** 7g | **Total Carbs** 12g

# BISTRO SALAD WITH SALMON AND AVOCADO

### Why This Recipe Works

In a composed salad, ingredients are usually laid out on a platter or individual plate to highlight colors and textures. In a tossed salad, they are tossed together in a bowl with dressing. For this keto-friendly salmon salad, we blended the tossed and composed salad styles into an edible still life. First, we tossed fresh, slightly bitter watercress and frisée in a Dijon and shallot vinaigrette. They formed the backdrop on which we arranged wholesome and colorful salmon, avocado, pomegranate seeds, and hazelnuts. For optimal flavor, instead of simply poaching the salmon, we roasted it using our unique method, starting off with a very hot oven and reducing the heat before adding the salmon to guarantee the silkiest fish. We flaked it into chunks and added thin yellow-green slices of buttery avocado for creamy richness and fat. Fresh pomegranate seeds, mint leaves, and crunchy toasted hazelnuts added the pops of sweet pink, cool green, and golden brown that turned this bistro favorite into a colorful bowl. We prefer the richness of farm-raised salmon for this recipe; however, wild salmon can be substituted. If using wild salmon, which contains less fat, cook the fish to 120 degrees (for medium-rare) and be aware that the nutritional information for this recipe will change.

1 (12-ounce) skin-on farm-raised salmon fillet, 1 to 1½ inches thick
½ teaspoon plus ⅛ teaspoon table salt, divided
½ teaspoon pepper
1 tablespoon white wine vinegar
1 tablespoon minced shallot
1 teaspoon Dijon mustard
2 tablespoons extra-virgin olive oil
4 ounces (4 cups) watercress, torn into 1½-inch pieces
½ head (3 ounces) frisée, torn into 1½-inch pieces
2 tablespoons coarsely chopped fresh mint
½ avocado (4 ounces), sliced ¼ inch thick
2 tablespoons blanched hazelnuts, toasted and chopped
2 tablespoons pomegranate seeds

**1.** Adjust oven rack to lowest position, place aluminum foil–lined rimmed baking sheet on rack, and heat oven to 500 degrees.

**2.** Pat salmon dry with paper towels and sprinkle with ½ teaspoon salt and pepper. Reduce oven to 275 degrees and carefully place fish skin side down on prepared sheet. Roast until center is still translucent when checked with tip of paring knife and registers 125 degrees (for medium-rare), 13 to 15 minutes. Transfer salmon to cutting board, let cool slightly, then flake into large pieces using 2 forks; discard skin.

**3.** Whisk vinegar, shallot, mustard, and remaining ⅛ teaspoon salt together in large bowl. While whisking constantly, slowly drizzle in oil until emulsified.

**4.** Add watercress, frisée, and mint to bowl with dressing and gently toss to coat. Divide salad between individual plates and top evenly with salmon, avocado, hazelnuts, and pomegranate seeds. Serve.

### Keto Meal Prep

» Salmon and dressing, prepared through step 3, can be refrigerated separately for up to 2 days. Bring salmon and dressing to room temperature and whisk dressing to recombine.

# CLASSIC TUNA SALAD

1 shallot, minced
2 tablespoons extra-virgin olive oil
3 (6-ounce) cans solid white tuna in water
2 teaspoons lemon juice
½ teaspoon table salt
½ teaspoon pepper
½ cup plus 2 tablespoons mayonnaise
1 celery rib, minced

**1.** Microwave shallot and oil in bowl until shallot begins to soften, about 2 minutes. Let cool slightly, about 5 minutes.

**2.** Place tuna in fine-mesh strainer and press dry with paper towels. Transfer tuna to medium bowl and mash with fork until finely flaked. Stir in shallot mixture, lemon juice, salt, and pepper and let sit for 10 minutes.

**3.** Stir in mayonnaise and celery and season with salt and pepper to taste. Serve.

## Tuna Salad with Eggs, Radishes, and Capers
Substitute 6 tablespoons extra-virgin olive oil for mayonnaise. Add 2 chopped Easy-Peel Hard-Cooked Eggs (page 37); 2 radishes, halved and thinly sliced; and ¼ cup capers, minced, to salad.
**Per ½-cup Serving** Cal 410; Total Fat 33g; Protein 24g; Net Carbs 2g; Fiber 1g; Total Carbs 3g

## Tuna Salad with Walnuts and Tarragon
Add ½ cup walnuts, toasted and chopped coarse, and 1 tablespoon minced fresh tarragon to salad.
**Per ½-cup Serving** Cal 490; Total Fat 43g; Protein 22g; Net Carbs 3g; Fiber 1g; Total Carbs 4g

### *Keto Meal Prep*
» Salad can be refrigerated for up to 2 days; stir to recombine before serving.

**Makes** 2 cups
**Total Time**: 25 minutes

## PER ½-CUP SERVING
**Cal** 410 | **Total Fat** 35g
**Protein** 20g | **Net Carbs** 2g
**Fiber** 0g | **Total Carbs** 2g

### Why This Recipe Works
We all remember this lunch box staple but often tuna salad doesn't hold up to our nostalgic memories. It can be watery, chalky, bland, or all three. Our grown-up keto tuna salad recipes show that it doesn't have to be. We found that the key to great tuna salad was to thoroughly drain chunked tuna and dry it with paper towels to remove the excess moisture that dilutes a dressing. Mashing the tuna with a fork gave it a uniform consistency, allowing the fish to effectively absorb the simple dressing's flavors so every mouthful was delicious. We infused olive oil with minced shallot, heating it briefly in the microwave. After it cooled, we combined it with the tuna, letting it rest for 10 minutes so the flavors could meld. Then we added lemon juice for tartness, silky mayo, and crunchy celery to complete the salad. Our variations replace mayo with more olive oil, adding eggs, crunchy radishes, and salty capers in one version, and walnuts accentuated by tarragon in another. Keep canned tuna handy; then grab mayo, lemon juice, and celery to mix with the fish to prepare a make-ahead lunch. Serve this tuna salad on its own, in lettuce cups, or on Seeded Bread (page 23).

**PER SERVING**
**Cal** 780 | **Total Fat** 58g
**Protein** 51g | **Net Carbs** 8g
**Fiber** 7g | **Total Carbs** 15g

## Why This Recipe Works

If you love sushi, you'll love this keto bowl reminiscent of sushi flavors, without the carb-heavy rice. We wanted it to be hearty enough for a meal so we combined tuna with cauliflower rice, adding cucumber, seaweed, scallion, and Japanese-inspired seasonings for satisfying taste. We made our sauce first to give the flavors of the mayo, sriracha, and vinegar time to meld. Then we cooked cauliflower rice, seasoning it with a dressing of rice vinegar, soy, and ginger. Finally it was the star's turn. Although sushi traditionally uses fish in its raw form, we found that briefly searing the tuna gave it a crisp, browned exterior we liked, while the interior stayed tender and juicy. Most cooked proteins need time to rest before slicing, but cutting the tuna immediately prevented carryover cooking and kept it at our preferred rare to medium-rare. For toppings, we loved sliced cucumber for its fresh crunch, creamy ripe avocado, and our simple, spicy mayo drizzled on top. If you prefer your tuna steaks cooked medium, observe the timing for medium-rare and tent the cooked steaks with foil for 5 minutes before slicing.

# SEARED TUNA SUSHI BOWL

¼ cup mayonnaise
1 tablespoon sriracha
4 teaspoons unseasoned rice vinegar, divided
2 teaspoons soy sauce
1 teaspoon grated fresh ginger
8 ounces cauliflower florets, cut into 1-inch pieces
¼ cup extra-virgin olive oil, divided
1 (12-ounce) tuna steak, 1 inch thick
¼ teaspoon table salt
¼ teaspoon pepper
⅓ English cucumber (5 ounces), halved lengthwise and sliced ¼-inch thick on bias
½ avocado (4 ounces), sliced ¼ inch thick
1 scallion, sliced thin
1 sheet toasted nori, halved lengthwise and sliced into thin strips (optional)
1 teaspoon toasted sesame seeds

**1.** Combine mayonnaise, sriracha, and 1 teaspoon vinegar in bowl; set aside. In medium bowl, whisk soy sauce, ginger, and remaining 1 tablespoon vinegar together; set aside.

**2.** Pulse cauliflower in food processor until chopped into ¼- to ⅛-inch pieces, 6 to 8 pulses, scraping down sides of bowl as needed.

**3.** Bring ¼ cup water to simmer in large saucepan over medium-high heat. Stir in cauliflower. Reduce heat to medium-low, cover, and cook, stirring occasionally, until cauliflower is tender, about 12 minutes. Stir in 2 tablespoons oil and half of soy sauce mixture and continue to cook, uncovered, stirring occasionally, until cauliflower rice is almost completely dry, about 3 minutes. Divide cauliflower mixture evenly between individual serving bowls; set aside.

**4.** Pat tuna dry with paper towels and sprinkle with salt and pepper. Heat 1 tablespoon oil in 12-inch nonstick skillet over medium-high heat until just smoking. Cook steak until opaque at perimeter, translucent red at center when checked with tip of paring knife, and registers 110 degrees (for rare), or reddish pink at center when checked with tip of paring knife and registers 125 degrees (for medium-rare), 1 to 2 minutes per side. Transfer tuna to cutting board and immediately cut into 1-inch pieces.

**5.** Add cucumber and remaining 1 tablespoon oil to bowl with remaining soy sauce mixture and toss to coat. Top prepared serving bowls evenly with tuna, cucumber, and avocado. Drizzle with mayonnaise sauce and sprinkle with scallion; nori, if using; and sesame seeds. Serve.

### *Keto Meal Prep*

» Sauce and cauliflower, prepared through step 3, can be refrigerated separately for up to 3 days. Bring to room temperature before serving.

# GRILLED SOUTHWESTERN SALMON BURGERS

½ cup mayonnaise

1 tablespoon minced canned chipotle chile in adobo sauce

1 teaspoon grated lime zest plus 2 teaspoons juice

1¼ pounds skinless farm-raised salmon, cut into 1-inch pieces

2 scallions, sliced thin

½ teaspoon salt

¼ teaspoon pepper

8 large iceberg lettuce leaves

1 tomato (6 ounces), cored and sliced thin

1 avocado (8 ounces), halved, pitted, and sliced thin

**1.** Combine mayonnaise, chipotle, and lime zest and juice in bowl. Working in 3 batches, pulse salmon in food processor until chopped into ¼-inch pieces, about 2 pulses, transferring each batch to large bowl.

**2.** Add 2 tablespoons mayonnaise sauce and scallions to chopped salmon and gently knead with your hands until well combined. Lightly moisten your hands, divide salmon mixture into 4 equal portions, then gently shape each portion into 1-inch-thick patty. Place patties on parchment paper–lined rimmed baking sheet and refrigerate for 15 minutes.

**3A. For a charcoal grill** Open bottom vent completely. Light large chimney starter filled with charcoal briquettes (6 quarts). When top coals are partially covered with ash, pour evenly over grill. Set cooking grate in place, cover, and open lid vent completely. Heat grill until hot, about 5 minutes.

**3B. For a gas grill** Turn all burners to high, cover, and heat grill until hot, about 15 minutes. Leave burners on high.

**4.** Clean cooking grate, then repeatedly brush grate with well-oiled paper towels until black and glossy, 5 to 10 times. Sprinkle patties with salt and pepper. Using spatula, place patties on grill and cook until well browned on first side and patties easily release from grill, 3 to 5 minutes. Gently flip patties and continue to cook until well browned on second side, centers are still translucent when checked with tip of paring knife, and burgers register 125 degrees (for medium-rare), 3 to 5 minutes.

**5.** Stack lettuce leaves together to create 4 lettuce wraps. Serve burgers on wraps, topped evenly with remaining mayonnaise sauce, tomato, and avocado.

## Keto Meal Prep

» Mayonnaise sauce and salmon patties, prepared through step 2, can be refrigerated for up to 24 hours.

**Serves** 4
**Total Time** 45 minutes

### PER SERVING
**Cal** 570 | **Total Fat** 47g
**Protein** 31g | **Net Carbs** 4g
**Fiber** 4g | **Total Carbs** 8g

## Why This Recipe Works

These craveworthy, tender salmon burgers are made with keto-friendly fatty farm-raised salmon but we also bulked up the fat content with mayo in the sauce and the patties. To prevent our burgers from drying out as they grilled, we needed to add moisture without overpowering the fish's rich flavor with mayo. We made a mayonnaise sauce, adding bright lime juice and chipotle, and used 2 tablespoons of this in our patties, which gave us the creaminess and moisture we were after. We used the remaining sauce to spread on the cooked burgers. We pulsed the salmon in a food processor for a texture that was good for making cohesive patties. We found that refrigerating the formed patties for at least 15 minutes ensured that the burgers would hold their shape when grilled. If using wild salmon, which contains less fat, cook the burgers to 120 degrees (for medium-rare) and be aware that the nutritional information for this recipe will change.

**Serves** 2
**Total Time** 45 minutes

## PER SERVING

**Cal** 580 | **Total Fat** 42g
**Protein** 45g | **Net Carbs** 3g
**Fiber** 2g | **Total Carbs** 5g

### Why This Recipe Works

What's not to love about fried fish tacos? Only the keto-unfriendly flour, bread-crumb coating, and tortillas that makes them so tasty! We were debating what we could use instead for the kind of crunch that bread crumbs give, and a colleague came up with the brilliant idea of using fried pork rinds, or *chicharones*. They contain plenty of fat, but the fact that they also have zero carbs makes them the perfect crunchy keto coating. And much to our delight, we discovered that they neither soaked up extra oil nor tasted greasy. We first dredged pieces of cod in almond flour, then dipped them in egg, and covered them in finely ground pork rinds. The coated fish fried up beautifully in coconut oil, giving us crispy, well-seasoned, golden-brown pieces. Bibb lettuce worked as taco shells. Our toppings were quick-pickled radishes, spicy jalapeño, and a creamy, garlicky mayonnaise sauce. We used coconut oil for frying, rather than olive oil, because it has a higher smoke point and its flavor was not overpowering. For more spicy heat, reserve, mince, and add the chile ribs and seeds to the pickling vinegar. Halibut and striped bass are good substitutes for the cod. Be aware that nutritional information will change. Feel free to sub in our Keto Tortillas (page 20) for the lettuce.

# FISH TACOS

- ½  cup distilled white vinegar
- ⅛  teaspoon plus ¼ teaspoon table salt, divided
- 2  radishes (2 ounces), trimmed and sliced thin
- ½  jalapeño chile, stemmed, seeded, and sliced thin
- 3  tablespoons mayonnaise
- 1  teaspoon water
- 1  garlic clove, minced
- 1  ounce pork rinds (3 cups)
- ¼  cup blanched, finely ground almond flour
- 1  large egg
- ⅛  teaspoon pepper
- 1  (12-ounce) skinless cod fillet, 1 to 1½ inches thick, sliced crosswise into 6 pieces
- ¼  cup coconut oil
- 6  large Bibb lettuce leaves
- ¼  cup fresh cilantro leaves

**1.** Microwave vinegar and ⅛ teaspoon salt in medium bowl until steaming, 1 to 2 minutes. Add radishes and jalapeño and let sit, stirring occasionally, for 45 minutes. Drain vegetable mixture and return to now-empty bowl; set aside for serving. Combine mayonnaise, water, and garlic in second bowl. Season with salt and pepper to taste; set aside for serving.

**2.** Process pork rinds in food processor to fine crumbs, about 20 seconds; transfer to shallow dish. Place almond flour in second shallow dish. Beat egg, remaining ¼ teaspoon salt, and pepper in third shallow dish.

**3.** Pat cod dry with paper towels. Working with 1 piece of cod at a time, dredge in flour; dip in egg mixture, letting excess drip off; then coat with pork rind crumbs, pressing gently to adhere, and transfer to plate.

**4.** Heat oil in 12-inch nonstick skillet over medium heat until shimmering. Cook cod until deep golden brown and crisp on all sides, about 5 minutes. Transfer cod to paper towel–lined plate and let drain briefly. Place one piece of cod in each lettuce leaf and top with pickled vegetables, mayonnaise sauce, and cilantro. Serve.

### *Keto Meal Prep*

» Pickled vegetables and mayonnaise sauce, prepared through step 1, can be refrigerated for up to 24 hours.

# PAN-SEARED SALMON WITH CUCUMBER-GINGER RELISH

**Serves** 2
**Total Time** 45 minutes

## PER SERVING
**Cal** 490 | **Total Fat** 37g
**Protein** 30g | **Net Carbs** 3g
**Fiber** 2g | **Total Carbs** 5g

RELISH

- 3 tablespoons extra-virgin olive oil
- 2 tablespoons unseasoned rice vinegar
- 2 tablespoons lime juice
- 1 tablespoon whole-grain mustard
- 1½ teaspoons grated fresh ginger
- ⅛ teaspoon table salt
- ½ English cucumber (8 ounces), cut into ¼-inch pieces
- ½ cup minced fresh mint
- ½ cup minced fresh cilantro
- ½ serrano chile, minced

SALMON

- ¼ teaspoon plus ⅛ teaspoon kosher salt, divided, plus salt for brining salmon
- ¼ teaspoon plus ⅛ teaspoon pepper, divided
- 2 (6-ounce) skin-on farm-raised salmon fillets, 1 to 1½ inches thick

**1. For the relish** Whisk oil, vinegar, lime juice, mustard, ginger, and salt in bowl until smooth. Stir in cucumber, mint, cilantro, and chile. Season with salt and pepper to taste. Set aside for serving.

**2. For the salmon** Dissolve ¼ cup salt in 1 quart water in large container. Submerge salmon in brine and let sit at room temperature for 15 minutes. Remove salmon from brine and pat dry with paper towels.

**3.** Sprinkle bottom of 10-inch nonstick skillet evenly with ¼ teaspoon salt and ¼ teaspoon pepper. Place fillets, skin side down, in skillet and sprinkle tops of fillets with remaining ⅛ teaspoon salt and remaining ⅛ teaspoon pepper. Heat skillet over medium-high heat and cook fillets without moving them until fat begins to render, skin begins to brown, and bottom ¼ inch of fillets turns opaque, 6 to 8 minutes.

**4.** Using tongs, flip fillets and continue to cook without moving them until centers are still translucent when checked with tip of paring knife and register 125 degrees (for medium-rare), 6 to 8 minutes. Transfer fillets, skin side down, to plate and let rest for 5 minutes before serving with cucumber-ginger relish.

## Why This Recipe Works

Pan-seared salmon is naturally keto and simply delicious so it makes a quick, easy, and flavorful weeknight supper. For this recipe, we brined our salmon to season it and keep it moist because we cooked it quickly. While the fish soaked in salt water, we had time to make a salad or side. We also paired our fish with a crisp cucumber-ginger relish, which added fat from olive oil to the meal. When we were ready to cook the salmon, we placed it skin side down in a cold, dry nonstick skillet. The skillet and fish heated at the same time and we used just the fat under the salmon skin to help cook the fish. If we had added fish to a hot pan without oil in it, the skin would burn. This way the skin slowly rendered its fat as the salmon cooked. The fat later helped sear the second side till it was golden brown and crisp. It also protected the fish from drying out during cooking. We prefer the richness of farm-raised salmon for this recipe; however, wild salmon can be substituted. If using wild salmon, which contains less fat, cook the fillets to 120 degrees (for medium-rare) and be aware that the nutritional information for this recipe will change. If you don't want to eat the salmon skin, it can be easily peeled off and discarded once the salmon is done. For a spicier relish, reserve, mince, and add the ribs and seeds from the chile.

## PER SERVING

**Cal** 480 | **Total Fat** 37g
**Protein** 34g | **Net Carbs** 2g
**Fiber** 2g | **Total Carbs** 4g

# PAN-ROASTED STRIPED BASS WITH RED PEPPER–HAZELNUT RELISH

## Why This Recipe Works

When you feel like eating fish for dinner instead of a fatty cut of meat, how do you ensure that you're getting enough fat for keto? White fish offers enough protein for the diet; to add fat, we chose a cooking method that used a little oil and added more oil in the guise of a colorful relish with red peppers to serve alongside. We decided to pan-roast the fish, which sounds easy enough but in reality it takes some practice to get it right. At home, many attempts result in dry, overbaked fish, often because the fillets are too thin and overcook by the time they can achieve a serious sear in the pan. To develop a foolproof recipe for moist, flavorful fillets, we used striped bass, a thick, semi-firm fish, and turned to a common restaurant method to cook it quickly—we seared the fillets in a hot pan, flipped them and then transferred the pan to the oven to finish cooking. The result was well-browned fillets that tasted juicy and firm. For relish with bold flavor, we chose roasted red peppers, hazelnuts, garlic, and lemon zest and whirled them together in the food processor before stirring in olive oil, fresh parsley, and thyme. Cod and snapper are good substitutes for the striped bass. Be aware that nutritional information will change.

½ cup hazelnuts, toasted and skinned

½ cup jarred roasted red peppers, rinsed, patted dry, and chopped coarse

1 garlic clove, minced

½ teaspoon grated lemon zest plus 4 teaspoons juice, divided

5 tablespoons extra-virgin olive oil, divided

2 tablespoons chopped fresh parsley

1 teaspoon minced fresh thyme

¼ teaspoon smoked paprika

½ teaspoon table salt

½ teaspoon pepper

4 (6-ounce) skinless striped bass fillets, 1 to 1½ inches thick

**1.** Adjust oven rack to middle position and heat oven to 425 degrees. Pulse hazelnuts, red peppers, garlic, and lemon zest in food processor until finely chopped, 10 to 12 pulses. Transfer to bowl and stir in ¼ cup oil, parsley, thyme, paprika, and lemon juice. Season with salt and pepper to taste; set aside for serving.

**2.** Pat striped bass dry with paper towels and sprinkle with salt and pepper. Heat remaining 1 tablespoon oil in 12-inch ovensafe skillet over medium-high heat until just smoking. Place fillets skinned side up in skillet and press lightly to ensure even contact with skillet. Cook until browned on first side, about 2 minutes. Gently flip striped bass using 2 spatulas, transfer skillet to oven, and roast until fish flakes apart when gently prodded with paring knife and registers 140 degrees, 7 to 10 minutes. Serve with red pepper–hazelnut relish.

### *Keto Meal Prep*

» Red pepper–hazelnut relish can be refrigerated for up to 2 days; bring to room temperature and whisk to recombine before serving.

# GRILLED BACON-WRAPPED SCALLOPS WITH CELERY SALAD

Serves 4
Total Time 1 hour

## PER SERVING
Cal 420 | Total Fat 30g
Protein 25g | Net Carbs 6g
Fiber 2g | Total Carbs 8g

5 tablespoons extra-virgin olive oil, divided

3 tablespoons cider vinegar

4 teaspoons Dijon mustard

8 celery ribs (1¼ pounds), sliced thin on bias

¼ cup fresh parsley leaves

1 shallot, sliced thin

12 slices bacon (12 ounces)

24 large sea scallops (1 pound), tendons removed

½ teaspoon table salt

½ teaspoon pepper

**1.** Whisk 3 tablespoons oil, vinegar, and mustard together in large bowl. Add celery, parsley, and shallot and toss to combine. Season with salt and pepper to taste; set aside for serving.

**2.** Place triple layer of paper towels on large plate and arrange 6 slices bacon in single layer on towels. Top with 3 more paper towels, remaining 6 slices bacon, and second plate. Microwave until bacon is slightly shriveled but still pliable, about 4 minutes.

**3.** Toss scallops with remaining 2 tablespoons oil, salt, and pepper. Press 2 scallops together, side to side, and wrap sides of bundle with 1 slice bacon. Thread onto 12-inch metal skewer through bacon. Repeat with remaining scallops and bacon, threading 3 bundles onto each of 4 skewers.

**4A. For a charcoal grill** Open bottom vent completely. Light large chimney starter filled with charcoal briquettes (6 quarts). When top coals are partially covered with ash, pour two-thirds evenly over half of grill, then pour remaining coals over other half of grill. Set cooking grate in place, cover, and open lid vent completely. Heat grill until hot, about 5 minutes.

**4B. For a gas grill** Turn all burners to high, cover, and heat grill until hot, about 15 minutes. Leave primary burner on high and turn other burner(s) to medium.

**5.** Clean and oil cooking grate. Place kebabs bacon side down on cooler side of grill. Cook (covered if using gas) until bacon is crisp on first side, about 4 minutes. Flip kebabs onto other bacon side and cook until crisp, about 4 minutes. Flip kebabs so one flat side of scallops is facing down and move to hotter side of grill. Grill until both sides of scallops are firm and centers are opaque, about 4 minutes. Serve with salad.

## Why This Recipe Works

Salty, smoky bacon and sweet, briny scallops are a perfect match on the grill. But they do present a delicious cooking problem. Delicate scallops are best when seared quickly over high heat. Bacon needs low, slow heat to render its fat before becoming crisp. Also, rendering bacon on the grill can cause flare-ups. We solved both problems by first microwaving bacon on a plate between layers of paper towels to absorb excess grease, weighing the bacon down with a second plate to prevent curling. We tossed the scallops with olive oil to encourage browning and prevent them from sticking to the grill grate. Using one piece of softened, slightly cooked bacon to bundle two scallops together gave us a perfect bacon-to-scallop ratio. A two-level grill fire, with a hotter and cooler side, allowed us to gently crisp the two bacon sides of the kebabs first and quickly finish cooking the scallops over high heat. A tart, crunchy celery and shallot salad was a much-needed fresh, light complement to the rich grilled kebabs. Be sure to purchase "dry" scallops, which don't have chemical additives. Dry scallops will look ivory or pinkish; "wet" scallops are bright white. You will need four 12-inch metal skewers for this recipe. Use a mandoline to thinly slice the celery. You should have about 12 ounces of celery after trimming.

## PER SERVING

**Cal** 610 | **Total Fat** 47g
**Protein** 33g | **Net Carbs** 7g
**Fiber** 8g | **Total Carbs** 15g

### Why This Recipe Works

Though named after the city-nation of
Singapore, this lightly sauced stir-fry
of vegetables, eggs, and shrimp is a
Hong Kong native. Typically, Singapore noodles are made with rice
vermicelli but for a keto-friendly
version, we chose *shirataki* noodles,
which have zero net carbohydrates.
Since ingredients cook at varying
rates, stir-frying them in batches
guaranteed a perfectly cooked dish.
We started with our shrimp and
beaten eggs. When they were just
done, we set them aside and cooked
the aromatics and bell pepper, removing them from the pan before adding
chicken broth, soy sauce, and curry
powder (a common ingredient in
Hong Kong) to the pan. We simmered
our savory sauce, then added the shirataki noodles to absorb its flavors and
tossed our shrimp mixture in. Shirataki noodles are often sold precooked
in 7- to 8-ounce packages. Thoroughly
drain and rinse the noodles before
using them. You can find shirataki
noodles in the international aisle of
most well-stocked supermarkets or
at your local Asian market.

# SINGAPORE NOODLES

- 5 tablespoons coconut oil, divided
- 12 ounces large shrimp (26 to 30 per pound), peeled, deveined, tails removed, and cut into ½-inch pieces
- 4 large eggs, lightly beaten
- ½ red bell pepper (4 ounces), cut into ¼-inch-wide strips
- 2 scallions, whites minced, greens sliced thin on bias
- 1 teaspoon grated fresh ginger
- 1 tablespoon curry powder
- ⅛ teaspoon cayenne pepper (optional)
- ½ cup chicken broth
- 4 teaspoons soy sauce
- 2 (7- to 8-ounce) packages shirataki noodles, rinsed and drained well
- 2 ounces (1 cup) bean sprouts
- 1 tablespoon lime juice

**1.** Heat 1 tablespoon oil in 12-inch
nonstick skillet over medium-high
heat until shimmering. Add shrimp
in even layer and cook without
moving until browned on bottom,
about 90 seconds. Stir and continue
to cook until just cooked through,
about 90 seconds. Push shrimp to
sides of skillet. Add 1 tablespoon
oil to center, then add eggs. Using
rubber spatula, stir eggs gently and
cook until set but still wet, about
1 minute. Stir eggs into shrimp and
continue to cook, breaking up large
pieces of egg, until eggs are fully
cooked, about 30 seconds. Transfer
shrimp-egg mixture to bowl.

**2.** Heat 1 tablespoon oil in
now-empty skillet over medium
heat until shimmering. Add bell
pepper and cook until crisp-tender,
about 2 minutes. Stir in scallion
whites and ginger and cook until
fragrant, about 30 seconds; transfer
to bowl with shrimp.

**3.** Return now-empty skillet to
medium-high heat, and heat
remaining 2 tablespoons oil, curry
powder, and cayenne, if using, stirring occasionally, until fragrant,
about 2 minutes. Off heat, add
chicken broth and soy sauce. Return
to medium-high heat and bring to
simmer. Add noodles and cook,
stirring frequently, until liquid is
absorbed, 5 to 7 minutes. Add
shrimp and vegetable mixture and
toss to combine. Add bean sprouts,
scallion greens, and lime juice, and
toss to combine. Serve immediately.

# SHRIMP SCAMPI

5  zucchini (8 ounces each), ends trimmed
3  tablespoons extra-virgin olive oil, divided
¼  teaspoon table salt
8  garlic cloves, sliced thin
½  teaspoon red pepper flakes
¼  teaspoon minced fresh thyme
1  (8-ounce) bottle clam juice
2  pounds large shrimp (26 to 30 per pound), peeled, deveined, and tails removed
6  tablespoons unsalted butter, cut into 6 pieces and chilled
2  tablespoons lemon juice
1  tablespoon chopped fresh parsley

**1.** Using spiralizer, cut zucchini into ⅛-inch-thick noodles, then cut noodles into 12-inch lengths. (You should have 2 pounds zucchini noodles after spiralizing; reserve any extra noodles for another use.)

**2.** Adjust oven rack to middle position and heat oven to 375 degrees. Toss zucchini noodles with 1 tablespoon oil and salt on rimmed baking sheet and spread into even layer. Roast until zucchini is tender, 20 to 25 minutes. Transfer zucchini to colander and shake to remove any excess liquid.

**3.** Meanwhile, heat remaining 2 tablespoons oil, garlic, pepper flakes, and thyme in 12-inch nonstick skillet over medium heat, stirring occasionally, until garlic is fragrant and just beginning to brown at edges, 3 to 5 minutes. Add clam juice and bring to simmer. Add shrimp, cover, and cook, stirring occasionally, until just opaque, 3 to 5 minutes. Off heat, transfer shrimp to bowl using slotted spoon and cover to keep warm.

**4.** Return sauce to simmer over medium-high heat and cook until reduced to ½ cup, about 5 minutes. Off heat, whisk in butter, 1 piece at a time, until combined. Whisk in lemon juice and parsley and season with salt and pepper to taste. Add shrimp and any accumulated juices and zucchini and gently toss to coat. Serve.

## *Keto Meal Prep*

» Spiralized zucchini, prepared through step 1, can be placed in zipper-lock bag and refrigerated for up to 5 days.

**Serves** 4
**Total Time** 50 minutes

## PER SERVING
**Cal** 420 | **Total Fat** 30g
**Protein** 27g | **Net Carbs** 9g
**Fiber** 2g | **Total Carbs** 11g

## Why This Recipe Works

For a keto version of classic Italian shrimp scampi, we wanted to find a good substitute for wheat-based pasta and retain all of the rich garlic and seafood flavors of the original recipe. As we have in other keto pasta recipes, we swapped in long strands of spiralized zucchini; their mild flavor allowed the shrimp and garlic to be the stars of the dish, and their texture closely resembled that of conventional pasta. For the sauce, we first infused our cooking oil with minced garlic, red pepper flakes, and thyme. We stirred in clam juice to reinforce the seafood flavor before cooking the shrimp in the liquid and setting it aside. Reducing the sauce before whisking in butter gave it a classic, rich finish. The sauce was deliciously garlicky but the first time we stirred zucchini noodles directly into it, their moisture diluted the flavor of the sauce. So we roasted the spiralized zucchini first. Once our sauce was thick, we tossed the shrimp and roasted noodles into it to coat and serve. If possible, use smaller, in-season zucchini, which have thinner skins and fewer seeds. We prefer to spiralize our own zucchini, but you can substitute 2 pounds of store-bought spiralized zucchini, though they tend to be drier and less flavorful. Avoid buying large zucchini, which have thicker skins and more seeds.

# VEGETABLE MAINS

**Serves** 4
**Total Time** 45 minutes

## PER SERVING

**Cal** 360 | **Total Fat** 29g
**Protein** 13g | **Net Carbs** 8g
**Fiber** 5g | **Total Carbs** 13g

### Why This Recipe Works

A composed Cobb salad is very much about appearance—not surprising, given that its birthplace is Hollywood! Created in the 1920s at LA's famed Brown Derby restaurant, the Cobb is about substance too. A well-executed Cobb assembles a large cast of flavored and textured ingredients that look and taste superb together: crunchy greens; tender chicken; buttery avocado; juicy tomato; hard-cooked eggs; crispy, smoky bacon; and tangy blue cheese. But we wanted a Cobb salad for the 21st century—a beautiful vegetarian keto superhero. So we took the chicken out but kept the protein-rich hard-cooked eggs. And we replaced bacon's smoky flavor with sautéed shiitake mushrooms, which we spiced with smoked paprika and chili powder. To up the nutritional ante, we used kale as the greens instead of romaine, and we added radicchio for lovely color and a slight bitter edge. We tossed some dressing with our greens and drizzled the rest over our still-classic yet modern vegetarian keto Cobb. You should have 4 ounces of kale after stemming. Feel free to substitute 4 ounces of baby kale for the mature kale; if using, skip step 1.

# SUPER COBB SALAD

8 ounces kale, stemmed and cut into 1-inch pieces
¼ cup extra-virgin olive oil, divided
8 ounces shiitake mushrooms, stemmed and sliced thin
½ teaspoon table salt, divided
⅛ teaspoon smoked paprika
⅛ teaspoon chili powder
⅛ teaspoon pepper
½ cup plain whole-milk yogurt
3 tablespoons crumbled blue cheese
1 garlic clove, minced
1 teaspoon lemon juice
½ small head radicchio (3 ounces), cored and cut into ½-inch pieces
2 recipes Easy-Peel Hard-Cooked Eggs (page 37), quartered
1 avocado (8 ounces), halved, pitted, and cut into ½-inch pieces
4 ounces cherry tomatoes, halved

**1.** Place kale in large bowl and cover with warm tap water (110 to 115 degrees). Swish kale around to remove grit. Let kale sit in warm water bath for 10 minutes. Remove kale from water and spin dry in salad spinner in multiple batches. Pat leaves dry with paper towels if still wet.

**2.** Meanwhile, heat 1 tablespoon oil in 12-inch nonstick skillet over medium heat until shimmering. Add mushrooms and ¼ teaspoon salt, cover, and cook until mushrooms have released their liquid, 4 to 6 minutes. Uncover and increase heat to medium-high. Stir in paprika, chili powder, and pepper and cook until mushrooms are golden, 4 to 6 minutes. Transfer to plate and let cool.

**3.** Whisk yogurt, blue cheese, garlic, lemon juice, remaining 3 tablespoons oil, and remaining ¼ teaspoon salt together in bowl until well combined. Season with salt and pepper to taste. Toss kale with ½ cup dressing, cover, and refrigerate for 20 minutes.

**4.** Add radicchio to kale and toss to combine. Transfer greens to four individual serving plates and arrange cooled mushrooms, eggs, avocado, and tomatoes evenly over top. Drizzle remaining dressing over salads. Serve.

### Keto Meal Prep

» Mushrooms, dressing, and dressed kale, prepared through step 3, can be refrigerated separately for up to 24 hours. Let mushrooms come to room temperature and whisk dressing to recombine before serving.

# ZUCCHINI NOODLE SALAD WITH PEANUT-GINGER DRESSING

- 3 zucchini (8 ounces each), ends trimmed
- ¼ cup unsweetened, creamy peanut butter
- 2 tablespoons soy sauce
- 1 tablespoon unseasoned rice vinegar
- 1 tablespoon toasted sesame oil
- 1 tablespoon coconut oil, melted
- 2 teaspoons grated fresh ginger
- 1 teaspoon sriracha
- 1 small garlic clove, minced
- ½ red bell pepper (4 ounces), stemmed, seeded, and cut into ¼-inch-wide strips
- 2 teaspoons sesame seeds, toasted

**1.** Using spiralizer, cut zucchini into ⅛-inch-thick noodles, then cut noodles into 12-inch lengths. (You should have 1 pound of zucchini noodles after spiralizing; reserve extra noodles for another use.)

**2.** Whisk peanut butter, soy sauce, vinegar, sesame oil, coconut oil, ginger, sriracha, and garlic in large bowl until smooth. Add zucchini noodles and bell pepper to bowl with dressing and toss to combine. Sprinkle with sesame seeds. Serve.

## Keto Meal Prep

» Spiralized zucchini, prepared through step 1, can be placed in zipper-lock bag and refrigerated for up to 5 days.

**Serves** 2
**Total Time** 30 minutes

### PER SERVING
**Cal** 470g | **Total Fat** 40g
**Protein** 14g | **Net Carbs** 10g
**Fiber** 6g | **Total Carbs** 16g

## Why This Recipe Works

With their bold, Asian-inspired flavors and bountiful crisp-tender vegetables, cool noodle salads make perfect umami-laden vegetarian lunches or dinners. Since we have plenty of successful recipes utilizing spiralized zucchini in place of traditional wheat or rice noodles, we decided to use them again here. Focusing first on how the noodles would be treated, we initially tried boiling them, but they absorbed too much water that diluted our finished dish. Stir-frying the noodles proved no better. In the end, leaving the zucchini noodles raw gave us a texture closer to that of real noodles; plus, tasters enjoyed their delicate, fresh taste accentuated by sesame oil and sriracha. Red bell pepper gave us color and textural contrast, and for a flavorful dressing, we built a base with peanut butter and soy sauce, adding ginger, rice vinegar, and garlic to round out the flavors. We prefer to spiralize our own zucchini, but you can substitute 1 pound of store-bought spiralized zucchini, though they tend to be drier and less flavorful. Avoid buying large zucchini, which have thicker skins and more seeds.

## PER SERVING

**Cal** 340 | **Total Fat** 30g
**Protein** 10g | **Net Carbs** 10g
**Fiber** 4g | **Total Carbs** 14g

### Why This Recipe Works

The best falafel are moist, tender, and packed with flavor, with a satisfyingly crunchy crust. They are traditionally made with chickpeas, with flour to bind everything together. This wouldn't work for keto, naturally. Most keto versions of falafel use cauliflower but we were disappointed by the soggy, distinctly vegetal fritters cauliflower produced. Someone suggested mushrooms instead. We gave them a shot and were amazed by the similarity of our faux-lafel to the real thing. The mushrooms added bulk and mimicked the earthy savoriness of this popular Middle Eastern street food. Almond flour and an egg white bound our fritters together and an abundance of herbs and spices (cilantro, cumin, coriander) mimicked falafel flavor. The falafel looked and tasted great but stayed soggy in the middle and lacked a distinctive crust. The culprit? The moisture of the mushrooms. Would evaporating more liquid help? We processed the mushrooms in a food processor and cooked them covered so they released water. Then we cooked them uncovered until they were quite dry. Now we could easily flavor, shape, and fry them into fritters that were crispy all the way through. No falafel is complete without toppings—we accompanied ours with a naturally low-carb tahini sauce and a no-sugar radish pickle and topped off the dish with refreshing, crunchy cucumber.

# MEDITERRANEAN "FALAFEL" WRAPS

- ½ cup white wine vinegar
- ⅛ teaspoon plus ¼ teaspoon table salt, divided
- ⅛ teaspoon plus ¼ teaspoon cayenne pepper, divided
- 4 radishes (4 ounces), trimmed and sliced thin
- 1 pound cremini mushrooms, trimmed and halved
- 5 tablespoons extra-virgin olive oil, divided
- ¾ cup fresh cilantro leaves
- ¾ cup fresh parsley leaves
- 1½ teaspoons ground coriander
- 1 teaspoon ground cumin
- 1 garlic clove, minced
- ¼ cup blanched, finely ground almond flour
- 1 large egg white
- 12 large Bibb lettuce leaves
- ¼ English cucumber (4 ounces), halved lengthwise and sliced thin
- ¼ cup Tahini Sauce (page 28)

**1.** Microwave vinegar, ⅛ teaspoon salt, and ⅛ teaspoon cayenne in medium bowl until steaming, 1 to 2 minutes. Add radishes and let sit, stirring occasionally, for 45 minutes. Drain radishes and return to now-empty bowl; set aside for serving.

**2.** Pulse mushrooms in food processor until finely chopped, about 25 pulses, scraping down sides of bowl as needed. Heat 2 tablespoons oil in 12-inch nonstick skillet over medium heat until shimmering. Add mushrooms and remaining ¼ teaspoon salt, cover, and cook until mushrooms have released their liquid, about 5 minutes. Uncover and continue to cook, stirring occasionally, until mushrooms are lightly browned and dry, about 10 minutes; transfer to large bowl.

**3.** Process cilantro, parsley, coriander, cumin, garlic, and remaining ¼ teaspoon cayenne in now-empty processor until finely ground, about 30 seconds, scraping down sides of bowl as needed. Stir herb mixture, flour, and egg white into mushrooms until combined. Cover and let sit at room temperature for 15 minutes.

**4.** Pinch off and roll mushroom mixture into 1½ tablespoon-size balls (you should have 12 balls). Flatten balls into ¾-inch-thick patties.

**5.** Heat remaining 3 tablespoons oil in now-empty skillet over medium heat until shimmering. Cook patties until deep golden brown, 3 to 5 minutes per side. Transfer patties to paper towel–lined plate and let drain briefly. Divide patties evenly among lettuce leaves and top with cucumber, radishes, and tahini sauce. Serve.

### Keto Meal Prep

» Pickled radishes and patties, prepared through step 5, can be refrigerated separately for up to 24 hours. To reheat patties, place on greased, foil-lined baking sheet and bake in 350-degree oven for 10 minutes or place on large plate and microwave for 45 to 60 seconds.

# KETO PIZZA WITH MOZZARELLA, TOMATOES, AND BASIL PESTO

6 tablespoons Basil Pesto (page 26)

1 recipe Pizza Crust (page 24), fully baked and still warm

4 ounces fresh mozzarella cheese, torn into bite-size pieces

3 ounces cherry tomatoes, quartered

Spread pesto over pizza crust, leaving ½-inch border. Top with mozzarella and tomatoes. Serve.

### Keto Pizza with Prosciutto, Arugula, and Ricotta

Stir ¾ cup whole-milk ricotta cheese, 1 tablespoon extra-virgin olive oil, ½ teaspoon lemon zest plus 1 teaspoon juice, ¼ teaspoon pepper, and ⅛ teaspoon salt together in bowl. Substitute ricotta mixture for pesto, 2 ounces thinly sliced prosciutto for mozzarella, and 1 cup (1 ounce) baby arugula for tomatoes. Sprinkle pizza with 2 tablespoons finely chopped jarred hot cherry peppers and drizzle with additional 1 tablespoon extra-virgin olive oil before serving.

**Per Serving** Cal 470; Total Fat 37g; Protein 29g; Net Carbs 5g; Fiber 2g; Total Carbs 7g

### Keto Pizza with Fennel, Mushrooms, and Hazelnut Romesco

Substitute Hazelnut Romesco (page 28) for pesto. Substitute 3 ounces trimmed and thinly sliced cremini mushrooms for mozzarella and 3 ounces thinly sliced fennel for tomatoes. Sprinkle pizza with 2 tablespoons chopped fresh parsley before serving.

**Per Serving** Cal 390; Total Fat 31g; Protein 21g; Net Carbs 7g; Fiber 3g; Total Carbs 10g

**Serves** 4
**Total Time** 15 minutes

## PER SERVING
**Cal** 530 | **Total Fat** 46g
**Protein** 26g | **Net Carbs** 6g
**Fiber** 3g | **Total Carbs** 9g

## Why This Recipe Works

We worked hard at developing a keto pizza crust that would be crisp on the outside and chewy within, truly satisfying to bite into. Then we wanted to find an easy way to turn the crust into a complete pizza or flatbread with minimal effort. Tomato sauces are often spread on pizza crusts before other toppings are added and the pizza is baked. But since tomato sauce is generally excluded from the keto diet because of its high carb content, we decided to take a different approach. We worked on a series of no-cook toppings so that the keto crust wouldn't require double baking and could stay crisp. We riffed on the flavors of a classic Neapolitan pizza, replacing them with a handful of fresh cherry tomatoes, mozzarella, and a pesto base for that signature basil flavor. For a non-vegetarian version, we combined ricotta with some olive oil and lemon for a zesty, creamy base to prosciutto and peppery arugula, topped off with hot cherry peppers—their sweet-savory heat elevated the dish. Our second variation was inspired by Spanish flavors: We topped the flatbread with romesco, a sauce made from roasted peppers and nuts, and sprinkled some shaved mushrooms and fennel over the top.

**Serves** 4
**Total Time** 45 minutes

## PER SERVING

**Cal** 590 | **Total Fat** 55g
**Protein** 17g | **Net Carbs** 9g
**Fiber** 7g | **Total Carbs** 16g

### Why This Recipe Works

It's a commonly held belief that those on the keto diet can't enjoy a really full plate of vegetables. With this simple but mouthwateringly satisfying dish, we dispel that idea for good. The most keto-friendly of all vegetables is broccoli rabe—a full pound contains less than 2 grams of net carbs. So naturally we turned to broccoli rabe for this recipe, grilling it to pick up some toasty char that balanced its strangely pleasing bitterness. We contrasted its vegetal quality with the creamy center and sweet-savory exterior of grilled eggplant, and tied the two vegetables together with an herby pistachio-tarragon pesto, purposely leaving it chunky for its satisfying crunch. We grilled a lemon too; it contributed a caramelized citrus tang. We finished the dish with a fresh sliced jalapeño—its green, fresh heat mimicked hot Italian pepperoncini which are not widely available. Some sweet, creamy burrata served with the vegetables turned a beautiful plate into a full meal. You can substitute fresh mozzarella for the burrata. You should have about 12 ounces broccoli rabe after trimming.

# GRILLED VEGETABLE PLATE WITH BURRATA AND PISTACHIO-TARRAGON PESTO

- 1 **pound broccoli rabe**
- 1 **pound eggplant, sliced into ¼-inch thick slices**
- 6 **tablespoons extra-virgin olive oil, divided**
- ½ **teaspoon salt, divided**
- 1 **lemon, quartered**
- 2 **(4-ounce) burrata cheese balls, room temperature**
- 6 **tablespoons Pistachio-Tarragon Pesto (page 26)**
- ¼ **cup fresh tarragon and/or parsley leaves**
- 2 **tablespoons chopped toasted pistachios**
- 1 **jalapeño, sliced thin (optional)**

**1.** Trim and discard bottom 1 inch of broccoli rabe stems. Wash broccoli rabe with cold water, then dry with clean dish towel.

**2A. For a charcoal grill** Open bottom vent completely. Light large chimney starter filled with charcoal briquettes (6 quarts). When top coals are partially covered with ash, pour evenly over grill. Set cooking grate in place, cover, and open lid vent completely. Heat grill until hot, about 5 minutes.

**2B. For a gas grill** Turn all burners to high, cover, and heat grill until hot, about 15 minutes. Turn all burners to medium-high.

**3.** Clean and oil cooking grate. Toss broccoli rabe with 2 tablespoons oil and ¼ teaspoon salt. Brush eggplant with remaining ¼ cup oil and sprinkle with remaining ¼ teaspoon salt. Arrange eggplant and lemon cut side down on grill and cook, turning as needed, until eggplant is tender and lightly browned and lemon is lightly charred, 8 to 10 minutes. Transfer eggplant and lemon to platter as they finish cooking and tent with aluminum foil.

**4.** Arrange broccoli rabe on grill and cook, turning as needed, until tender and lightly charred, 8 to 10 minutes; transfer to platter with eggplant.

**5.** Place burrata on plate and cut into 4 pieces, collecting creamy liquid. Arrange vegetables evenly on individual plates and top with burrata, pesto, tarragon, pistachios, and jalapeño, if using. Serve with grilled lemon.

# CAULIFLOWER STEAKS WITH CHIMICHURRI

1 head cauliflower (2 pounds)
2 tablespoons extra-virgin olive oil
½ teaspoon table salt
¼ teaspoon pepper
6 tablespoons Chimichurri (page 27)

**1.** Adjust oven rack to lowest position and heat oven to 500 degrees. Discard outer leaves of cauliflower and trim stem flush with bottom florets. Halve cauliflower lengthwise through core. Cut one 1½-inch-thick slab lengthwise from each half, trimming any florets not connected to core. (You should have two 10-ounce steaks; reserve remaining cauliflower for another use.)

**2.** Place steaks on rimmed baking sheet and drizzle with 1 tablespoon oil. Sprinkle with ¼ teaspoon salt and ⅛ teaspoon pepper and rub to distribute. Flip steaks and repeat.

**3.** Cover sheet tightly with aluminum foil and roast for 5 minutes. Remove foil and continue to roast until bottoms of steaks are well browned, 8 to 10 minutes. Gently flip and continue to roast until tender and second sides are well browned, 6 to 8 minutes. Serve with chimichurri.

**Serves** 2
**Total Time** 45 minutes

### PER SERVING
**Cal** 400 | **Total Fat** 36g
**Protein** 6g | **Net Carbs** 10g
**Fiber** 6g | **Total Carbs** 16g

## Why This Recipe Work

Humble cauliflower gets a major upgrade when it's cut into thick slabs, deeply browned, and served with a pungent, vibrant chimichurri. This is the perfect dish for anyone looking for a break from meat. The cauliflower is hearty, flavorful, and satisfying. For perfectly cooked cauliflower steaks, we opted for two cooking methods—steaming and roasting in a scorching oven. Steaming the cauliflower briefly under foil followed by uncovered roasting under high heat produced well-caramelized steaks with tender interiors, ready for a generous slathering of sauce. Look for a fresh, firm, bright white head of cauliflower that feels heavy for its size and is free of blemishes or soft spots; florets are more likely to separate from older heads of cauliflower. We also enjoy using Salsa Verde (page 27) or Chermoula (page 28) on the cauliflower steaks in place of the chimichurri.

**Serves** 4
**Total Time** 1 hour

## PER SERVING

**Cal** 380 | **Total Fat** 36g
**Protein** 7g | **Net Carbs** 7g
**Fiber** 2g | **Total Carbs** 9g

## Why This Recipe Works

Grilled portobello burgers are a great vegetarian alternative to traditional meats, but they can easily fall flat. Though the grill adds delicious char, plain grilled mushrooms can be boring. We wanted boldly flavored grilled portobello burgers that were easy to make. The first thing to do was marinate our mushrooms in olive oil and red wine vinegar seasoned with garlic, salt, and pepper. The second was to create a tangy, cheesy filling that would fit into the domed shape of a portobello that is perfect for stuffing. Then, while the mushrooms marinated, we set up the grill. Once the mushrooms were nicely charred, we packed them with our feta and sun-dried tomato mixture and put them back on the grill until the filling was warmed through. We served these hearty burgers on keto-friendly lettuce wraps. And we didn't stop there: A summery lemon-basil mayonnaise finished this rich, satisfying dish with hints of tart and sweet. Use portobello mushroom caps measuring 4 to 5 inches in diameter. We find it best to use a spoon to scrape the gills off the underside of the portobellos.

# GRILLED PORTOBELLO BURGERS

- 4 portobello mushroom caps (3 ounces each), gills removed
- ¼ cup extra-virgin olive oil
- 2 tablespoons red wine vinegar
- 1 garlic clove, minced
- ¾ teaspoon salt
- ½ teaspoon pepper
- 4 ounces feta cheese, crumbled (1 cup)
- ½ cup oil-packed sun-dried tomatoes, patted dry and chopped
- ⅓ cup mayonnaise
- ⅓ cup chopped fresh basil
- 1 tablespoon lemon juice
- 8 large iceberg lettuce leaves

**1.** Using sharp knife, cut ¼-inch slits, spaced ½ inch apart, in crosshatch pattern on surface (non-cupped side) of mushrooms. Combine oil, vinegar, garlic, salt, and pepper in 1-gallon zipper-lock bag. Add mushrooms, press out air, seal bag, turn bag to coat mushrooms, and let sit for 15 minutes.

**2.** Combine feta and tomatoes in bowl. Whisk mayonnaise, basil, and lemon juice together in separate bowl.

**3A. For a charcoal grill** Open bottom vent completely. Light large chimney starter filled with charcoal briquettes (6 quarts). When top coals are partially covered with ash, pour evenly over grill. Set cooking grate in place, cover, and open lid vent completely. Heat grill until hot, about 5 minutes.

**3B. For a gas grill** Turn all burners to high, cover, and heat grill until hot, about 15 minutes. Leave all burners on high.

**4.** Clean and oil cooking grate. Remove mushrooms from marinade, reserving any excess marinade. Place mushrooms cupped side up on grill and cook until mushrooms have released their liquid and are charred on first side, 4 to 6 minutes. Flip mushrooms, brush with reserved marinade, and continue to cook until charred on second side, 3 to 5 minutes.

**5.** Transfer mushrooms cupped side up to plate and divide feta mixture evenly among caps, packing it down with your hand. Return mushrooms to grill, feta side up, and cook, covered, until heated through, about 3 minutes.

**6.** Stack lettuce leaves together to create 4 lettuce wraps. Serve mushrooms on wraps, topped evenly with sauce.

### Keto Meal Prep

» Mushrooms, prepared through step 1, can be refrigerated for up to 24 hours.
» Grilled, filled mushrooms and sauce can be refrigerated for up to 3 days. To reheat mushrooms, place on greased, foil-lined baking sheet and bake in 350-degree oven for 10 minutes or place on large plate and microwave for 45 to 60 seconds.

# GREEN SHAKSHUKA

**Serves** 4
**Total Time** 1 hour

- 2 pounds Swiss chard, stems removed and reserved, leaves chopped
- 6 tablespoon extra-virgin olive oil, divided
- ½ teaspoon table salt, divided
- 4 garlic cloves, minced
- 2 teaspoons ground coriander
- 11 ounces (11 cups) baby spinach, chopped
- ½ cup vegetable broth
- 1½ tablespoons lemon juice
- 8 large eggs
- ½ teaspoon ground dried Aleppo pepper
- 2 ounces feta cheese, crumbled (½ cup)
- 2 tablespoons chopped fresh dill
- 2 tablespoons chopped fresh mint

**1.** Slice 4 ounces chard stems thin; discard remaining stems or reserve for another use. Heat 2 tablespoons oil in Dutch oven over medium heat until shimmering. Add chard stems and ¼ teaspoon salt and cook until softened and lightly browned, 5 to 7 minutes. Stir in garlic and coriander and cook until fragrant, about 1 minute.

**2.** Add chard leaves and spinach. Increase heat to medium-high, cover, and cook, stirring occasionally, until wilted but still bright green, 3 to 5 minutes. Off heat, transfer 1 cup chard mixture to blender. Add broth and 2 tablespoons oil and process until smooth, about 45 seconds, scraping down sides of blender jar as needed. Stir chard mixture and lemon juice into pot.

**3.** Make 4 shallow indentations (about 2 inches wide) in surface of greens using back of spoon. Crack 2 eggs into each indentation and sprinkle with Aleppo pepper and remaining ¼ teaspoon salt. Cover and cook over medium-low heat until edges of egg whites are just set, 5 to 10 minutes. Off heat, let sit, covered, until whites are fully set and yolks are still runny, 2 to 4 minutes. Sprinkle with feta, dill, and mint and drizzle with remaining 2 tablespoons oil. Serve immediately.

## PER SERVING

**Cal** 420 | **Total Fat** 34g
**Protein** 18g | **Net Carbs** 6g
**Fiber** 4g | **Total Carbs** 10g

## Why This Recipe Works

The classic Tunisian dish *shakshuka* is a humble, satisfying one-pot meal of eggs in a long-simmered tomato and pepper sauce. We swapped out the red sauce for a fresh, vibrant mix of greens. For an easy one-pot keto meal, we chose savory Swiss chard and tender baby spinach. First, we cooked the sliced chard stems; then we stirred in garlic and coriander to create an aromatic base in which we cooked the chopped chard leaves and spinach. A roomy Dutch oven allowed us to wilt the large volume of greens easily. We blended a cup of the cooked greens with broth to give the sauce a creamy, cohesive texture. To finish, we poached eight eggs, sprinkled with Aleppo pepper and salt, directly in the sauce, covering the pot to contain the heat for efficient, even cooking. We served our green shakshuka with a sprinkle of fragrant fresh dill and mint and salty, creamy feta cheese. If you can't find Aleppo pepper, you can substitute ⅛ teaspoon paprika and ⅛ teaspoon finely chopped red pepper flakes. You should have about 12 ounces Swiss chard leaves after stemming. The Dutch oven will seem crowded when you first add the greens, but they will quickly wilt down. Avoid removing the lid during the first 5 minutes of cooking in step 3; it will increase the total cooking time of the eggs.

**Serves** 2
**Total Time** 30 minutes

## PER SERVING

**Cal** 580 | **Total Fat** 52g
**Protein** 15g | **Net Carbs** 6g
**Fiber** 5g | **Total Carbs** 11g

## Why This Recipe Works

A richly comforting bowl of cheesy, creamy noodles oddly seemed like it might be out of the scope of the keto diet, because of the pasta. We tried subbing no-carb *shirataki* noodles for regular pasta to make a simple *cacio e pepe* (cheese and pepper) pasta; this failed spectacularly, becoming a watery, cheesy mess. We learned that the starch exuded by regular noodles is what helps bind and emulsify a cheesy sauce. We didn't have that here so we turned to a combination of heavy cream and cream cheese for their emulsifying and binding properties, keeping a healthy dose of Pecorino to thicken and season the sauce. This worked well but the sauce was still watery. Then we found that dry-frying the noodles first in an empty skillet drove off excess moisture successfully. To make a fully composed dish, we added crispy mushroom nuggets and savory baby spinach. Shirataki noodles are often sold precooked in 7- to 8-ounce packages. Thoroughly drain and rinse the noodles before using them. You can find shirataki noodles in the international aisle of most well-stocked supermarkets or at your local Asian market. You will need a 12-inch nonstick skillet with a lid for this recipe. To quickly soften the cream cheese, microwave it for 20 to 30 seconds.

# CREAMY SHIRATAKI NOODLES WITH SPINACH, MUSHROOMS, AND PECORINO

- 2 tablespoons extra-virgin olive oil
- 4 ounces cremini mushrooms, trimmed and chopped
- ⅛ teaspoon table salt
- 2 (7- to 8-ounce) packages shirataki noodles, rinsed and drained well
- 2 ounces Pecorino Romano, grated (1 cup), divided
- ½ cup heavy cream
- 2 ounces cream cheese, softened
- ½ teaspoon pepper
- 2 ounces (2 cups) baby spinach, chopped

**1.** Heat oil in 12-inch nonstick skillet over medium heat until shimmering. Add mushrooms and salt, cover, and cook until mushrooms have released their liquid, about 5 minutes.

**2.** Uncover and continue to cook until mushrooms are well browned and crisp, 6 to 8 minutes. Using slotted spoon, transfer mushrooms to bowl. Wipe skillet clean with paper towels.

**3.** Add noodles to now-empty skillet and cook over medium heat until dry, about 3 minutes; transfer to bowl. Add ½ cup Pecorino, cream, cream cheese, and pepper to now-empty skillet and cook, stirring frequently, over medium-low heat until fully combined, 3 to 5 minutes. Gently fold in noodles and spinach and cook until heated through and spinach is wilted, about 2 minutes. Season with salt and pepper to taste and adjust consistency with hot water as needed. Sprinkle individual portions evenly with mushrooms and remaining ½ cup Pecorino before serving.

# VEGETABLE SIDES

**Serves** 2
**Total Time** 25 minutes

## PER SERVING

**Cal** 160 | **Total Fat** 15g
**Protein** 3g | **Net Carbs** 3g
**Fiber** 2g | **Total Carbs** 5g

### Why This Recipe Works

Finding vegetables to eat on a keto diet can be challenging, but asparagus is a no-brainer. Low in carbs, asparagus has other healthy properties—it's high in fiber, folate, and antioxidants and has anti-inflammatory benefits. Best of all, it tastes great in this no-fuss, quick side dish. To avoid overcooking the asparagus, we started with thicker spears. To help them release moisture, encouraging caramelization and better flavor, we parcooked the spears covered, with butter and oil. The water evaporating from both the butter and asparagus helped them steam cook through evenly. Then we removed the lid and turned up the heat to brown the spears. We preferred the flavor of stalks that had been browned on only one side, keeping the other side green and crisp-tender. This also allowed us to skip the tedious step of rotating individual spears. Some toasted garlic or lemon juice and fruity lemon zest with fresh tarragon brightened the vegetable's natural sweetness in our simple variations. This recipe works best with asparagus that is at least ½ inch thick near the base. Do not use pencil-thin asparagus; it will overcook. You should have about 8 ounces of asparagus after trimming.

# PAN-ROASTED ASPARAGUS

1  tablespoon unsalted butter
4  teaspoons extra-virgin olive oil, divided
12  ounces thick asparagus, trimmed
⅛  teaspoon table salt
1  teaspoon lemon juice

**1.** Heat butter and 2 teaspoons oil in 12-inch skillet over medium heat until butter is melted. Add half of asparagus to skillet with tips pointed in 1 direction and add remaining asparagus with tips pointed in opposite direction. Sprinkle with salt. Using tongs, distribute spears in even layer, cover, and cook until asparagus is bright green and still crisp, about 7 minutes.

**2.** Uncover, increase heat to medium-high, and cook until asparagus is tender and well browned on 1 side, 3 to 4 minutes, using tongs to transfer spears from center of skillet to edge of skillet to ensure even browning. Drizzle with lemon juice and remaining 2 teaspoons oil. Season with salt and pepper to taste. Serve.

### Pan-Roasted Asparagus with Toasted Garlic

Cook 1 thinly sliced garlic clove and 2 teaspoons oil in 12-inch skillet over medium heat until garlic is crisp and golden, about 4 minutes. Transfer garlic to paper towel–lined plate and set aside, leaving oil in skillet. Add butter to garlic oil left in skillet and proceed with recipe. Sprinkle toasted garlic over asparagus before serving.
**Per Serving** Cal 160; Total Fat 15g; Protein 3g; Net Carbs 3g; Fiber 2g; Total Carbs 5g

### Pan-Roasted Asparagus with Tarragon and Lemon

Combine 1 tablespoon minced fresh tarragon, 1 teaspoon grated lemon zest, 1 small minced garlic clove, and pinch cayenne in bowl; set aside. Sprinkle tarragon mixture over asparagus before serving.
**Per Serving** Cal 160; Total Fat 15g; Protein 3g; Net Carbs 3g; Fiber 2g; Total Carbs 5g

# ROASTED BROCCOLI SALAD

1¼ pounds broccoli

5 tablespoons extra-virgin olive oil, divided

2 avocados (1 pound), halved, pitted, and cut into ½-inch pieces

1 tablespoon white wine vinegar

1 garlic clove, minced

½ teaspoon table salt

½ teaspoon pepper

4 ounces cherry tomatoes, quartered

¼ cup chopped fresh basil

**1.** Adjust oven rack to lowest position, place rimmed baking sheet on rack, and heat oven to 500 degrees. Cut broccoli horizontally at juncture of crowns and stalks. Cut crowns into 4 wedges if 3 to 4 inches in diameter or 6 wedges if 4 to 5 inches in diameter. Trim tough outer peel from stalks, then cut into ½-inch-thick planks about 2 to 3 inches long.

**2.** Toss broccoli with 3 tablespoons oil. Working quickly, lay broccoli in single layer, flat sides down, on preheated sheet. Roast until stalks are well browned and tender and florets are lightly browned, 9 to 11 minutes. Transfer broccoli to cutting board, let cool slightly, then cut into 1½-inch pieces.

**3.** Process remaining 2 tablespoons oil, half of avocado, vinegar, garlic, salt, and pepper in food processor until smooth, scraping down sides of bowl as needed; transfer to large serving bowl. Add broccoli, remaining avocado, tomatoes, and basil and toss to combine. Season with salt and pepper to taste. Serve.

**Serves** 6
**Total Time** 45 minutes

## PER SERVING
**Cal** 240 | **Total Fat** 22g
**Protein** 4g | **Net Carbs** 5g
**Fiber** 7g | **Total Carbs** 12g

## Why This Recipe Works

Broccoli, high in fiber, vitamins A and C, and potassium, is also low in carbs, making it just right for keto eating. We love this versatile vegetable in stir-fries and in salads like this one, which pairs beautifully with chicken or meat. To heighten its flavor, we roasted thick-cut broccoli, using high heat and a preheated baking sheet to get a sweet char; because it's only cooked on one side, the broccoli stays tender and bright green. We found that a mayonnaise-based dressing, which is often used for broccoli salads, overwhelmed the taste of the vegetable. But we wanted to enhance the salad's keto fat requirements so, inspired by the creamy, mild-flavored avocado in our salad, we tried blending some of it into our dressing. It worked, lending a delicate avocado flavor to the slight bitterness of the roasted broccoli. Aromatic garlic and white wine vinegar were counterpoints to the avocado's sweetness. A topping of cherry tomatoes packed a tart punch, and though basil is an unusual herb to pair with broccoli, it added a fresh finish to the salad. We start with 1¼ pounds broccoli, which is trimmed to 1 pound after cutting off the tough outer part of the stalk and the base.

**PER SERVING**
**Cal** 150 | **Total Fat** 14g
**Protein** 3g | **Net Carbs** 1g
**Fiber** 2g | **Total Carbs** 3g

## Why This Recipe Works

Broccoli rabe is another delicious vegetable that works well with keto eating plans because its complex, nuanced flavor makes it a great low-carb side to serve with rich, hearty meat preparations. Most recipes call for blanching and shocking the green before cooking in order to tame its bitterness—a fussy method that washes out its distinctive flavor. When we learned that most of the vegetable's bitterness comes from an enzymatic reaction triggered when the florets are cut or chewed, we decided to simply keep the leafy parts of the broccoli rabe whole. Because the heat from cooking deactivated the enzyme, much of the bitterness was tamed. We also skipped stovetop methods and broiled the rabe, which created deep caramelization without overcooking the pieces. Plus, broiling took just minutes and required nothing more than a rimmed baking sheet. Since the heat generated by a broiler varies from oven to oven, we recommend keeping an eye on the broccoli rabe as it cooks. If the leaves are getting too dark or not browning in the time specified in the recipe, adjust the distance of the oven rack from the broiler element. The variation with olives and garlic is fresh and light-tasting; for a rich version, try the creamy Gruyère sauce. You should have about 12 ounces of broccoli rabe after trimming.

# BROILED BROCCOLI RABE

¼ cup extra-virgin olive oil, divided
1 pound broccoli rabe
¼ teaspoon table salt
2 teaspoons lemon juice

**1.** Adjust oven rack 4 inches from broiler element and heat broiler. Brush rimmed baking sheet with 1 tablespoon oil.

**2.** Trim and discard bottom 1 inch of broccoli rabe stems. Wash broccoli rabe with cold water, then dry with clean dish towel. Cut tops (leaves and florets) of broccoli rabe from stalks, keeping tops whole, then cut stalks into 1-inch pieces; transfer to prepared sheet. Drizzle with remaining 3 tablespoons oil, sprinkle with salt, and toss to coat.

**3.** Broil until exposed half of leaves are well browned, 2 to 2½ minutes. Using tongs, toss to expose un-browned leaves. Return sheet to oven and continue to broil until most leaves are lightly charred and stalks are crisp-tender, 2 to 2½ minutes. Transfer to serving platter, drizzle with lemon juice, and season with salt and pepper to taste. Serve.

### Broiled Broccoli Rabe with Olives and Garlic

While broccoli rabe cooks, combine 2 tablespoons extra-virgin olive oil, 1 minced garlic clove, and ¼ teaspoon pepper flakes in small bowl and microwave until fragrant, about 30 seconds. Reduce lemon juice to 1 teaspoon. Stir 2 tablespoons chopped pitted kalamata olives and lemon juice into oil mixture. Toss broccoli rabe with olive mixture before serving.
**Per Serving** Cal 210; Total Fat 22g; Protein 3g; Net Carbs 1g; Fiber 2g; Total Carbs 3g

### Broiled Broccoli Rabe with Creamy Gruyère Sauce

Omit lemon juice. Bring ½ cup of heavy cream to boil over medium-high heat in small saucepan and cook until reduced to ¼ cup, 2 to 3 minutes. Off heat, whisk in 2 ounces shredded Gruyère cheese and ½ teaspoon Dijon mustard. Over low heat, continue to cook, whisking constantly until completely smooth, about 2 minutes. Pour sauce over broccoli rabe just before serving.
**Per Serving** Cal 310; Total Fat 30g; Protein 8g; Net Carbs 1g; Fiber 2g; Total Carbs 3g

# CAULIFLOWER RICE

1 pound cauliflower florets, cut into 1-inch pieces
5 tablespoons extra-virgin olive oil, divided
½ shallot, minced
¼ cup chicken broth
¼ teaspoon table salt
1 tablespoon minced fresh parsley

**1.** Pulse cauliflower in food processor in batches until chopped into ⅛- to ¼-inch pieces, 6 to 8 pulses, scraping down sides of bowl as needed.

**2.** Heat 2 tablespoons oil in large saucepan over medium-low heat until shimmering. Add shallot and cook until softened, about 2 minutes. Stir in cauliflower, broth, and salt. Cover and cook, stirring occasionally, until cauliflower is tender, 12 to 15 minutes.

**3.** Uncover and continue to cook, stirring occasionally, until cauliflower rice is almost completely dry, about 3 minutes. Stir in remaining 3 tablespoons oil and parsley and season with salt and pepper to taste. Serve.

### Mexican Cauliflower Rice
*For a spicier rice, include a portion of the chile seeds.*
Substitute ½ minced jalapeño and 1 small minced garlic clove for shallot. Substitute cilantro for parsley. Add ½ teaspoon ground cumin and ½ teaspoon ground coriander to saucepan with jalapeño and add ½ teaspoon lime juice to cauliflower with cilantro.
**Per Serving** Cal 190; Total Fat 18g; Protein 2g; Net Carbs 4g; Fiber 2g; Total Carbs 6g

### Cauliflower-Almond Rice Pilaf
Substitute mint for parsley. Add ⅛ teaspoon ground cardamom, ¼ teaspoon ground cinnamon, and ⅛ teaspoon ground turmeric to saucepan with shallot. Add 2 tablespoons toasted sliced almonds to cauliflower with mint.
**Per Serving** Cal 190g; Total Fat 19g; Protein 3g; Net Carbs 4g; Fiber 3g; Total Carbs 7g

### *Keto Meal Prep*
» Rice can be refrigerated for up to 3 days. To reheat, microwave in covered bowl until heated through, 1 to 3 minutes, fluffing with fork halfway through microwaving.

**Serves** 4
**Total Time** 40 minutes

## PER SERVING
**Cal** 190 | **Total Fat** 18g
**Protein** 2g | **Net Carbs** 4g
**Fiber** 2g | **Total Carbs** 6g

## Why This Recipe Works
Cauliflower has become a popular low-carb replacement for foods like pizza crust, but this shape-shifter of a vegetable can even approximate cooked white rice surprisingly well, providing a neutral-flavored companion to all sorts of dishes. Perfectly suited to the keto diet, it pairs well with recipes like our Seared Tuna Sushi Bowl (page 138) and One-Pan Steak Fajitas (page 109). Of course it's also delicious eaten on its own as a pilaf. To make our cauliflower rice, we found that the key was to blitz the florets in a food processor until transformed into perfect rice-size granules. We made it foolproof, working in batches so all of the florets broke down evenly. Next, we wanted to boost our cauliflower flavor; a shallot and a small amount of broth did the trick. To ensure that the vegetable was tender but still maintained a rice-like chew, we first steamed the "rice" in a covered pot and finished cooking it uncovered to evaporate any remaining moisture. Our faux rice cooked up pleasantly fluffy. For variety, you can spice it up with cumin and coriander or increase your fat, protein, and fiber by adding almonds to the dish. This recipe can easily be doubled using a Dutch oven in place of the saucepan.

**Serves** 4
**Total Time** 40 minutes

## PER SERVING
**Cal** 150 | **Total Fat** 14g
**Protein** 2g | **Net Carbs** 4g
**Fiber** 2g | **Total Carbs** 6g

### Why This Recipe Works
The very words mashed potatoes make you feel comforted, don't they? But their high carb content, which is what makes them soothing and delicious, is also what makes them unavailable for the keto diet. No matter; you will not miss them because at the test kitchen, we've developed a recipe to replace mashed potatoes with low-carb cauliflower, which has the added benefit of being rich in vitamins and potassium. What's more, this dish really resembles the original—just take a look at the next page. And the low starch content of cauliflower means it purees like a dream. We first tried mashing steamed cauliflower, but ended up with a wet, sloppy mess. When we ditched the potato masher and pureed cauliflower in the food processor instead, we got a smooth, velvety-textured dish that makes a delightful accompaniment to steak, chicken, or fish. You can add crunch and extra protein to the puree with bacon, cheddar, and scallions or enhance cauliflower's neutral taste with the distinctive licorice flavor of fennel. This recipe can easily be doubled using a Dutch oven in place of the saucepan.

# WHIPPED CAULIFLOWER

- 1 pound cauliflower florets, cut into 1-inch pieces
- 5 tablespoons unsalted butter
- ¼ teaspoon table salt

**1.** Bring 1 cup water to boil in large saucepan oven over high heat, then add cauliflower. Cover, reduce heat to medium, and cook until tender, 14 to 16 minutes, stirring once halfway through cooking.

**2.** Drain cauliflower and transfer to food processor. Add butter and salt and process until completely smooth, about 4 minutes, scraping down sides of bowl as needed. Adjust consistency with hot water as needed. Season with salt and pepper to taste. Serve.

### Whipped Cauliflower with Crispy Bacon, Cheddar, and Scallions
Cook 2 ounces chopped bacon in 10-inch skillet over medium heat until crispy and well rendered, 5 to 7 minutes; transfer to paper towel–lined plate. Reduce salt to ⅛ teaspoon. Add ½ cup shredded sharp cheddar cheese to food processor with cauliflower. Stir bacon and 1 thinly sliced scallion into whipped cauliflower before serving.
**Per Serving** Cal 240; Total Fat 21g; Protein 8g; Net Carbs 4g; Fiber 2g; Total Carbs 6g

### Whipped Cauliflower with Fennel, Garlic, and Lemon
Melt butter in 8-inch nonstick skillet over medium heat until shimmering. Add 2 minced garlic cloves, ½ teaspoon ground fennel, and ⅛ teaspoon red pepper flakes and cook until fragrant, about 30 seconds; set aside. Add spiced butter and 1 teaspoon grated lemon zest to food processor with cauliflower.
**Per Serving** Cal 160; Total Fat 14g; Protein 2g; Net Carbs 4g; Fiber 2g; Total Carbs 6g

### *Keto Meal Prep*
» Whipped cauliflower can be refrigerated for up to 3 days. To reheat, microwave in covered bowl until heated through, 1 to 3 minutes, stirring halfway through microwaving.

# CUCUMBER SALAD WITH CHILE AND MINT

**Serves** 2
**Total Time** 35 minutes

**PER SERVING**
**Cal** 210 | **Total Fat** 21g
**Protein** 1g | **Net Carbs** 3g
**Fiber** 1g | **Total Carbs** 4g

2 small cucumbers (12 ounces), peeled, halved lengthwise, seeded, and sliced thin

2½ tablespoons white wine vinegar

1 Thai chile, stemmed, seeded, and minced

2 tablespoons extra-virgin olive oil

1 tablespoon toasted sesame oil

1½ teaspoons fish sauce

¾ teaspoon lime juice

2 tablespoons minced fresh mint

**1.** Line rimmed baking sheet with paper towels and evenly spread cucumber slices on sheet. Refrigerate while preparing dressing.

**2.** Bring vinegar to simmer in small saucepan and cook until reduced to 1 tablespoon, 3 to 5 minutes. Transfer to large bowl and let cool to room temperature, about 5 minutes. Whisk in chile, olive oil, sesame oil, fish sauce, and lime juice until well combined. Add chilled cucumbers and mint and toss to combine. Let sit for 5 minutes, then toss to redistribute dressing. Season with salt and pepper to taste. Serve.

## Why This Recipe Works

Cucumbers make a cool, crisp salad to serve at lunch or dinner, especially when keto eaters crave a light complement to a heartier meat course. But we didn't want cucumbers that got soggy from their own moisture; cucumber liquid can mute flavor and texture, and dilute the dressing. To ensure good crunch, we let the sliced cucumbers drain on paper towels and chill in the fridge while we made the dressing. For this, we combined olive oil and sesame oil with white wine vinegar that had been simmered for a few minutes to concentrate its flavor and keep it from tasting harsh. Inspired by Asian salads, we also added fish sauce, lime juice, and a Thai chile to the dressing. When tossed with the cucumbers, this potent oil mixture retained its salty brightness. You should have about 8 ounces of cucumber after prepping. The texture of this salad depends upon thinly sliced cucumbers; be sure to slice them as thin as possible. This salad is best served within 1 hour of being dressed.

**Serves** 2
**Total Time** 25 minutes

## PER SERVING

**Cal** 240 | **Total Fat** 22g
**Protein** 2g | **Net Carbs** 6g
**Fiber** 3g | **Total Carbs** 9g

### Why This Recipe Works

A classic vegetable side, green beans pair well with meat, chicken, and fish so this is a great, simple recipe to have in your back pocket to whip up quickly. Green beans are low-carb, keto-friendly, and delicious when crunchy, but they run the risk of getting overcooked fast. We wanted fresh-tasting and flavorful green beans that stayed crisp-tender when cooked quickly. So we added some water directly to a covered skillet so the beans steamed gently for a few minutes. Then we simply uncovered the pan to brown them. A dressing made with whole-grain mustard and red wine vinegar highlighted their sweetness. Chipotle-lime and sesame-miso vinaigrettes are deeply flavorful dressing variations that also work with the crisp beans. Both the cooked beans and the dressing can be refrigerated, so they make a great addition to a keto lunch box.

# SAUTÉED GREEN BEANS WITH MUSTARD VINAIGRETTE

3 tablespoons extra-virgin olive oil, divided
1 small shallot, minced
1½ teaspoons whole-grain mustard
¾ teaspoon red wine vinegar
¼ teaspoon minced fresh thyme
⅛ teaspoon table salt
Pinch pepper
8 ounces green beans, trimmed

**1.** Whisk 2 tablespoons oil, shallot, mustard, vinegar, thyme, salt, and pepper together in bowl; set aside.

**2.** Heat remaining oil in 12-inch nonstick skillet over medium heat until shimmering. Add green beans and 2 tablespoons water. Cover and cook, without stirring, until green beans are bright green and almost tender, about 5 minutes.

**3.** Uncover and continue to cook, stirring occasionally, until green beans are spotty brown, 3 to 4 minutes; transfer to serving platter. Whisk vinaigrette to recombine, then drizzle over green beans. Season with salt and pepper to taste. Serve.

### Sautéed Green Beans with Chipotle-Lime Vinaigrette

Omit thyme and pepper. Substitute 1½ teaspoons minced canned chipotle chile in adobo sauce for mustard and lime juice for vinegar. Whisk 1 tablespoon minced fresh cilantro into dressing.
**Per Serving** Cal 230; Total Fat 21g; Protein 2g; Net Carbs 6g; Fiber 3g; Total Carbs 9g

### Sautéed Green Beans with Sesame-Miso Vinaigrette

Omit shallot, thyme, salt, and pepper. Substitute 1 tablespoon toasted sesame oil for 1 tablespoon olive oil, white miso paste for mustard, and 1½ teaspoons rice vinegar for red wine vinegar in step 1.
**Per Serving** Cal 230; Total Fat 21g; Protein 2g; Net Carbs 6g; Fiber 3g; Total Carbs 9g

### *Keto Meal Prep*

» Green beans and vinaigrette can be refrigerated separately for up to 2 days. To reheat, bring vinaigrette to room temperature and whisk to recombine. Microwave beans in covered bowl until steaming, 1 to 2 minutes; drain away any accumulated liquid before drizzling with vinaigrette.

# QUICK COLLARD GREENS

**Serves** 4
**Total Time** 35 minutes

## PER SERVING

**Cal** 170 | **Total Fat** 15g
**Protein** 4g | **Net Carbs** 2g
**Fiber** 6g | **Total Carbs** 8g

¼ teaspoon table salt, plus salt for cooking collard greens
2½ pounds collard greens, stemmed and halved lengthwise
¼ cup extra-virgin olive oil
2 garlic cloves, minced
¼ teaspoon red pepper flakes

**1.** Bring 4 quarts water to boil in large pot over high heat. Stir in 1 tablespoon salt, then add collard greens, 1 handful at a time. Cook until tender, 4 to 5 minutes. Drain and rinse with cold water until greens are cool, about 1 minute. Press greens with rubber spatula to release excess liquid. Place greens on dish towel and compress into 10-inch log. Roll up towel tightly, then remove greens from towel. Cut greens crosswise into ¼-inch slices.

**2.** Heat oil in 12-inch nonstick skillet over medium heat until shimmering. Scatter greens in skillet and cook, stirring frequently, until heated through, about 5 minutes. Stir in garlic, pepper flakes, and ¼ teaspoon salt and cook until fragrant, about 1 minute. Season with salt and pepper to taste. Serve.

## Quick Collard Greens with Chorizo

Reduce oil to 2 tablespoons and omit salt in step 2. Add 4 ounces Spanish chorizo sausage, halved lengthwise and sliced ¼ inch thick, to hot oil in step 2 before greens. Cook until lightly browned, 3 to 5 minutes. Scatter greens over chorizo and proceed with recipe as directed.
**Per Serving** Cal 240; Total Fat 19g; Protein 11g; Net Carbs 3g; Fiber 6g; Total Carbs 9g

## Quick Collard Greens with Coconut and Curry

Substitute 2 teaspoons grated fresh ginger and 1 teaspoon curry powder for garlic and pepper flakes. Once ginger and curry powder are fragrant, stir in 1 cup coconut milk and cook until thickened slightly, about 5 minutes.
**Per Serving** Cal 190; Total Fat 16g; Protein 4g; Net Carbs 3g; Fiber 6g; Total Carbs 9g

## *Keto Meal Prep*

» Collard greens can be refrigerated for up to 3 days. To reheat, microwave in covered bowl until steaming, 1 to 3 minutes.

### Why This Recipe Works

Collard greens belong to the cabbage and kale family and share their heartiness and complex flavor. Packed with phytonutrients and vitamins, collards are the perfect keto vegetable. Our blanch-and-sauté recipe quickly yields the same tender results as long braising. Stemming the greens was a necessary first step, and blanching the leaves in salted water tenderized them quickly and neutralized their bitter qualities. To remove excess water left from blanching, we used a spatula to press on the drained greens and then rolled them up in a dish towel to dry them further. We chopped the compressed collards and sautéed them with pungent, aromatic garlic and spicy red pepper flakes. The addition of chorizo or coconut milk and ginger also makes a tasty, rich counterpoint to the high-fiber, low-carb greens. You should have about 1¼ pounds of collard greens after stemming.

## PER SERVING

**Cal** 420 | **Total Fat** 38g
**Protein** 13g | **Net Carbs** 4g
**Fiber** 2g | **Total Carbs** 6g

# KALE CAESAR SALAD

## Why This Recipe Works

Romaine is the Caesar salad green of choice but we wanted a heartier leaf that would give us more nutrients per carb, so important for the keto diet where every carb counts. Kale, with its pungent earthiness, was our natural choice: it's nutrient-dense, and it paired beautifully with the tangy Caesar dressing—perhaps even better than romaine. And though using raw kale sounds like it would be healthiest, we learned that soaking the greens in warm water first helped to break down the fibrous cell walls and made nutrients such as iron and vitamins A and C more available for absorption. A 10-minute soak did the trick and also tenderized the kale. For the dressing, initially a traditional Caesar egg-based dressing seemed the way to go, but a thicker mayonnaise-based dressing stood up better to the greens. To the mayonnaise, we added Parmesan and three anchovy fillets, which brought savoriness and healthy omega-3 fats. With our dressing reworked, the salad was ready to toss; we then gave it a 20-minute rest to blend the flavors before serving, and topped the salad with Parmesan frico chips to replace traditional croutons. You should have about 4 ounces of kale after stemming.

### FRICO

- 1 ounce Parmesan cheese, shredded (¼ cup)

### SALAD

- 6 ounces curly kale, stemmed and cut into 1-inch pieces
- ¼ cup grated Parmesan cheese
- 3 tablespoons extra-virgin olive oil
- 2 tablespoons mayonnaise
- 1 tablespoon lemon juice
- 2 teaspoons Dijon mustard
- 3 anchovy fillets, rinsed and minced
- 1 garlic clove, minced to paste

**1. For the frico**  Adjust oven rack to middle position and heat oven to 400 degrees. Line rimmed baking sheet with parchment paper.

**2.** Spread Parmesan into 5-inch circle in center of prepared sheet. Bake until light golden, 7 to 9 minutes. Let frico cool on sheet for 5 minutes. Transfer frico to plate, discarding parchment, and let cool completely. Break frico into 1½-inch-wide pieces; set aside for serving.

**3. For the salad**  Place kale in large bowl and cover with warm tap water (110 to 115 degrees). Swish kale around to remove grit. Let kale sit in warm water bath for 10 minutes. Remove kale from water and spin dry in salad spinner in multiple batches. Pat leaves dry with paper towels if still wet.

**4.** Whisk Parmesan, oil, mayonnaise, lemon juice, mustard, anchovies, and garlic together in bowl. Add kale and toss to coat. Cover and refrigerate for 20 minutes. Season with salt and pepper to taste. Serve, topped with frico chips, if desired.

### Keto Meal Prep

» Frico and dressed kale can be refrigerated separately for up to 24 hours. To serve, bring frico and kale to room temperature, then sprinkle with Parmesan.

# SAUTÉED SUMMER SQUASH

1  teaspoon grated lemon zest plus 2 teaspoons juice
1  small garlic clove, minced
2  yellow squashes and/or zucchini (8 ounces each), ends trimmed
2  tablespoons extra-virgin olive oil, divided
¼  teaspoon table salt
⅛  teaspoon pepper
1½ tablespoons chopped fresh parsley, divided

**1.** Combine lemon juice and garlic in large bowl and set aside for at least 10 minutes. Using vegetable peeler, shave each squash lengthwise into ribbons: Peel off 3 ribbons from 1 side, then turn squash 90 degrees and peel off 3 more ribbons. Continue to turn and peel squash until you reach seeds. Discard core.

**2.** Whisk 5 teaspoons oil, salt, pepper, and lemon zest into garlic mixture. Heat remaining 1 teaspoon oil in 12-inch nonstick skillet over medium-high heat until just smoking. Add squash and cook, tossing occasionally with tongs, until squash has softened and is translucent, 3 to 4 minutes. Transfer squash to bowl with dressing, add 1 tablespoon parsley, and toss to coat. Season with salt and pepper to taste. Transfer to serving platter and sprinkle with remaining 1½ teaspoons parsley. Serve immediately.

## Sautéed Summer Squash with Mint and Pistachios

Omit lemon zest and substitute 1 teaspoon cider vinegar for lemon juice. Substitute 2 tablespoons chopped fresh mint for parsley and sprinkle squash with 1 tablespoon chopped toasted pistachios before serving.

**Per Serving** Cal 170; Total Fat 16g; Protein 3g; Net Carbs 4g; Fiber 2g; Total Carbs 6g

## Sautéed Summer Squash with Oregano and Red Pepper Flakes

Omit lemon zest. Add ¼ teaspoon red pepper flakes to heated oil in step 2 and substitute 2 teaspoons minced fresh oregano for parsley.

**Per Serving** Cal 150; Total Fat 14g; Protein 2g; Net Carbs 4g; Fiber 2g; Total Carbs 6g

**Serves** 2
**Total Time** 25 minutes

## PER SERVING
**Cal** 150 | **Total Fat** 14g
**Protein** 2g | **Net Carbs** 4g
**Fiber** 2g | **Total Carbs** 6g

### Why This Recipe Works
Tracking keto macros on a daily basis can be time-consuming so we focused on developing delicious, no-fuss recipes like this one that save you time in the kitchen instead. This dish makes the most of summer squash and zucchini—two vegetables that can overrun your garden, leaving you at a loss for what to do with them. For this recipe, we wanted the squash to cook quickly, without going through the usual salting, shredding, and draining process that prevents the vegetable from getting too liquidy. The solution was quite simple—instead of cutting or grating the squash, we peeled it with a vegetable peeler, discarding the seedy cores. The result was thin, even strips that cooked up quickly into a dish that looked and tasted like summer. Cooking the squash in a single layer over moderately high heat allowed the translucent ribbons to become crisp-tender without browning, which would mask their fresh flavor and appearance. Pairing the vegetable with herbs and lemon or vinegar gave the squash a light brightness we liked. One variation with oregano and red pepper flakes evoked Italian sunshine while another with mint and pistachios was a cool summer dish. You should have about 10 ounces of squash after peeling in step 1. Be sure to start checking for doneness at the lower end of the cooking time.

CHAPTER 8

# SNACKS

**Serves** 15 (Makes 30 balls)
**Total Time** 30 minutes, plus
2 hours chilling time

**PER 2-BALL SERVING**
**Cal** 190 | **Total Fat** 16g
**Protein** 9g | **Net Carbs** 1g
**Fiber** 1g | **Total Carbs** 2g

## Why This Recipe Works

Keto eaters often lament that there are not enough savory snacks to eat on their diet, so we developed snack recipes that are easy to put together and have on hand for whenever a little nibble is wanted. Here we took the flavors of a make-ahead party recipe for a cheese ball and shrank it down into a delicious little keto snack. We processed cheddar cheese and cream cheese for a firm yet creamy consistency, adding mayonnaise for silky richness. Onion powder added zing, while fresh parsley and dill, which feature in classic ranch dressing, lent the snack a pleasant green color. To make individual servings, we shaped the mixture into 30 bite-size balls. We covered the balls with a mixture of crisp bacon bits and finely ground almonds to enhance their fat content and give them some crunch. These mini cheese balls are also delicious spread on Seeded Crackers (page 206) or eaten with Seeded Bread (page 23). To quickly soften the cream cheese, microwave it for 20 to 30 seconds.

# BACON-RANCH CHEESE BALLS

12  ounces extra-sharp cheddar cheese, shredded (3 cups)
4  ounces cream cheese, softened
2  tablespoons mayonnaise
2  tablespoons chopped fresh parsley
2  tablespoons chopped fresh dill
½  teaspoon onion powder
8  ounces sliced bacon, chopped
¾  cup slivered almonds, toasted

**1.** Process cheddar, cream cheese, mayonnaise, parsley, dill, and onion powder in food processor until smooth, about 1 minute, scraping down sides of bowl as needed. Transfer cheese mixture to bowl, cover, and refrigerate until firm, about 2 hours.

**2.** Cook bacon in 12-inch nonstick skillet over medium heat until crispy, 5 to 7 minutes. Using slotted spoon, transfer bacon to clean, dry food processor. Add almonds and pulse until mixture is finely ground, about 8 pulses, scraping down sides of bowl as needed; transfer to shallow dish.

**3.** Divide cheese mixture into 30 equal pieces, about 1 tablespoon each. Using your hands, roll mixture into balls, then roll each ball in bacon-almond mixture, pressing gently to adhere; transfer to serving platter. Serve.

### *Keto Meal Prep*

» Cheese balls can be refrigerated for up to 1 week or frozen for up to 1 month. To serve from frozen, let cheese balls thaw overnight in refrigerator.

# CLASSIC DEVILED EGGS

- 2 recipes Easy-Peel Hard-Cooked Eggs (page 37)
- 3 tablespoons mayonnaise
- 1 tablespoon minced fresh parsley
- 1 teaspoon cider vinegar
- 1 teaspoon Dijon mustard
- ¼ teaspoon Worcestershire sauce
  Pinch cayenne pepper

**1.** Peel eggs and halve lengthwise with paring knife. Transfer yolks to bowl; arrange whites on plate. Mash yolks with fork until no large lumps remain. Add mayonnaise and use rubber spatula to smear mixture against side of bowl until thick, smooth paste forms, 1 to 2 minutes. Stir in parsley, vinegar, mustard, Worcestershire, and cayenne until fully incorporated.

**2.** Transfer yolk mixture to small heavy-duty plastic bag. Press mixture into 1 corner and twist top of bag. Using scissors, snip ½ inch off filled corner. Squeezing bag, pipe yolk mixture into egg white halves. Serve.

## Chipotle Deviled Eggs with Radishes and Cilantro

Omit Worcestershire and cayenne. Substitute cilantro for parsley, 1½ teaspoons lime juice for vinegar, and 2 teaspoons minced canned chipotle chile in adobo for mustard. Add 2 finely chopped radishes to filling.

**Per Serving** Cal 290; Total Fat 25g; Protein 13g; Net Carbs 2g; Fiber 0g; Total Carbs 2g

## Deviled Eggs with Tuna, Capers, and Chives

Omit Worcestershire. Add 6 tablespoons drained and finely chopped canned tuna, 1 tablespoon rinsed and chopped capers, and 1 tablespoon minced fresh chives to filling.

**Per Serving** Cal 360; Total Fat 26g; Protein 26g; Net Carbs 1g; Fiber 0g; Total Carbs 1g

## *Keto Meal Prep*

» Deviled eggs can be refrigerated for up to 2 days.

**Serves** 2 (Makes 8 egg halves)
**Total Time** 20 minutes

### PER SERVING
**Cal** 280 | **Total Fat** 25g
**Protein** 13g | **Net Carbs** 6g
**Fiber** 0g | **Total Carbs** 6g

### Why This Recipe Works

The best deviled eggs start with the best hard-cooked eggs. Conventional wisdom insists that older eggs peel more easily than fresh ones. But we wanted to be able to start with eggs of any age and still end up with flawlessly smooth peeled results. Instead of a cold-water start, we used our recipe for Easy-Peel Hard-Cooked Eggs (page 37), which calls for placing cold eggs directly into hot steam. This denatures the outermost egg white proteins quickly, causing them to shrink away from the shell membrane, making it easy to slip off the eggshells after cooking. Then it was a question of making a devilishly good filling, which deviled eggs often lack. Since combining egg yolks with mayonnaise is traditional, we were glad we could use 3 tablespoons of mayo for a smooth, rich, keto-friendly filling. To add tart, punchy flavor we stirred fresh parsley, cider vinegar, Dijon mustard, Worcestershire sauce (for umami), and cayenne into the egg yolk–mayo mixture. For one variation, heat and texture came from chipotle, cilantro, and radishes. For the other, canned tuna enhanced protein, while capers and chives gave crunch and freshness. This recipe can be easily doubled. If you prefer, use a pastry bag fitted with a large plain or star tip to fill the egg halves.

**Makes** 3 cups
**Total Time** 1 hour 10 minutes, plus 30 minutes cooling time

---

### PER ¼-CUP SERVING

**Cal** 230 | **Total Fat** 22g
**Protein** 6g | **Net Carbs** 2g
**Fiber** 4g | **Total Carbs** 6g

---

## Why This Recipe Works

Crunchy, aromatic spiced nuts make a craveworthy snack for anyone, but they are especially great for keto eaters—healthy, filling, and suited to the keto diet. We wanted to create an easy recipe that allowed the flavor of different nuts to shine through. Our spice combination of cinnamon, ginger, coriander, and cumin worked well to complement the natural sweetness of walnuts, pecans, and almonds. We also tested a variety of zero net carb sweeteners for the mix but tasters preferred a more natural, unsweetened mixture. To help spices stick to the nuts, recipes sometimes call for butter or syrup. Our fats were already just right and syrup increased the carb content of our recipe too much. So we used beaten egg whites, which created a crunchy shell around each nut without making them sticky. For a savory-sweet variation, we added ground fennel and orange zest; for another, we turned to cayenne pepper and cocoa powder for slightly spicy, earthy flavor. You can use any combination of raw pecans, walnuts, or whole unblanched almonds here; we prefer an equal combination of nuts, but any ratio will work. Just be sure to use 3 cups (15 ounces) of nuts. Nutritional values will vary based on the combination of nuts you choose.

# SPICED NUT MIX

- 2 large egg whites
- 2 teaspoons ground cinnamon
- 1 teaspoon ground ginger
- 1 teaspoon ground coriander
- 1 teaspoon table salt
- ½ teaspoon ground cumin
- 1 cup walnuts
- 1 cup pecans
- 1 cup whole almonds

**1.** Adjust oven racks to upper-middle and lower-middle positions and heat oven to 275 degrees. Line 2 rimmed baking sheets with parchment paper.

**2.** Whisk egg whites, cinnamon, ginger, coriander, salt, and cumin together in bowl. Add nuts and toss to coat. Spread nuts evenly over prepared sheets. Bake, stirring occasionally, until nuts are dry and crisp, 45 to 50 minutes, switching and rotating sheets halfway through baking.

**3.** Let nuts cool completely on sheets, about 30 minutes. Break apart any large clumps of nuts. Serve.

### Spicy Cocoa Nut Mix

Substitute 1 tablespoon unsweetened Dutch cocoa powder and ¼ teaspoon cayenne for cinnamon, ginger, coriander, and cumin.
**Per ¼-cup Serving** Cal 230; Total Fat 22g; Protein 6g; Net Carbs 3g; Fiber 3g; Total Carbs 6g

### Fennel and Orange Nut Mix

Substitute 2 teaspoons ground fennel and 2 teaspoons grated orange zest for cinnamon, ginger, coriander, and cumin.
**Per ¼-cup Serving** Cal 230; Total Fat 22g; Protein 6g; Net Carbs 2g; Fiber 4g; Total Carbs 6g

### *Keto Meal Prep*

» Nuts can be stored in airtight container for up to 2 weeks.

# SNACK BARS

1½ cups whole almonds, chopped coarse

½ cup raw pepitas

¾ cup sugar-free dark chocolate chips, divided

¼ cup (2 ounces) granulated erythritol

3 tablespoons creamy, unsweetened almond butter

1 large egg

1 teaspoon vanilla extract

½ teaspoon table salt

½ cup unsweetened shredded coconut

**1.** Adjust oven rack to middle position and heat oven to 350 degrees. Make foil sling for 8-inch square baking pan by folding 2 long sheets of aluminum foil so each is 8 inches wide. Lay sheets of foil in pan perpendicular to each other, with extra foil hanging over edges of pan. Push foil into corners and up sides of pan, smoothing foil flush to pan; lightly spray with olive oil spray and set aside.

**2.** Spread almonds and pepitas on rimmed baking sheet and toast until lightly browned and fragrant, 10 to 12 minutes, stirring occasionally. Transfer almond mixture to large bowl, add ¼ cup chocolate chips, and stir until chocolate is melted and evenly coats almonds and pepitas.

**3.** Whisk erythritol, almond butter, egg, vanilla, and salt together in second bowl. Stir erythritol mixture, coconut, and remaining ½ cup chocolate chips into almond mixture until combined. Transfer almond mixture to prepared pan and spread into even layer. Place 9-inch sheet of parchment paper or waxed paper on top of almond mixture and press and smooth very firmly with your hands, especially at edges and corners, until mixture is level and compact. Remove parchment and bake until bars are fragrant and just beginning to brown around edges, about 15 minutes. Transfer pan to wire rack and let cool for 1 hour. Using foil overhang, lift bars out of pan. Return to wire rack and let cool completely, about 30 minutes.

**4.** Discard foil and transfer bars to cutting board. Using sharp chef's knife, quarter bars to create four 4-inch squares. Cut each square into 3 equal strips. Serve.

## *Keto Meal Prep*

» Snack bars can be stored in airtight container for up to 1 week or frozen for up to 1 month. Thaw frozen bars in refrigerator overnight before serving.

**Makes** 12 bars
**Total Time** 50 minutes, plus 1½ hours cooling time

### PER BAR

**Cal** 250 | **Total Fat** 21g
**Protein** 9g | **Net Carbs** 6g
**Fiber** 4g | **Sugar Alcohols** 8g
**Total Carbs** 18g

## Why This Recipe Works

Granola bars often contain oats and grains that are high in carbohydrates. But we wanted an easy, portable, keto-friendly snack bar so we experimented with different ingredients to create a really delicious option. Anyone will want to dig into a jar of these treats for a quick bite. Hearty almonds and healthy pepitas provided the base for our bars. Toasting the nuts and seeds gave the snack a pleasant, well-rounded flavor. Erythritol added slight sweetness and almond butter, along with one egg, helped bind the bars. Tossing some chocolate chips with the warm nut-seed mixture melted the chocolate slightly for a pleasing texture while still allowing the nuts and seeds to remain crisp. We stirred the remaining chocolate chips and shredded coconut into the nut-seed mixture later for textural contrast; tasters liked the little bursts of sweetness from the chips. After baking the mixture in an 8-inch square baking pan, we let it cool in the pan for 1½ hours before cutting it into 12 bars. Be sure not to overcook the nuts and seeds in step 2; they will continue to toast while the bars bake. Erythritol is our preferred low-carb sweetener here; see page 14 for more information on low-carb sweeteners and substitutions.

**PER 4-CRACKER SERVING**
Cal 170 | Total Fat 13g
Protein 11g | Net Carbs 1g
Fiber 1g | Total Carbs 2g

## Why This Recipe Works

We wanted to create a keto cracker that could accompany our keto dips and spreads and was easy to make, requiring just one kind of flour. Our first attempt was for crackers made with almond flour. But using just almond flour produced a dense, boring result. After testing several alternatives, we decided to stick with almond flour but add grated Parmesan cheese. The cheese added structure and flavor to the crackers. Two tablespoons of olive oil and one egg brought the dough together while providing richness—the egg also helped with the structure without making the crackers eggy. A mix of toasted sesame, poppy, and caraway seeds gave our crackers a complex savory taste. To make shaping easier and keep the dough from sticking to the rolling pin, we rolled the dough between two greased sheets of parchment. We pricked the rolled dough with a fork to prevent it from puffing during baking and baked the crackers twice; first to set the cracker dough and then to finish drying the crackers out after they were cut. A simple egg wash gave the crackers both an alluring sheen and a pleasing snap, and it helped anchor a light sprinkling of coarse sea salt.

# SEEDED CRACKERS

½ cup (2 ounces) blanched, finely ground almond flour

1½ ounces Parmesan cheese, grated (¾ cup)

1 large egg, plus 1 large egg white lightly beaten with 1 tablespoon water

2 tablespoons extra-virgin olive oil

1 teaspoon toasted sesame seeds

1 teaspoon poppy seeds

1 teaspoon caraway seeds

¼ teaspoon table salt

½ teaspoon coarse sea salt (optional)

**1.** Adjust oven rack to middle position and heat oven to 425 degrees. Stir almond flour, Parmesan, whole egg, oil, sesame seeds, poppy seeds, caraway seeds, and table salt together in bowl. Press and roll dough between 2 sheets of greased parchment paper into 11 by 9-inch rectangle, about ⅛ inch thick. Remove top piece of parchment and trim edges to remove any tapering.

**2.** Slide dough, still on parchment, onto baking sheet. Brush with egg white mixture, then poke at 2-inch intervals using fork. Sprinkle with sea salt, if using. Bake until dough is set and edges are beginning to brown, about 7 minutes, rotating sheet halfway through baking. Slide cracker, still on parchment, onto cutting board. Reduce oven temperature to 350 degrees.

**3.** Cut cracker lengthwise into four even strips, then cut crosswise into 1-inch-wide crackers. Carefully arrange crackers evenly on now-empty sheet, discarding parchment. Bake until golden brown and crisp, 4 to 6 minutes, rotating sheet halfway through baking. Transfer crackers to wire rack and let cool completely, about 30 minutes. Serve.

### Black Pepper–Rosemary Crackers

Substitute 2 teaspoons coarsely ground pepper and 1 teaspoon minced fresh rosemary for sesame seeds, poppy seeds, and caraway seeds.
**Per 4-Cracker Serving** Cal 160; Total Fat 12g; Protein 11g; Net Carbs 1g; Fiber 1g; Total Carbs 2g

### Sesame Crackers

Omit poppy seeds and caraway seeds and increase sesame seeds to 1 tablespoon.
**Per 4-Cracker Serving** Cal 160; Total Fat 13g; Protein 11g; Net Carbs 1g; Fiber 1g; Total Carbs 2g

### *Keto Meal Prep*

» Crackers can be stored in airtight container for up to 1 week.

# HERBED SPINACH DIP

- 10 ounces frozen chopped spinach, thawed and squeezed dry
- ½ red bell pepper (4 ounces), chopped fine
- ½ cup sour cream
- ½ cup mayonnaise
- ½ cup fresh parsley leaves
- 3 scallions, sliced thin
- 1 tablespoon fresh dill or 1 teaspoon dried
- 1 garlic clove, minced
- ½ teaspoon table salt
- ¼ teaspoon hot sauce
- ¼ teaspoon pepper

Process all ingredients in food processor until well combined, about 1 minute. Transfer to serving bowl, cover, and refrigerate until flavors meld, at least 1 hour. Season with salt and pepper to taste. Serve.

## Keto Meal Prep

» Dip can be refrigerated for up to 5 days; bring to room temperature and stir to recombine before serving.

**Makes** about 2 cups
**Total Time** 15 minutes, plus 1 hour chilling time

## PER ¼-CUP SERVING

**Cal** 140 | **Total Fat** 13g
**Protein** 2g | **Net Carbs** 3g
**Fiber** 1g | **Total Carbs** 4g

## Why This Recipe Works

We packed tons of flavor, fat, and fiber into this simple spinach dip, combining sour cream and mayonnaise with spinach, herbs, red bell pepper, scallions, garlic, and even a little kick of hot sauce. The food processor helped distribute the spinach evenly throughout the base of mayonnaise and sour cream and gave the dip a smooth texture. The dip pairs well with crudités, our Seeded Crackers (page 206), or chips made from Keto Tortillas (page 20). The garlic must be minced or pressed before going into the food processor or the dip will contain large chunks of garlic.

**Makes** about 2 cups
**Total Time** 15 minutes

---

## PER ¼-CUP SERVING

**Cal** 280 | **Total Fat** 26g
**Protein** 8g | **Net Carbs** 3g
**Fiber** 0g | **Total Carbs** 3g

---

### Why This Recipe Works

To make another keto-friendly dip, we turned to feta cheese, which we love and which was a natural fit for this Greek-style dip. But rather than using true Greek sheep's- or goat's-milk feta, we chose cow's-milk feta. Why? Cow's-milk feta produces a firmer dip that holds up well at room temperature but is still loose enough to easily scoop up. Since feta can be salty, we started by rinsing it in water to remove as much extra salt as we could. Rinsing also softened the cheese, making it easier to process. Adding a little extra water to the processor while combining ingredients smoothed it out further. So did olive oil, which we also used to bump up the fat content. Dill and parsley added fresh grassiness; a little garlic and lemon juice rounded out the flavors. This dip is great for a crowd; spread it evenly in a wide, shallow bowl, drizzle with an extra 1 tablespoon of olive oil, and sprinkle with an extra 1 tablespoon of parsley before serving with our Seeded Crackers (page 206) or crudités.

# WHIPPED FETA DIP WITH DILL AND PARSLEY

1 tablespoon lemon juice
1 small garlic clove, minced
1 pound cow's-milk feta cheese
¼ cup water
½ cup extra-virgin olive oil
2 tablespoons minced fresh dill or mint
2 tablespoons minced fresh parsley

**1.** Combine lemon juice and garlic in small bowl and set aside. Break feta into rough ½-inch pieces and place in medium bowl. Add water to cover, then swish briefly to rinse. Transfer to fine-mesh strainer and drain well.

**2.** Transfer feta to food processor. Add ¼ cup water and reserved lemon juice mixture and process until feta mixture resembles ricotta cheese, about 15 seconds. With processor running, slowly drizzle in oil. Continue to process until mixture has Greek yogurt–like consistency (some small lumps will remain), about 2 minutes, stopping once to scrape down bottom and sides of bowl. Add dill and parsley and pulse to combine. Serve.

### *Keto Meal Prep*

» Dip can be refrigerated for up to 5 days; bring to room temperature and stir to recombine before serving.

# MEDITERRANEAN WHIPPED ALMOND DIP

5 ounces blanched whole, slivered, or sliced almonds

6 tablespoons extra-virgin olive oil

¼ cup tahini

1 tablespoon lemon juice

1 garlic clove, minced

½ teaspoon table salt

⅛ teaspoon pepper

**1.** Place almonds in bowl and add water to cover by 1 inch. Soak almonds at room temperature for at least 8 hours or up to 24 hours. Drain and rinse well.

**2.** Process soaked almonds, ⅔ cup water, oil, tahini, lemon juice, garlic, salt, and pepper in blender until smooth, about 2 minutes, scraping down sides of blender jar as needed. Adjust consistency as needed with extra water. Season with salt and pepper to taste. Serve.

### Mediterranean Whipped Almond Dip with Lemon and Fresh Herbs

*We prefer a combination of herbs here, but you can use a single herb, if desired.*

Increase lemon juice to 2 tablespoons and add ½ cup chopped fresh basil, chives, dill and/or parsley and 1 teaspoon lemon zest to blender with almonds.

**Per ¼-cup Serving** Cal 280; Total Fat 27g; Protein 6g; Net Carbs 3g; Fiber 3g; Total Carbs 6g

### Smoky Mediterranean Whipped Almond Dip

Combine oil and 1 teaspoon smoked paprika in small bowl and microwave until fragrant, about 30 seconds; let cool slightly. Substitute infused oil for olive oil in step 2.

**Per ¼-cup Serving** Cal 280, Total Fat 27g; Protein 6g; Net Carbs 3g; Fiber 3g; Total Carbs 6g

## *Keto Meal Prep*

» Dip can be refrigerated for up to 5 days; bring to room temperature and adjust consistency with water before serving.

**Makes** about 1¾ cups
**Total Time** 15 minutes, plus 8 hours soaking time

### PER ¼-CUP SERVING
**Cal** 280 | **Total Fat** 27g
**Protein** 6g | **Net Carbs** 4g
**Fiber** 2g | **Total Carbs** 6g

### Why This Recipe Works

Do you miss hummus on the keto diet? We wanted to create a foolproof recipe for a hummus-like dip that you could enjoy instead and also serve to your friends. Since chickpeas were obviously unsuitable, we turned to that great keto lifesaver—the nut. First, we experimented with a test kitchen recipe for cashew dip but cashews were too carb-heavy for keto. Would almonds work? We were skeptical but they worked really well. When soaked to soften and pureed with water, almonds took on a creaminess not unlike chickpeas. And because of their neutral flavor, the addition of tahini and garlic steered the puree in the flavor direction of hummus, while extra-virgin olive oil and lemon juice boosted the taste and thinned the dip to a spreadable consistency. With an almond "hummus" to rival the chickpea original, we focused on creating flavor variations. Tasters liked the mildly smoky flavor of smoked paprika; for a fresh, herby spread, we used parsley, basil, chives, and dill with lemon juice and zest. Serve with Seeded Crackers (page 206), chips made from our Keto Tortillas (page 20), or crudités. This dip is great for a crowd; spread it evenly in a wide, shallow bowl, drizzle with an extra 1 tablespoon oil, and sprinkle with 1 tablespoon of your favorite minced fresh herb before serving.

CHAPTER 9

# SWEET TREATS

**Serves** 6 (Makes 12 clusters)
**Total Time** 50 minutes

## PER SERVING
**Cal** 170 | **Total Fat** 15g
**Protein** 3g | **Net Carbs** 2g
**Fiber** 5g | **Sugar Alcohols** 3g
**Total Carbs** 10g

### Why This Recipe Works

These make-ahead chocolate clusters are great to grab as you head out the door to work. They will satisfy any mid-afternoon sweet craving. Our version starts with tempered chocolate. Untempered chocolate can look dull and taste chewy. Tempering gives a sheen and snap, but the process is typically finicky. So we developed an easy microwave method, quickly heating and then cooling chocolate to create snappy texture and shine. To balance the intense bitterness of unsweetened chocolate, we added powdered erythritol; it dissolves faster than granulated. Then we played with toppings to press onto the tempered disks for flavor and crunch. Toasted macadamia nuts and coconut were a match made in heaven. For another variation, we finely chopped 1 tablespoon of unsweetened dried cherries and tossed them with toasted pepitas. Even the small amount of cherries added intense sweet flavor. Orange zest and toasted pecans made a delicious third option. A sprinkle of sea salt brings out the flavors of our toppings and reduces the chocolate's bitterness. Erythritol is our preferred low-carb sweetener here; however, you can substitute your favorite low-carb sweetener. Be aware that not all low-carb sweeteners can be substituted 1:1 for erythritol. See page 14 for more information on low-carb sweeteners and substitutions. Do not make these in a room that is warmer than 80 degrees.

# DARK CHOCOLATE CLUSTERS WITH MACADAMIA NUTS AND COCONUT

¼ cup macadamia nuts, toasted and chopped

2 tablespoons unsweetened flaked coconut, toasted

¼ teaspoon coarse sea salt

4 ounces unsweetened chocolate (3 ounces chopped fine, 1 ounce grated)

2 tablespoons powdered erythritol

**1.** Line baking sheet with parchment paper. Combine macadamia nuts, coconut, and salt in small bowl. Microwave chopped chocolate in medium bowl at 50 percent power, stirring every 15 seconds, until two-thirds melted (chocolate should not be much warmer than body temperature; check by holding bowl in palm of your hand), 45 to 60 seconds. Remove melted chocolate from microwave and stir in remaining grated chocolate and erythritol until smooth, returning to microwave for no more than 5 seconds at a time to finish melting if necessary.

**2.** Working quickly, spoon 1 tablespoon of melted chocolate onto prepared sheet and spread into 2½ inch wide circle using back of spoon. Sprinkle with 1 tablespoon macadamia nut mixture and press gently to adhere. Repeat with remaining melted chocolate and macadamia nut mixture, spacing circles 1½ inches apart. Let clusters cool until firm, about 30 minutes. Serve.

### Dark Chocolate Clusters with Pepitas and Dried Cherries

Substitute toasted pepitas for macadamia nuts and 1 tablespoon finely chopped unsweetened dried cherries for coconut.

**Per Serving** Cal 150; Total Fat 12g; Protein 4g; Net Carbs 3g; Fiber 4g; Sugar Alcohols 3g; Total Carbs 10g

### Dark Chocolate Clusters with Pecans and Orange

Omit coconut. Substitute 6 tablespoons pecans for macadamia nuts. Toss pecans with 1 tablespoon grated orange zest before sprinkling over melted chocolate.

**Per Serving** Cal 170; Total Fat 14g; Protein 3g; Net Carbs 2g; Fiber 5g; Sugar Alcohols 3g; Total Carbs 10g

### *Keto Meal Prep*

» Clusters can be stored in airtight container for up to 2 weeks.

# CHOCOLATE-COVERED PEANUT BUTTER BITES

**Serves** 16 (Makes 16 bites)
**Total Time** 45 minutes, plus
1½ hours chilling time

## PER SERVING
**Cal** 110 | **Total Fat** 11g
**Protein** 3g | **Net Carbs** 3g
**Fiber** 0g | **Sugar Alcohols** 14g
**Total Carbs** 17g

½ cup unsweetened creamy peanut butter

4 tablespoons unsalted butter, cut into 4 pieces, softened

⅛ teaspoon table salt

1 cup (4 ounces) plus 2 tablespoons powdered erythritol, divided

6 ounces unsweetened chocolate (4 ounces chopped fine, 2 ounces grated)

**1.** Using stand mixer fitted with paddle, mix peanut butter, butter, and salt on medium speed until mixture is nearly combined with some visible pieces of butter remaining, about 30 seconds. Reduce speed to low and slowly add 1 cup erythritol. Mix until just combined, scraping down sides of bowl as needed. Cover bowl, transfer to refrigerator, and let dough chill for 15 minutes.

**2.** Line 2 large plates with parchment paper. Divide dough into 16 portions, about 1 tablespoon each. Using your hands, roll dough into balls, and arrange evenly on prepared plates. Insert 1 toothpick three-quarters of the way into each ball. Freeze balls until firm, about 1 hour.

**3.** Microwave chopped chocolate in medium bowl at 50 percent power, stirring every 15 seconds, until two-thirds melted (chocolate should not be much warmer than body temperature; check by holding bowl in palm of your hand), 2 to 3 minutes. Remove melted chocolate from microwave and stir in remaining grated chocolate and remaining 2 tablespoons erythritol until smooth, returning to microwave for no more than 5 seconds at a time to finish melting if necessary.

**4.** Tilt bowl slightly so chocolate pools on 1 side. Working with 1 plate of balls at a time (keeping second plate in freezer), grasp toothpicks and dip balls in chocolate until covered by two-thirds. Allow excess to drip off, then return balls to prepared plate. Refrigerate balls, uncovered, until chocolate is set and peanut butter mixture is no longer frozen, about 30 minutes. Remove toothpicks and serve.

## Chocolate-Covered Almond Butter Bites

Substitute unsweetened almond butter for peanut butter.
**Per Serving** Cal 110; Total Fat 10g; Protein 3g; Net Carbs 2g; Fiber 1g; Sugar Alcohols 14g; Total Carbs 17g

## *Keto Meal Prep*

» Peanut butter bites can be refrigerated for up to 1 week or frozen for up to 1 month.

» To serve from frozen, let peanut butter bites soften in refrigerator for at least 1 hour.

## Why This Recipe Works

A peanut butter–based sweet treat is a great source of natural fat for the keto diet. Covered in chocolate, one peanut butter bite is also enough to be a quick sweet fix. But store-bought keto chocolate–peanut butter candies are often dry and chalky in texture and either cloyingly sweet or overly bitter. So we used less sweetener than most recipes and a better-controlled mixing technique to turn these dense sweets into soft, creamy, balanced morsels. In non-keto versions of peanut butter bites (often called buckeyes), the dough is typically held together by large amounts of confectioners' sugar, which we couldn't use. Instead we achieved the right amount of sweetness using powdered erythritol, which combines with the softened butter more easily than granulated. Mixing the ingredients until the dough just formed and then refrigerating it made the candy easier to roll. A dip in unsweetened tempered chocolate was the perfect indulgent finish. Erythritol is our preferred low-carb sweetener here; however, you can substitute your favorite low-carb sweetener. Be aware that not all low-carb sweeteners can be substituted 1:1 for erythritol. See page 14 for more information on low-carb sweeteners and substitutions. Do not make these in a room that is warmer than 80 degrees.

**Serves** 16 (Makes 16 cookies)
**Total Time** 1 hour

---

## PER SERVING

**Cal** 170 | **Total Fat** 14g
**Protein** 4g | **Net Carbs** 5g
**Fiber** 2g | **Sugar Alcohols** 9g
**Total Carbs** 16g

---

### Why This Recipe Works

A good chocolate chip cookie is moist and chewy, with crisp edges and deep toffee and butterscotch notes. To mimic that keto-style, we swapped in almond flour for a tender crumb, coconut flour for its high absorbency power to bind the cookies together, and xanthan gum for structure. In initial testing, our cookies baked up flat and greasy, but adding baking powder and baking soda helped them rise more. The lack of starch meant the dough needed more time to hydrate and soften, so we rested it for 30 minutes. This gave the sweetener time to dissolve, leading to faster caramelization in the oven. Melting the butter and adding almond butter resulted in cookies with the right chewy texture, crisp edges, and a complex, toffee-like flavor. Cookies continue to firm up as they cool so we bake them till just golden brown and set, but still soft in the center. This recipe yields two fully baked cookies and 14 frozen dough disks for later baking. Feel free to add up to six more dough disks, spaced evenly apart, to the baking sheet in step 3, if desired, and increase baking time to 12 to 14 minutes. Erythritol is our preferred low-carb sweetener here; you can substitute your favorite low-carb sweetener. Be aware that not all low-carb sweeteners can be substituted 1:1 for erythritol. See page 14 for more information on low-carb sweeteners and substitutions.

# CHOCOLATE CHIP COOKIES

- 1 cup (4 ounces) blanched, finely ground almond flour
- ¼ cup (1 ounce) coconut flour
- 1 teaspoon baking powder
- ½ teaspoon baking soda
- ½ teaspoon xanthan gum (optional)
- ¼ teaspoon table salt
- ½ cup (3½ ounces) granulated erythritol
- 6 tablespoons unsalted butter, melted and cooled
- ¼ cup creamy almond butter
- 2 large eggs
- 4 teaspoons vanilla extract
- 1 cup (6 ounces) sugar-free dark chocolate chips

**1.** Whisk almond flour, coconut flour, baking powder, baking soda, xanthan gum, if using, and salt together in bowl. Whisk erythritol, melted butter, almond butter, eggs, and vanilla in large bowl until well combined. Stir flour mixture into erythritol mixture until just combined, then fold in chocolate chips. Cover and let dough rest at room temperature for 30 minutes.

**2.** Adjust oven rack to middle position and heat oven to 350 degrees. Line 2 rimmed baking sheets with parchment paper. Divide dough into 16 portions, about 2 tablespoons each, and roll into balls using your hands. Arrange 14 balls on 1 prepared sheet spaced 2 inches apart. Using damp fingers, flatten dough balls until 3 inches in diameter. Freeze dough disks until firm, about 1 hour, then transfer to zipper-lock bag and return to freezer.

**3.** Meanwhile, arrange remaining 2 dough balls on second sheet and press into 3-inch disks. Bake until light golden brown and edges have begun to set but centers are still soft, 8 to 10 minutes, rotating sheet halfway through baking. Let cookies cool completely on sheet. Serve.

### Keto Meal Prep

» Dough disks can be frozen for up to 1 month. To bake, arrange desired number on parchment-lined baking sheet, place on top of second baking sheet (to prevent bottoms from burning), and increase baking time to 15 to 20 minutes.

» Cookies can be stored at room temperature for up to 2 days.

# MINI LEMON CHEESECAKE CUPS
*good.*

⅓ cup (1⅓ ounces) blanched, finely ground almond flour

2 teaspoons powdered erythritol, plus ⅓ cup (1⅓ ounces), divided

1 tablespoon unsalted butter, melted

8 ounces cream cheese, softened

1 teaspoon grated lemon zest plus 2 teaspoons juice

⅛ teaspoon table salt

1 large egg, room temperature

1 teaspoon vanilla extract

1. Adjust oven rack to middle position and heat oven to 300 degrees. Line middle 6 cups of 12-cup nonstick muffin tin with paper or foil liners.

2. Stir almond flour, 2 teaspoons erythritol, and melted butter in bowl until combined. Divide almond mixture among prepared muffin cups and press into even layer using your fingers. Bake until crust is golden brown and set, 12 to 14 minutes. Transfer to wire rack and let cool while making batter.

3. Using stand mixer fitted with paddle, beat cream cheese and lemon zest on medium-high speed until light and fluffy, about 2 minutes. Reduce speed to low, add remaining ⅓ cup erythritol and salt, and mix until incorporated, about 1 minute, scraping down sides of bowl as needed. Add egg, vanilla, and lemon juice; increase speed to medium, and beat until smooth, about 1 minute.

4. Divide batter evenly among muffin cups. Bake until set, about 20 minutes. Let cheesecakes cool in muffin tin on wire rack for 30 minutes. Wrap muffin tin with plastic wrap and refrigerate until cheesecakes are chilled and firm, at least 1 hour. Serve.

## Keto Meal Prep

» Cheesecake cups can be refrigerated for up to 1 week or frozen for up to 1 month.

» To serve from frozen, let cheesecake cups soften in refrigerator overnight.

**Serves** 6 (Makes 6 cups)
**Total Time** 45 minutes, plus 1½ hours chilling time

## PER SERVING
**Cal** 190 | **Total Fat** 17g
**Protein** 5g | **Net Carbs** 3g
**Fiber** 1g | **Sugar Alcohols** 9g
**Total Carbs** 13g

### Why This Recipe Works
Cheesecakes look impressive and taste satisfyingly indulgent but seem daunting to make. Our mini versions couldn't be simpler, however, and the fact that they use keto-friendly ingredients like cream cheese and eggs makes them accessible to anyone on the diet. Our goal for this dessert was to find a grain-free flour crust to support our lemon-flavored cream cheese filling. We used almond flour to replace the traditional graham cracker crust, baking it briefly before filling it. Lining the muffin tin with cupcake liners proved to be essential for getting the cheesecakes out of the muffin tin without breaking them in the process. (It also makes cleanup easier.) If you make these desserts a day ahead, note that the crust will have a much softer texture. The cheesecake cups are great on their own or sprinkled with a few fresh berries. This recipe can easily be doubled. You will need a 12-cup nonstick muffin tin for this recipe. Erythritol is our preferred low-carb sweetener here; however, you can substitute your favorite low-carb sweetener. Be aware that not all low-carb sweeteners can be substituted 1:1 for erythritol. See page 14 for more information on low-carb sweeteners and substitutions.

## PER SERVING

**Cal** 350 | **Total Fat** 31g
**Protein** 10g | **Net Carbs** 6g
**Fiber** 5g | **Sugar Alcohols** 8g
**Total Carbs** 19g

### Why This Recipe Works

Other than its warm chocolatiness, the best part of a mug cake is how quickly it comes together and how easy it is to eat—the perfect treat when you crave something decadent. We started by melting butter with keto-friendly chocolate chips. We then added some cocoa powder, powdered erythritol to balance the bitterness of the cocoa, and an egg to emulsify. We mixed in heavy cream too, not only to add fat to our cake but also to give it buttery tenderness. A little vanilla extract helped highlight subtle caramel notes, salt took the cake from flat to robust and baking powder lifted the almond flour. In less than 20 minutes we had a satisfying chocolate treat. We developed this recipe in a full-size, 1200-watt microwave. If you're using a compact microwave with 800 watts or fewer, you may need to increase the microwaving times. This recipe can be easily doubled; cook both cakes in the microwave at the same time and increase microwaving times to 80 seconds and 60 seconds respectively in step 2. You will need a 12-ounce straight-sided microwave-safe coffee mug for this recipe. Erythritol is our preferred low-carb sweetener here; however, you can substitute your favorite low-carb sweetener. Be aware that not all low-carb sweeteners can be substituted 1:1 for erythritol. See page 14 for more information on low-carb sweeteners and substitutions.

# CHOCOLATE MUG CAKE

- 1 tablespoon unsalted butter
- 4 teaspoons sugar-free dark chocolate chips, divided
- 1 egg, room temperature
- 1 tablespoon heavy cream
- 1½ teaspoons unsweetened cocoa powder
- 1½ teaspoons granulated erythritol
- ¼ teaspoon vanilla extract
- ⅛ teaspoon baking powder
  Pinch table salt
- 1 tablespoon blanched, finely ground almond flour

**1.** Microwave butter and 1 tablespoon chocolate chips in medium bowl at 50 percent power, stirring occasionally, until melted, 1 to 2 minutes. Whisk in egg, cream, cocoa, erythritol, vanilla, baking powder, and salt until smooth. Whisk in almond flour until combined. Transfer to 12-ounce microwave-safe coffee mug.

**2.** Microwave at 50 percent power for 45 seconds. Stir batter, then press remaining 1 teaspoon chocolate chips into center of cake. Microwave at 50 percent power for 20 seconds (cake should be slightly wet around edges of mug and somewhat firmer towards center). Let cake cool in mug for 2 minutes before serving.

# COCONUT PALETAS

1 cup unsweetened canned
  coconut milk
1 cup heavy cream
3 tablespoons powdered
  erythritol
1½ tablespoons vanilla extract
⅛ teaspoon table salt
3 tablespoons unsweetened
  flaked coconut

**1.** Whisk coconut milk, cream, erythritol, vanilla, and salt in 4-cup liquid measuring cup until erythritol has dissolved. Stir in flaked coconut.

**2.** Divide coconut mixture evenly among six 3-ounce Popsicle molds. Insert Popsicle stick in center of each mold, cover, and freeze until firm, at least 6 hours. Let paletas sit at room temperature for 15 minutes before serving. If necessary, hold mold under warm running water for 30 seconds to remove paleta.

### Horchata Paletas

Add ½ teaspoon ground cinnamon and ⅛ teaspoon ground cloves to coconut mixture in step 1. Substitute 3 tablespoons toasted sliced almonds for flaked coconut.
**Per Serving** Cal 170; Total Fat 17g; Protein 2g; Net Carbs 4g; Fiber 0g; Sugar Alcohols 5g; Total Carbs 9g

### Coconut, Lime, and Cardamom Paletas

Add 2 teaspoons grated lime zest, 1 tablespoon lime juice, and ½ teaspoon cardamom to coconut mixture in step 1.
**Per Serving** Cal 170; Total Fat 17g; Protein 1g; Net Carbs 4g; Fiber 0g; Sugar Alcohols 5g; Total Carbs 9g

### *Keto Meal Prep*

» Paletas can be frozen for up to 1 month.

**Serves** 6 (Makes 6 paletas)
**Total Time** 25 minutes, plus 6 hours freezing time

## PER SERVING

**Cal** 170 | **Total Fat** 17g
**Protein** 1g | **Net Carbs** 3g
**Fiber** 0g | **Sugar Alcohols** 5g
**Total Carbs** 8g

### Why This Recipe Works

*Paletas* are a creamy, Mexican frozen treat often filled with chunks of fruits, textured with rice pudding, or flavored with spices. We wanted to create a keto version that was easy and satisfying. Since we couldn't use fruit or fruit juice, we opted for richly flavored, naturally sweet coconut milk mixed with heavy cream. We sweetened it further with powdered erythritol, adding vanilla extract to enhance the coconut milk and salt to balance the paletas' taste. We still wanted some textural contrast, and unsweetened flaked coconut gave that to our paletas. In one version we used almonds and the warm flavors of cinnamon and cloves to give the paletas an *horchata* taste. In another, we added floral brightness to the paletas with cardamom and lime zest and juice. Erythritol is our preferred low-carb sweetener here; however, you can substitute your favorite low-carb sweetener. Be aware that not all low-carb sweeteners can be substituted 1:1 for erythritol. See page 14 for more information on low-carb sweeteners and substitutions. This recipe was developed using 3-ounce Popsicle molds.

**Serves** 4
**Total Time** 50 minutes, plus
4 hours chilling time

## PER SERVING
**Cal** 320 | **Total Fat** 33g
**Protein** 3g | **Net Carbs** 4g
**Fiber** 0g | **Sugar Alcohols** 9g
**Total Carbs** 13g

## Why This Recipe Works

Panna cotta is an elegant, refined dessert made with sugar and gelatin melted in cream and milk. The mixture is chilled in individual ramekins and thanks to its ingredients, it's a natural choice for an easy keto sweet. We set out to create a simple method that would guarantee a pudding with the delicate texture and rich flavor of cream and vanilla that could be served to family or friends at a dinner party. The amount of gelatin proved critical; we used a light hand, adding just enough to make the dessert firm enough to unmold. For sweetness, we opted for powdered erythritol, as it dissolves in the milk mixture much more easily than granular. A vanilla bean gives the panna cotta the deepest flavor, but 1 teaspoon of vanilla extract can be used instead. To serve this dessert unmolded, you'll need four 4- to 5-ounce ramekins. Panna cotta may also be chilled and served in wineglasses. Erythritol is our preferred low-carb sweetener here; however, you can substitute your favorite low-carb sweetener. Be aware that not all low-carb sweeteners can be substituted 1:1 for erythritol. See page 14 for more information on low-carb sweeteners and substitutions. You should have about 1½ ounces strawberries after hulling.

# VANILLA BEAN PANNA COTTA WITH STRAWBERRIES

½  vanilla bean
1½  cups cold heavy cream
1½  teaspoons unflavored gelatin
½  cup water
3  tablespoons granulated
   erythritol
   Pinch table salt
3  ounces strawberries, hulled
   and cut into ½-inch pieces
2  tablespoons shredded
   fresh mint

**1.** Cut vanilla bean in half lengthwise. Using tip of paring knife, scrape out vanilla seeds. Combine vanilla bean and seeds and cream in medium saucepan and bring to simmer over medium heat. Off heat, cover, and let sit until flavors meld, about 10 minutes.

**2.** Sprinkle gelatin over water in bowl and let sit until gelatin softens, about 5 minutes. Fill large bowl halfway with ice and water. Set four 4-to 5-ounce ramekins on rimmed baking sheet.

**3.** Whisk gelatin mixture, erythritol, and salt into cream until dissolved. Transfer mixture to bowl and set over prepared ice water bath. Stir mixture often until slightly thickened and mixture register 50 degrees, about 20 minutes. Strain mixture through fine-mesh strainer into 2-cup liquid measuring cup, then divide evenly among ramekins. Cover all ramekins on baking sheet with plastic wrap and refrigerate until panna cottas are just set and wobble when shaken gently, at least 4 hours or up to 12 hours.

**4.** To unmold, run paring knife around perimeter of each ramekin. (If shape of ramekin makes this difficult, quickly dip ramekin into hot water bath to loosen panna cotta.) Hold serving plate over top of each ramekin and invert; set plate on counter and gently shake ramekin to release panna cotta. Top with strawberries and mint. Serve.

## *Keto Meal Prep*
» Panna cotta can be refrigerated
   for up to 1 day.

# NUTRITIONAL INFORMATION FOR OUR RECIPES

To calculate the nutritional values of our recipes per serving, we used The Food Processor SQL by ESHA research. When using this program, we entered all the ingredients, using weights wherever possible. We also used our preferred brands in these analyses. Any ingredient listed as "optional" was excluded from the analyses. If there is a range in the serving size, we used the highest number of servings to calculate nutritional values.

Total sugars are natural sugars found in ingredients and are calculated in net carbs.
***Net Carbs** = Total Carbs - (Fiber + Sugar Alcohols)

| | Cal | Total Fat (g) | Sat Fat (g) | Chol (mg) | Sodium (mg) | *Net Carbs (g) | Total Carbs (g) | Fiber (g) | Total Sugars (g) | Added Sugars (g) | Sugar Alcohols (g) | Protein (g) |
|---|---|---|---|---|---|---|---|---|---|---|---|---|
| **KETO ESSENTIALS** | | | | | | | | | | | | |
| Keto Tortillas | 110 | 9 | 1 | 30 | 115 | 1 | 4 | 3 | 0 | 0 | 0 | 5 |
| Spinach-Herb Tortillas | 110 | 9 | 1 | 30 | 115 | 1 | 4 | 3 | 0 | 0 | 0 | 5 |
| Smoky Chipotle Tortillas | 110 | 9 | 1 | 30 | 115 | 2 | 5 | 3 | 0 | 0 | 0 | 5 |
| Seeded Bread | 210 | 16 | 4.5 | 75 | 330 | 4 | 10 | 6 | 1 | 0 | 0 | 7 |
| Cheddar-Caraway Bread | 230 | 18 | 6 | 85 | 400 | 4 | 10 | 6 | 1 | 0 | 0 | 9 |
| Cinnamon-Pecan Bread | 220 | 18 | 4.5 | 75 | 330 | 5 | 14 | 6 | 1 | 0 | 3 | 7 |
| Pizza Crust | 150 | 12 | 5 | 45 | 240 | 2 | 3 | 1 | 1 | 0 | 0 | 10 |
| Basil Pesto | 120 | 12 | 2 | 0 | 40 | 1 | 1 | 0 | 0 | 0 | 0 | 2 |
| Pistachio-Tarragon Pesto | 120 | 12 | 1.5 | 0 | 25 | 1 | 2 | 1 | 0 | 0 | 0 | 1 |
| Salsa Verde | 70 | 7 | 1 | 0 | 80 | 0 | 1 | 1 | 0 | 0 | 0 | 1 |
| Chimichurri | 70 | 7 | 1 | 0 | 100 | 1 | 1 | 0 | 0 | 0 | 0 | 0 |
| Chermoula | 70 | 7 | 1 | 0 | 50 | 1 | 1 | 0 | 0 | 0 | 0 | 0 |
| Hazelnut Romesco | 50 | 5 | 0.5 | 0 | 85 | 1 | 1 | 0 | 1 | 0 | 0 | 0 |
| Tahini Sauce | 40 | 3.5 | 0 | 0 | 25 | 2 | 2 | 0 | 0 | 0 | 0 | 1 |
| Avocado Crema | 45 | 3.5 | 1.5 | 10 | 10 | 1 | 2 | 1 | 1 | 0 | 0 | 1 |
| Horseradish–Sour Cream Sauce | 20 | 1.5 | 1 | 5 | 130 | 1 | 1 | 0 | 1 | 0 | 0 | 0 |
| **BREAKFAST** | | | | | | | | | | | | |
| Breakfast Scramble with Gruyère and Herbs | 420 | 35 | 18 | 620 | 600 | 1 | 1 | 0 | 1 | 0 | 0 | 23 |
| with Feta and Spinach | 410 | 34 | 17 | 615 | 660 | 2 | 3 | 1 | 1 | 0 | 0 | 22 |
| with Cheddar and Bacon | 520 | 44 | 17 | 605 | 650 | 2 | 2 | 0 | 1 | 0 | 0 | 28 |
| Muffin Tin Frittatas with Sausage, Bell Pepper, and Cheddar | 530 | 40 | 19 | 460 | 890 | 5 | 6 | 1 | 3 | 0 | 0 | 36 |
| with Asparagus and Fontina | 410 | 33 | 15 | 440 | 780 | 3 | 4 | 1 | 2 | 0 | 0 | 25 |
| with Mushrooms and Gruyère | 430 | 33 | 15 | 435 | 750 | 5 | 6 | 1 | 3 | 0 | 0 | 28 |
| Smoked Salmon Brunch Plate | 470 | 39 | 11 | 230 | 800 | 7 | 10 | 3 | 6 | 0 | 0 | 22 |
| Hard-Cooked Eggs | 70 | 5 | 1.5 | 185 | 70 | 0 | 0 | 0 | 0 | 0 | 0 | 6 |

| | Cal | Total Fat (g) | Sat Fat (g) | Chol (mg) | Sodium (mg) | *Net Carbs (g) | Total Carbs (g) | Fiber (g) | Total Sugars (g) | Added Sugars (g) | Sugar Alcohols (g) | Protein (g) |
|---|---|---|---|---|---|---|---|---|---|---|---|---|
| **BREAKFAST (CONT.)** | | | | | | | | | | | | |
| Pancakes | 420 | 37 | 8 | 160 | 440 | 6 | 17 | 5 | 2 | 0 | 6 | 15 |
| Keto Maple Syrup | 5 | 0 | 0 | 0 | 0 | 0 | 10 | 0 | 0 | 0 | 10 | 0 |
| Blueberry Muffins | 200 | 16 | 6 | 80 | 170 | 5 | 16 | 3 | 2 | 0 | 8 | 6 |
| Grain-Free Granola | 240 | 21 | 9 | 0 | 75 | 7 | 12 | 4 | 2 | 0 | 1 | 6 |
| Grain-Free Chocolate Granola | 290 | 26 | 10 | 0 | 75 | 6 | 15 | 6 | 2 | 0 | 3 | 5 |
| Grain-Free Chai Spice Granola | 250 | 21 | 10 | 0 | 75 | 8 | 13 | 4 | 2 | 0 | 1 | 8 |
| Toasted Coconut Porridge | 290 | 23 | 16 | 0 | 115 | 6 | 19 | 10 | 2 | 0 | 3 | 7 |
| Overnight Chia Pudding with Raspberries and Almonds | 380 | 33 | 15 | 70 | 170 | 6 | 22 | 10 | 4 | 0 | 6 | 7 |
| Green Smoothie | 370 | 38 | 5 | 0 | 310 | 3 | 15 | 4 | 0 | 0 | 8 | 2 |
| Chocolate-Almond Shake | 470 | 46 | 29 | 0 | 280 | 6 | 18 | 4 | 1 | 0 | 8 | 8 |
| **SOUPS AND STEWS** | | | | | | | | | | | | |
| Chicken Zoodle Soup | 470 | 35 | 6 | 130 | 1160 | 6 | 8 | 2 | 6 | 0 | 0 | 30 |
| Chipotle Chicken Zoodle Soup | 460 | 35 | 6 | 130 | 1120 | 5 | 6 | 1 | 4 | 0 | 0 | 30 |
| Miso Chicken Zoodle Soup | 470 | 35 | 6 | 130 | 1110 | 7 | 9 | 2 | 6 | 0 | 0 | 31 |
| Broccoli Cheddar Soup with Chicken | 650 | 47 | 13 | 165 | 1120 | 7 | 10 | 3 | 3 | 0 | 0 | 43 |
| Kimchi Beef Meatball Soup | 550 | 44 | 19 | 120 | 1060 | 2 | 4 | 2 | 1 | 0 | 0 | 34 |
| Thai Coconut Soup with Shrimp and Bok Choy | 330 | 25 | 19 | 160 | 930 | 8 | 9 | 1 | 2 | 0 | 0 | 20 |
| Hearty Spring Vegetable Soup | 300 | 25 | 4.5 | 5 | 810 | 8 | 12 | 4 | 6 | 0 | 0 | 8 |
| Roasted Eggplant and Kale Soup | 310 | 27 | 6 | 5 | 880 | 8 | 14 | 6 | 6 | 0 | 0 | 5 |
| Hearty Beef Stew with Cauliflower and Mushrooms | 610 | 47 | 16 | 125 | 1000 | 9 | 13 | 4 | 6 | 0 | 0 | 38 |
| Easy Ground Beef Chili | 640 | 50 | 16 | 130 | 630 | 8 | 14 | 6 | 4 | 0 | 0 | 35 |
| New England Seafood Chowder | 550 | 40 | 20 | 170 | 1110 | 6 | 8 | 2 | 4 | 0 | 0 | 40 |
| **POULTRY** | | | | | | | | | | | | |
| Chicken Salad with Fresh Herbs | 470 | 34 | 6 | 115 | 650 | 1 | 1 | 0 | 0 | 0 | 0 | 38 |
| Chicken Salad with Smoked Paprika and Almonds | 580 | 43 | 6 | 115 | 650 | 3 | 6 | 3 | 2 | 0 | 0 | 42 |
| Curried Chicken Salad with Pistachios | 570 | 42 | 7 | 115 | 650 | 4 | 7 | 3 | 2 | 0 | 0 | 42 |
| Green Goodness Bowl | 680 | 51 | 9 | 125 | 770 | 6 | 14 | 8 | 3 | 0 | 0 | 45 |
| Thai Chicken Lettuce Wraps | 600 | 45 | 9 | 155 | 640 | 8 | 11 | 3 | 4 | 0 | 0 | 40 |
| Turkey-Veggie Burgers | 540 | 43 | 10 | 65 | 500 | 6 | 11 | 5 | 4 | 0 | 0 | 34 |
| Chicken Baked in Foil with Fennel and Radishes | 650 | 47 | 7 | 125 | 790 | 8 | 13 | 5 | 5 | 0 | 0 | 43 |
| Prosciutto-Wrapped Chicken with Asparagus | 830 | 63 | 14 | 180 | 1120 | 5 | 8 | 3 | 3 | 0 | 0 | 57 |
| Oven-Roasted Chicken Thighs | 380 | 24 | 7 | 215 | 460 | 0 | 0 | 0 | 0 | 0 | 0 | 38 |
| Barbecue-Rubbed Oven-Roasted Chicken Thighs | 390 | 24 | 7 | 215 | 500 | 0 | 1 | 1 | 0 | 0 | 0 | 38 |
| Cajun-Rubbed Oven-Roasted Chicken Thighs | 390 | 24 | 7 | 215 | 460 | 0 | 1 | 1 | 0 | 0 | 0 | 38 |

| | Cal | Total Fat (g) | Sat Fat (g) | Chol (mg) | Sodium (mg) | *Net Carbs (g) | Total Carbs (g) | Fiber (g) | Total Sugars (g) | Added Sugars (g) | Sugar Alcohols (g) | Protein (g) |
|---|---|---|---|---|---|---|---|---|---|---|---|---|
| **POULTRY *(CONT.)*** | | | | | | | | | | | | |
| One-Pan Roast Chicken Thighs with Cauliflower and Tomatoes | 620 | 46 | 10 | 215 | 800 | 7 | 11 | 4 | 4 | 0 | 0 | 42 |
| Grilled Chicken Thighs with Shaved Zucchini Salad | 730 | 54 | 14 | 235 | 1160 | 5 | 7 | 2 | 4 | 0 | 0 | 52 |
| Chicken Mole Poblano | 500 | 33 | 8 | 180 | 750 | 7 | 10 | 3 | 3 | 0 | 0 | 38 |
| Indian Butter Chicken | 560 | 42 | 25 | 255 | 670 | 5 | 7 | 2 | 4 | 0 | 0 | 36 |
| Three-Cheese Zucchini Noodles with Chicken | 600 | 47 | 22 | 160 | 830 | 7 | 10 | 3 | 6 | 0 | 0 | 39 |
| Weeknight Skillet Roast Chicken with Lemon-Herb Pan Sauce | 660 | 49 | 15 | 210 | 1230 | 2 | 2 | 0 | 1 | 0 | 0 | 49 |
| **BEEF, PORK, AND LAMB** | | | | | | | | | | | | |
| Pan-Seared Steak Tips with Rosemary–Peppercorn Pan Sauce | 570 | 45 | 21 | 175 | 790 | 1 | 1 | 0 | 0 | 0 | 0 | 36 |
| with Mustard-Cream Pan Sauce | 580 | 45 | 21 | 180 | 1090 | 2 | 2 | 0 | 1 | 0 | 0 | 36 |
| with Porcini Mushroom–Sage Pan Sauce | 580 | 45 | 21 | 175 | 790 | 2 | 3 | 1 | 0 | 0 | 0 | 37 |
| Pan-Seared Strip Steak with Smashed Cucumber Salad | 650 | 53 | 28 | 195 | 950 | 2 | 4 | 2 | 2 | 0 | 0 | 37 |
| Butter-Basted Rib-Eye Steak | 650 | 57 | 26 | 160 | 670 | 1 | 1 | 0 | 0 | 0 | 0 | 31 |
| with Coffee-Chile Butter | 650 | 57 | 26 | 160 | 670 | 1 | 1 | 0 | 0 | 0 | 0 | 31 |
| with Rosemary-Orange Butter | 650 | 57 | 26 | 160 | 670 | 1 | 1 | 0 | 0 | 0 | 0 | 31 |
| One-Pan Steak Fajitas (with tortillas) | 900 | 68 | 13 | 180 | 910 | 11 | 27 | 16 | 5 | 0 | 0 | 49 |
| One-Pan Steak Fajitas (without tortillas) | 680 | 51 | 11 | 115 | 690 | 7 | 18 | 11 | 4 | 0 | 0 | 40 |
| Beef Stir-Fry with Bok Choy and Shiitakes | 820 | 75 | 37 | 130 | 850 | 5 | 8 | 3 | 3 | 0 | 0 | 29 |
| Grilled Beef and Vegetable Kebabs | 720 | 59 | 12 | 115 | 680 | 7 | 9 | 2 | 5 | 0 | 0 | 37 |
| Zucchini Noodles with Pesto Meatballs | 690 | 60 | 15 | 90 | 910 | 7 | 10 | 3 | 6 | 0 | 0 | 30 |
| Nut-Crusted Pork Chops | 670 | 53 | 28 | 145 | 600 | 5 | 9 | 4 | 2 | 0 | 0 | 42 |
| with Caraway and Dill | 670 | 53 | 28 | 145 | 650 | 5 | 10 | 5 | 2 | 0 | 0 | 43 |
| with Sesame and Scallion | 680 | 54 | 28 | 145 | 690 | 5 | 10 | 5 | 2 | 0 | 0 | 43 |
| Smothered Boneless Pork Ribs | 630 | 50 | 19 | 185 | 690 | 7 | 9 | 2 | 4 | 0 | 0 | 37 |
| Grilled Thin-Cut Pork Chops with Spicy Barbecue Coleslaw | 740 | 53 | 12 | 190 | 940 | 4 | 7 | 3 | 3 | 0 | 0 | 54 |
| Lemon-Thyme Pork Tenderloin with Green Beans | 630 | 47 | 9 | 115 | 670 | 5 | 9 | 4 | 4 | 0 | 0 | 41 |
| Vietnamese Pork and Noodle Bowls | 790 | 63 | 23 | 120 | 560 | 8 | 16 | 8 | 3 | 0 | 0 | 40 |
| Italian Eggplant Rolls | 520 | 44 | 14 | 80 | 670 | 8 | 12 | 4 | 5 | 0 | 0 | 23 |
| Pan-Roasted Lamb Chops with Brussels Sprouts and Chermoula | 800 | 69 | 24 | 135 | 660 | 7 | 11 | 4 | 3 | 0 | 0 | 33 |
| Greek-Style Lamb Wraps with Tzatziki | 630 | 51 | 23 | 145 | 710 | 5 | 7 | 2 | 4 | 0 | 0 | 35 |

| | Cal | Total Fat (g) | Sat Fat (g) | Chol (mg) | Sodium (mg) | *Net Carbs (g) | Total Carbs (g) | Fiber (g) | Total Sugars (g) | Added Sugars (g) | Sugar Alcohols (g) | Protein (g) |
|---|---|---|---|---|---|---|---|---|---|---|---|---|
| **SEAFOOD** | | | | | | | | | | | | |
| Bistro Salad with Salmon and Avocado | 610 | 46 | 7 | 100 | 910 | 5 | 12 | 7 | 3 | 0 | 0 | 39 |
| Classic Tuna Salad | 410 | 35 | 5 | 50 | 850 | 2 | 2 | 0 | 1 | 0 | 0 | 20 |
| Tuna Salad with Eggs, Radishes, and Capers | 410 | 33 | 5 | 130 | 860 | 2 | 3 | 1 | 1 | 0 | 0 | 24 |
| Tuna Salad with Walnuts and Tarragon | 490 | 43 | 6 | 50 | 850 | 3 | 4 | 1 | 1 | 0 | 0 | 22 |
| Seared Tuna Sushi Bowl | 780 | 58 | 9 | 85 | 1180 | 8 | 15 | 7 | 6 | 0 | 0 | 51 |
| Grilled Southwestern Salmon Burgers | 570 | 47 | 8 | 90 | 560 | 4 | 8 | 4 | 2 | 0 | 0 | 31 |
| Fish Tacos | 580 | 42 | 18 | 185 | 830 | 3 | 5 | 2 | 2 | 0 | 0 | 45 |
| Pan-Seared Salmon with Cucumber–Ginger Relish | 490 | 37 | 6 | 80 | 550 | 3 | 5 | 2 | 2 | 0 | 0 | 30 |
| Pan-Roasted Striped Bass with Red Pepper–Hazelnut Relish | 480 | 37 | 5 | 70 | 490 | 2 | 4 | 2 | 2 | 0 | 0 | 34 |
| Grilled Bacon-Wrapped Scallops with Celery Salad | 420 | 30 | 6 | 60 | 1140 | 6 | 8 | 2 | 2 | 0 | 0 | 25 |
| Singapore Noodles | 610 | 47 | 36 | 535 | 1250 | 7 | 15 | 8 | 5 | 0 | 0 | 33 |
| Shrimp Scampi | 420 | 30 | 13 | 260 | 540 | 9 | 11 | 2 | 5 | 0 | 0 | 27 |
| **VEGETABLE MAINS** | | | | | | | | | | | | |
| Super Cobb Salad | 360 | 29 | 6 | 195 | 480 | 8 | 13 | 5 | 5 | 0 | 0 | 13 |
| Zucchini Noodle Salad with Peanut-Ginger Dressing | 470 | 40 | 15 | 0 | 990 | 10 | 16 | 6 | 9 | 0 | 0 | 14 |
| Mediterranean "Falafel" Wraps | 340 | 30 | 4 | 0 | 230 | 10 | 14 | 4 | 4 | 0 | 0 | 10 |
| Keto Pizza with Mozzarella, Tomatoes, and Basil Pesto | 530 | 46 | 15 | 105 | 690 | 6 | 9 | 3 | 4 | 0 | 0 | 26 |
| with Prosciutto, Arugula, and Ricotta | 470 | 37 | 14 | 115 | 1090 | 5 | 7 | 2 | 3 | 0 | 0 | 29 |
| with Fennel, Mushrooms, and Hazelnut Romesco | 390 | 31 | 10 | 90 | 630 | 7 | 10 | 3 | 5 | 0 | 0 | 21 |
| Grilled Vegetable Plate with Burrata and Pistachio-Tarragon Pesto | 590 | 55 | 14 | 40 | 570 | 9 | 16 | 7 | 5 | 0 | 0 | 17 |
| Cauliflower Steaks with Chimichurri | 400 | 36 | 5 | 0 | 960 | 10 | 16 | 6 | 6 | 0 | 0 | 6 |
| Grilled Portobello Burgers | 380 | 36 | 9 | 30 | 860 | 7 | 9 | 2 | 4 | 0 | 0 | 7 |
| Green Shakshuka | 420 | 34 | 8 | 385 | 900 | 6 | 10 | 4 | 2 | 0 | 0 | 18 |
| Creamy Shirataki Noodles with Spinach, Mushrooms, and Pecorino | 580 | 52 | 27 | 130 | 630 | 6 | 11 | 5 | 4 | 0 | 0 | 15 |
| **VEGETABLE SIDES** | | | | | | | | | | | | |
| Pan-Roasted Asparagus | 160 | 15 | 5 | 15 | 150 | 3 | 5 | 2 | 2 | 0 | 0 | 3 |
| with Toasted Garlic | 160 | 15 | 5 | 15 | 150 | 3 | 5 | 2 | 2 | 0 | 0 | 3 |
| with Tarragon and Lemon | 160 | 15 | 5 | 15 | 150 | 3 | 5 | 2 | 2 | 0 | 0 | 3 |
| Roasted Broccoli Salad | 240 | 22 | 3 | 0 | 220 | 5 | 12 | 7 | 2 | 0 | 0 | 4 |

| | Cal | Total Fat (g) | Sat Fat (g) | Chol (mg) | Sodium (mg) | *Net Carbs (g) | Total Carbs (g) | Fiber (g) | Total Sugars (g) | Added Sugars (g) | Sugar Alcohols (g) | Protein (g) |
|---|---|---|---|---|---|---|---|---|---|---|---|---|
| **VEGETABLE SIDES _(CONT.)_** | | | | | | | | | | | | |
| Broiled Broccoli Rabe | 150 | 14 | 2 | 0 | 170 | 1 | 3 | 2 | 0 | 0 | 0 | 3 |
| with Olives and Garlic | 210 | 22 | 3 | 0 | 190 | 1 | 3 | 2 | 0 | 0 | 0 | 3 |
| with Creamy Gruyère Sauce | 310 | 30 | 12 | 50 | 290 | 1 | 3 | 2 | 1 | 0 | 0 | 8 |
| Cauliflower Rice | 190 | 18 | 2.5 | 0 | 220 | 4 | 6 | 2 | 3 | 0 | 0 | 2 |
| Mexican Cauliflower Rice | 190 | 18 | 2.5 | 0 | 220 | 4 | 6 | 2 | 2 | 0 | 0 | 2 |
| Cauliflower-Almond Rice Pilaf | 210 | 19 | 2.5 | 0 | 220 | 4 | 7 | 3 | 3 | 0 | 0 | 3 |
| Whipped Cauliflower | 150 | 14 | 9 | 40 | 180 | 4 | 6 | 2 | 2 | 0 | 0 | 2 |
| with Crispy Bacon, Cheddar, and Scallions | 240 | 21 | 13 | 60 | 280 | 4 | 6 | 2 | 2 | 0 | 0 | 8 |
| with Fennel, Garlic, and Lemon | 160 | 14 | 9 | 40 | 180 | 4 | 6 | 2 | 2 | 0 | 0 | 2 |
| Cucumber Salad with Chile and Mint | 210 | 21 | 3 | 0 | 210 | 3 | 4 | 1 | 2 | 0 | 0 | 1 |
| Sautéed Green Beans with Mustard Vinaigrette | 240 | 22 | 3 | 0 | 230 | 6 | 9 | 3 | 4 | 0 | 0 | 2 |
| with Chipotle-Lime Vinaigrette | 230 | 21 | 3 | 0 | 150 | 6 | 9 | 3 | 4 | 0 | 0 | 2 |
| with Sesame-Miso Vinaigrette | 230 | 21 | 3 | 0 | 125 | 6 | 9 | 3 | 4 | 0 | 0 | 2 |
| Quick Collard Greens | 170 | 15 | 2 | 0 | 210 | 2 | 8 | 6 | 1 | 0 | 0 | 4 |
| with Chorizo | 240 | 19 | 5 | 25 | 450 | 3 | 9 | 6 | 1 | 0 | 0 | 11 |
| with Coconut and Curry | 190 | 16 | 3 | 0 | 210 | 3 | 9 | 6 | 1 | 0 | 0 | 4 |
| Kale Caesar Salad | 420 | 38 | 8 | 25 | 830 | 4 | 6 | 2 | 1 | 0 | 0 | 13 |
| Sautéed Summer Squash | 150 | 14 | 2 | 0 | 300 | 4 | 6 | 2 | 3 | 0 | 0 | 2 |
| with Mint and Pistachios | 170 | 16 | 2.5 | 0 | 290 | 4 | 6 | 2 | 3 | 0 | 0 | 3 |
| with Oregano and Red Pepper Flakes | 150 | 14 | 2 | 0 | 290 | 4 | 6 | 2 | 3 | 0 | 0 | 2 |
| **SNACKS** | | | | | | | | | | | | |
| Bacon-Ranch Cheese Balls | 190 | 16 | 8 | 40 | 270 | 1 | 2 | 1 | 0 | 0 | 0 | 9 |
| Classic Deviled Eggs | 280 | 25 | 5 | 380 | 350 | 1 | 1 | 0 | 1 | 0 | 0 | 13 |
| Chipotle Deviled Eggs with Radishes and Cilantro | 290 | 25 | 5 | 380 | 290 | 2 | 2 | 0 | 1 | 0 | 0 | 13 |
| Deviled Eggs with Tuna, Capers, and Chives | 360 | 26 | 6 | 405 | 650 | 1 | 1 | 0 | 0 | 0 | 0 | 26 |
| Spiced Nut Mix | 230 | 22 | 2 | 0 | 200 | 2 | 6 | 4 | 1 | 0 | 0 | 6 |
| Spicy Cocoa Nut Mix | 230 | 22 | 2 | 0 | 200 | 3 | 6 | 3 | 1 | 0 | 0 | 6 |
| Fennel and Orange Nut Mix | 230 | 22 | 2 | 0 | 200 | 2 | 6 | 4 | 1 | 0 | 0 | 6 |
| Snack Bars | 250 | 21 | 4 | 15 | 105 | 6 | 18 | 4 | 1 | 0 | 8 | 9 |
| Seeded Crackers | 170 | 13 | 3.5 | 35 | 420 | 1 | 2 | 1 | 0 | 0 | 0 | 11 |
| Black Pepper–Rosemary Crackers | 160 | 12 | 3.5 | 35 | 410 | 1 | 2 | 1 | 0 | 0 | 0 | 11 |
| Sesame Crackers | 160 | 13 | 3.5 | 35 | 410 | 1 | 2 | 1 | 0 | 0 | 0 | 11 |
| Herbed Spinach Dip | 140 | 13 | 2.5 | 10 | 310 | 3 | 4 | 1 | 1 | 0 | 0 | 2 |
| Whipped Feta Dip with Dill and Parsley | 280 | 26 | 0 | 50 | 520 | 3 | 3 | 0 | 2 | 0 | 0 | 8 |

| | Cal | Total Fat (g) | Sat Fat (g) | Chol (mg) | Sodium (mg) | *Net Carbs (g) | Total Carbs (g) | Fiber (g) | Total Sugars (g) | Added Sugars (g) | Sugar Alcohols (g) | Protein (g) |
|---|---|---|---|---|---|---|---|---|---|---|---|---|
| **SNACKS (CONT.)** | | | | | | | | | | | | |
| Mediterranean Whipped Almond Dip | 280 | 27 | 3 | 0 | 170 | 4 | 6 | 2 | 1 | 0 | 0 | 6 |
| Mediterranean Whipped Almond Dip with Lemon and Fresh Herbs | 280 | 27 | 3 | 0 | 170 | 3 | 6 | 3 | 1 | 0 | 0 | 6 |
| Smoky Mediterranean Whipped Almond Dip | 280 | 27 | 3 | 0 | 170 | 3 | 6 | 3 | 1 | 0 | 0 | 6 |
| **SWEET TREATS** | | | | | | | | | | | | |
| Dark Chocolate Clusters with Macadamia Nuts and Coconut | 170 | 15 | 7 | 0 | 45 | 2 | 10 | 5 | 0 | 0 | 3 | 3 |
| with Pepitas and Dried Cherries | 150 | 12 | 7 | 0 | 50 | 3 | 10 | 4 | 1 | 0 | 3 | 4 |
| with Pecans and Orange | 170 | 14 | 6 | 0 | 45 | 2 | 10 | 5 | 0 | 0 | 3 | 3 |
| Chocolate Covered Peanut Butter Bites | 110 | 11 | 5 | 10 | 20 | 3 | 17 | 0 | 0 | 0 | 14 | 3 |
| Chocolate Covered Almond Butter Bites | 110 | 10 | 4.5 | 10 | 20 | 2 | 17 | 1 | 0 | 0 | 14 | 3 |
| Chocolate Chip Cookies | 170 | 14 | 3.5 | 35 | 120 | 5 | 16 | 2 | 1 | 0 | 9 | 4 |
| Mini Lemon Cheesecake Cups | 190 | 17 | 10 | 85 | 200 | 3 | 13 | 1 | 2 | 0 | 9 | 5 |
| Chocolate Mug Cake | 350 | 31 | 13 | 235 | 280 | 6 | 19 | 5 | 1 | 0 | 8 | 10 |
| Coconut Paletas | 170 | 17 | 11 | 45 | 60 | 3 | 8 | 0 | 2 | 0 | 5 | 1 |
| Horchata Paletas | 170 | 17 | 10 | 45 | 60 | 4 | 9 | 0 | 2 | 0 | 5 | 2 |
| Coconut, Lime, and Cardamom Paletas | 170 | 17 | 11 | 45 | 60 | 4 | 9 | 0 | 2 | 0 | 5 | 1 |
| Vanilla Bean Panna Cotta with Strawberries | 320 | 33 | 21 | 100 | 65 | 4 | 13 | 0 | 3 | 0 | 9 | 3 |

# CONVERSIONS AND EQUIVALENTS

The recipes in this book were developed using standard U.S. measures following U.S. government guidelines. The charts below offer equivalents for U.S. and metric measures. All conversions are approximate and have been rounded up or down to the nearest whole number.

**EXAMPLE**

1 teaspoon = 4.9292 milliliters, rounded up to 5 milliliters
1 ounce = 28.3495 grams, rounded down to 28 grams

## VOLUME CONVERSIONS

| U.S. | METRIC |
| --- | --- |
| 1 teaspoon | 5 milliliters |
| 2 teaspoons | 10 milliliters |
| 1 tablespoon | 15 milliliters |
| 2 tablespoons | 30 milliliters |
| ¼ cup | 59 milliliters |
| ⅓ cup | 79 milliliters |
| ½ cup | 118 milliliters |
| ¾ cup | 177 milliliters |
| 1 cup | 237 milliliters |
| 1¼ cups | 296 milliliters |
| 1½ cups | 355 milliliters |
| 2 cups (1 pint) | 473 milliliters |
| 2½ cups | 591 milliliters |
| 3 cups | 710 milliliters |
| 4 cups (1 quart) | 0.946 liter |
| 1.06 quarts | 1 liter |
| 4 quarts (1 gallon) | 3.8 liters |

## WEIGHT CONVERSIONS

| OUNCES | GRAMS |
| --- | --- |
| ½ | 14 |
| ¾ | 21 |
| 1 | 28 |
| 1½ | 43 |
| 2 | 57 |
| 2½ | 71 |
| 3 | 85 |
| 3½ | 99 |
| 4 | 113 |
| 4½ | 128 |
| 5 | 142 |
| 6 | 170 |
| 7 | 198 |
| 8 | 227 |
| 9 | 255 |
| 10 | 283 |
| 12 | 340 |
| 16 (1 pound) | 454 |

# CONVERSIONS FOR COMMON BAKING INGREDIENTS

Because measuring by weight is far more accurate than measuring by volume, and thus more likely to produce reliable results, in our recipes we provide ounce measures in addition to cup measures for many ingredients. Refer to the chart below to convert these measures into grams.

Note that not all alternative sweeteners have equivalent volume/weight. If using sweeteners other than erythritol or Swerve, make sure to sub based on the volume measurement not weight.

| INGREDIENT | OUNCES | GRAMS |
|---|---|---|
| **Flour Substitutes** | | |
| 1 cup blanched, finely ground almond flour | 4 | 113 |
| 1 cup coconut flour | 4 | 113 |
| **Erythritol** | | |
| 1 cup granulated erythritol | 7 | 198 |
| 1 cup powdered erythritol | 4 | 113 |
| **Cocoa Powder** | | |
| 1 cup (unsweetened) cocoa powder | 3 | 85 |
| **Butter†** | | |
| 4 tablespoons (½ stick or ¼ cup) | 2 | 57 |
| 8 tablespoons (1 stick or ½ cup) | 4 | 113 |
| 16 tablespoons (2 sticks or 1 cup) | 8 | 227 |

† In the United States, butter is sold both salted and unsalted. We recommend unsalted butter. If you are using salted butter, take this into consideration before adding salt to a recipe.

# OVEN TEMPERATURE

| FAHRENHEIT | CELSIUS | GAS MARK |
|---|---|---|
| 225 | 105 | ¼ |
| 250 | 120 | ½ |
| 275 | 135 | 1 |
| 300 | 150 | 2 |
| 325 | 165 | 3 |
| 350 | 180 | 4 |
| 375 | 190 | 5 |
| 400 | 200 | 6 |
| 425 | 220 | 7 |
| 450 | 230 | 8 |
| 475 | 245 | 9 |

# CONVERTING TEMPERATURES FROM AN INSTANT-READ THERMOMETER

We include doneness temperatures in many of the recipes in this book. We recommend an instant-read thermometer for the job. Refer to the table above to convert Fahrenheit degrees to Celsius. Or, for temperatures not represented in the chart, use this simple formula:

Subtract 32 degrees from the Fahrenheit reading, then divide the result by 1.8 to find the Celsius reading.

**To convert** 160°F to Celsius:
160°F − 32 = 128°
128° ÷ 1.8 = 71.11°C, rounded down to 71°C

# TAKING THE TEMPERATURE OF MEAT AND POULTRY

Since the temperature of beef and pork will continue to rise as the meat rests—an effect called carryover cooking—they should be removed from the oven, grill, or pan when they are 5 to 10 degrees below the desired serving temperature. Carryover cooking doesn't apply to poultry (it lacks the dense muscle structure of beef and pork and doesn't retain heat as well), so it should be cooked to the desired serving temperature. The following temperatures should be used to determine when to stop the cooking process.

| INGREDIENT | TEMPERATURE |
| --- | --- |
| **Beef/lamb** | |
| Rare | 115 to 120 degrees (120 to 125 degrees after resting) |
| Medium-rare | 120 to 125 degrees (125 to 130 degrees after resting) |
| Medium | 130 to 135 degrees (135 to 140 degrees after resting) |
| Medium-well | 140 to 145 degrees (145 to 150 degrees after resting) |
| Well-done | 150 to 155 degrees (155 to 160 degrees after resting) |
| **Pork** | |
| Chops and tenderloin | 145 degrees (150 degrees after resting) |
| Loin roasts | 140 degrees (145 degrees after resting) |
| **Chicken** | |
| White meat | 160 degrees |
| Dark meat | 175 degrees |

# INDEX

**Note:** Page references in *italics* indicate photographs.